POLICY DYNAMICS

POLICY DYNAMICS

Brian W. Hogwood

and

B. Guy Peters

ST. MARTIN'S PRESS

NEW YORK

St. Martin's Press, Inc., 175 Fifth Avenue, New York, NY 10010
Printed in Great Britain
First published in the United States of America in 1983

ISBN 0-312-62014-4

Library of Congress Cataloging in Publication Data
Hogwood, Brian W.
   Policy dynamics.
      1. Policy sciences. 2. Comparative government.
3. Public administration. I. Peters, B. Guy. II. Title.
H97.H63   1982   361.6′1   82-10330
ISBN 0-312-62014-4

CONTENTS

LIST OF TABLES

LIST OF FIGURES

PREFACE

> Let no one say that I have said nothing new; the
> arrangement of the subject is new.
>
> Pascal, *Pensées* (1670), 22

CHANGE is a universal phenomenon in politics and policy. Trite, isn't it? Yet despite the trite sayings about change, students of policy have largely managed to avoid following through the implications of the issue of change. In writing this book we are by no means claiming to be the first authors to have drawn attention to the facts that policy change can occur in a number of ways and that much policy change, and the process of securing it, is shaped by the characteristics of previous policies (see especially Rose, 1976b; Wildavsky, 1979; Lindblom, 1959; Hall *et al.*, 1975). However, it seemed to us that none of the previous writers had systematically followed through the implications of what we perceived to be the growing importance of replacement policies relative to genuine policy innovations in both Britain and the United States. In following through those implications ourselves, we found it necessary to broaden our discussion to present a framework for analyzing *all* forms of policy change in order to place our interest in policy replacement in perspective.

The origins of the idea for this book germinated on some obscure vine-covered slope in Algeria which produced the grapes which went into a bottle of red Algerian wine which the authors were consuming one evening when Guy Peters was staying with Brian Hogwood on a visit to the University of Strathclyde in Glasgow. Early on in the evening one of the authors asked the other whether anyone had ever written an article or book pointing out the significance of the apparently obvious fact that most policy changes in both Britain and the United States now involved the replacement of policies which already existed rather than the government entering into a new filed of activity in which it had not previously been engaged. Although each of us had read much on the themes of policymaking and policy change, neither of us could recall a book or article with this point as its primary focus. We started to jot down various points which we might make in a paper or article on this theme. The bottle of Algerian wine turned out to be fairly dire, so we adulterated it with various other liquids including some failed home-made strawberry wine and some brandy. Some time later in the evening our ability to make incisive intellectual points became attenuated and we were directed into the more enjoyable task of looking for appropriate epigraphs. All the epigraphs from *Alice in Wonderland* stem from that evening.

Since then we have pursued the twin tasks of writing up our ideas and finding appropriate epigraphs in a number of ways. Our first presentation of our ideas on what we had come to call 'policy succession' was made at the Annual Meeting of the American Political Science Association in Washington, DC in 1980. We received some useful feedback from that presentation, particularly from Deborah Stone. By that stage we felt that we should develop our theme in book form, since even our lengthy APSA paper proved too short to present all the interlocking themes which had to be tackled. Each of us has separately presented various aspects of our joint work at a number of conferences and seminars, and we would like to thank those who provided useful comments, particularly those who drew attention to points that required further thought: Department of Political Science, University of North Carolina; ECPR Workshop on 'Markets, Hierarchies and Politics' at Florence, 1980; Center for Public Policy Studies, Tulane University; Department of Politics, University of Edinburgh; Department of Political Science, York University, Toronto; CSPP/SSRC Conference on Problems of Intergovernmental Fiscal Relations in the 1980s, University of Strathclyde. David Beam, Richard Rose, Ed Page and Duncan McLean provided us with useful comments at various stages. Travel to these conferences and seminars and also to enable the authors to meet each other to work on the book was made possible by money from the Alfred P. Sloan Foundation and a Ford Foundation Grant to the Centre for the Study of Public Policy at the University of Strathclyde to promote the study of intergovernmental relations.

Such is the hectic pace of transatlantic book writing that on one occasion when Guy Peters was due to visit Glasgow, Brian Hogwood was due to attend a Christmas reunion in Cheshire. We would like to thank the Davnalls for resolving this dilemma by lending us their house for a day (and providing more wine) and thus enabling both of us to take in the reunion and do much useful work together on the book.

What final conclusion would we draw from our work on this book, which both of us found a stimulating intellectual voyage of discovery? During the process of work on this book we discussed it over many bottles of wine after that first evening, and all of them were better than the Algerian red.

Chapter 1

THE PERVASIVENESS OF POLICY SUCCESSION

> For all that moveth doth in change delight.
> Edmund Spenser, *The Faerie Queene*

MUCH of the language of policy analysis and the study of policymaking has a distinctly pristine air about it. We speak of 'creation', 'birth' and 'innovation' as though policies frequently came new into the world. In reality, 'new' policies are rarely written on a *tabula rasa*, but rather on a well-occupied or even crowded tablet of existing laws, organizations and clients. Thus, most policymaking is actually policy succession: the replacement of an existing policy, program or organization by another. The concentration of policy analysis on dramatic creation or termination events in public policy may therefore direct attention away from the more common and important phenomenon of policy succession.

This phenomenon poses some apparent paradoxes for the nature of policy change in the future. Although the rate of economic growth in Western countries may not be so fast in future as it was in the thirty years up to 1975, it is reasonable to predict that there will be a faster rate of change (and certainly increased unpredictability) in the social and economic environment in which government policies operate. Yet greater rigidities have been built into the policy system in its ability to respond, since the nature of the response will to a greater extent be about attempting to change the government policies which already exist rather than responding to change through complete innovation. There will also be a paradox of political effort: even if policy actors put as much or even more effort than in the past into seeking to secure change, the amount of substantive change achieved will be less than in periods of high policy innovation.

This book is about the way in which the contemporary dynamics of public policy has changed from the past, and also about the challenges for policymaking posed for the future.

1.1   The growing importance of policy succession

> There is no new thing under the sun.
>
> *Ecclesiastes*, 1 : 8

Our argument is not only that policy succession is a highly important feature of policymaking in Western societies but also that it will continue to grow in relative importance. We accept that there will continue to be new problems and new opportunities for government to engage in activities embodying a high degree of innovation. Some of these will reflect technological and social changes, many of which currently cannot be foreseen. Nevertheless, the dynamics of the evolution of government policy will require that governments devote an increasing proportion of their time and energy to concerns arising from existing policies.

The changing balance between innovation and succession will not be exactly the same for all countries and all policy areas. The timing of major innovations for, say, social security policy, will differ from that of energy policy, and consequently this will affect the distribution across time of replacements of those original policies. The total amount of policy change in any period and its relative distribution between innovation and succession varies among countries, reflecting distinctive features of their public policy history, such as the New Deal period in the United States. However, while these individual characteristics may affect the pattern of change in any particular decade or even the long-run rate of growth of policy succession, they do not alter the basic premise that in *all* Western societies the importance of policy succession relative to innovation has increased and will continue to do so.

There are three good reasons for expecting policy succession to occupy this growing role in the affairs of government.

1.1.1   *Crowding of the policy space*

The first of these reasons relates to the phenomenon, noted by a number of commentators, of the increased crowding of the 'policy space' (see, for example, Heidenheimer, Heclo and Adams, 1975, p. 220). In other words, over the years governments have gradually expanded their activity in particular fields of policy so that there are relatively few completely new activities in which they could be involved. For example, even though the United States has been in the throes of a political battle over the creation of a system of national health insurance, in many ways this system would be built upon existing programs of national health insurance for the elderly, of subsidized care for the indigent, and direct provision of medical care for groups such as veterans. By 1978 over 40 per cent of all medical care expenses in the United States were covered by the public sector. The magnitude of changes associated with national health insurance would be significant, but they would be changes occurring in a field in which government is already active rather than a leap into an entirely new policy area. Thus, Heidenheimer, Heclo and Adams (1975, p. 220) note of income maintenance policies in Western countries that: 'The frontiers of policy development no longer stretch towards the horizon allowing unimpeded expansion with cheap resources; they are now internal frontiers of integration, harmonization and trade-offs.'

Even where there are remaining interstices in the policy space which could be filled, it may make sense to deal with them simultaneously with altering existing legislation, although there would be no guarantees that this would be done. For example, the United States has no equivalent of the children's benefits common in European countries, but adopting that program might best be done while considering the inadequacies of the total social welfare system.

1.1.2 'Policy as its own cause'

Secondly, but related to the first point, existing policies themselves may create conditions requiring changes in policies or programs. In other words, the problem to be tackled by a 'new' policy proposal may not be the absence of policy in an area but problems resulting from existing policies or unforeseen adverse consequences arising from the interaction of different programs. Policy may be its own cause. (See the essay with this title in Wildavsky, 1979.) For example, the areas of income maintenance and taxation are both quite well populated with policies. However, the individual programs and their interaction have established conditions calling for substantial policy succession. In particular, the 'poverty trap' results from the interaction of tax and income maintenance provisions. (For a discussion of this in the British context see Sandford, 1977, chapter 10, especially pp. 161–2.) There are points on the earned-income scale where the imposition of tax and the withdrawal of means-tested benefits would result in a loss of disposable income for individuals earning additional gross income. This is hardly an esoteric point. Data on this are regularly published in the British government's annual compilation, *Social Trends* (see, for example, pp. 90–2 of the 1982 edition). Such a situation is clearly nonsensical and has been the object of several attempts at policy succession in both the United States and the United Kingdom. Thus, as May and Wildavsky (1978, p. 13) point out, 'past policies become an important (and sometimes the most important) part of the environment to which future policies must adapt'.

These past policies have implications both for the process by which new policies might come into being—because of the pre-existing interests of established clientele and service providers and their political spokesmen—and for the substance of future policy because of the inheritance of past policies. This is particularly the case where past policies result in the building up of stocks (see section 7.4). An obvious example of this is British housing policy (or rather the various programs which can collectively be labelled housing policy), which has resulted in a severe misallocation of resources to and within the housing sector (see Cullingworth, 1979; Webster, 1980). However, any replacement housing policy proposals would have to take account both of the political problems in succeeding with such proposals in the face of opposition from the substantial numbers who benefit from the existing provisions, and of the fact that the bulk of the housing stock for some period to come has been determined by past policies. In other cases, such as income maintenance, which is a policy with flow rather than stock implications, the problems posed by existing policies to replacement policies are mainly the political ones of successfully following through proposals for change.

1.1.3 *Resource constraints on policy innovation*

Thirdly, policy succession should be expected to become an even more common feature of the policy process as a consequence of the relationship between the rate of sustainable economic growth and the financial implications of existing policy commitments. Rose and Peters (1978) point out that because the costs of public policy represent a greater proportion of the national product than they did twenty-five years ago, a much higher rate of growth of the national product would be required to sustain the historical rates of growth of public policy without cutting into the real take-home pay of citizens. Thus, even in the absence of the crowding of a particular policy space, the latitude for avoiding the problems of policy termination or policy succession by instituting a new program without cutting the old is considerably reduced. As a Swedish academic and politician has written, we face a 'pre-planned society' in which current politicians have little latitude except to try to pay for the commitments made by their predecessors (Tarschys, 1977). The alternative is to undertake the difficult task of terminating or replacing these commitments.

The figures in Table 1.1 make this point dramatically. In all of the countries shown, the growth of public expenditure expressed as a percentage of the national product was substantially higher in the 1970s than in the 1950s. However, this difference was almost entirely accounted for by the fact that by the 1970s public expenditure was much higher in relation to total national product than it had been in the 1950s: just to maintain the same rate of growth of public expenditure would absorb a much larger proportion of total national product. Thus a constant growth rate of public expenditure would absorb an increasingly large proportion of a constant rate of growth of the economy. In fact, economic growth rates fell in the late 1970s, leading to the growth of public expenditure being greater in absolute terms than the growth of the economy in most industrial countries in the 1970s.

Table 1.1 The limited future scope for innovation through increasing public expenditure

	Public expenditure as percentage of national product		Annual growth of public expenditure as percentage of total national product		Annual growth of public expenditure as percentage of annual growth of national product	
	1950s	*1970s*	*1950s*	*1970s*	*1950s*	*1970s*
USA	27	36	1.3	1.8	54	62
UK	34	50	1.2	2.2	52	122
France	33	41	2.6	3.6	80	100
West Germany	31	46	2.5	3.7	37	142
Italy	23	47	1.7	5.2	32	200
Sweden	27	54	1.8	3.8	55	224

Sources: OECD (1969) and OECD (1981).

The final column of Table 1.1 shows just how far governments in the 1970s have already mortgaged the future scope for innovations involving new public expenditure. Even allowing for the fact that much of the increase in public expenditure in the 1970s was in transfer payments, it is clearly impossible to continue for long along a path where the absolute increase in public expenditure is twice the absolute increase in the size of the economic product (as in Italy and Sweden in the 1970s). Only in the United States was the ratio of public expenditure increase to economic growth less than unity: public expenditure growth was 'only' 62 per cent of total economic growth (compared to total public expenditure being 36 per cent as a ratio to total national product). However, in the United States ideological pressures against new expenditure programs are higher than elsewhere.

There may continue to be scope for new programs involving regulation rather than expenditure (though the late 1970s also saw an anti-regulatory backlash on both sides of the Atlantic), but Western governments in the 1980s and 1990s will be too concerned with coping with the consequences of the commitments of the 1960s and 1970s to embark on new expenditure programs which do not involve replacing old ones.

1.1.4   *Exaggerated rumors of policy death*

If the concept of policy birth is decreasingly appropriate unless we allude to the genealogy of the policy then so too are recent rumors of policy death much exaggerated. Interest has recently been taken in the policy analysis literature in the concept of policy termination (Bardach, 1976; Biller, 1976; Behn, 1978; Brewer, 1978; Bothun and Comer, 1979; de Leon, 1978). This literature has noted the relative infrequency of policy termination and indeed justifies the interest in the topic by its infrequency and the need to specify the conditions for successful termination. However, the writers on policy termination have been obliged to note that terminated policies are often succeeded by replacement policies. One writer even discusses termination in terms of adjustment, and notes that 'termination signals a beginning as much as it does an end' (Brewer, 1978, p. 38). To emphasize policy termination in such situations is rather like talking about the death of the caterpillar without noting the birth of the butterfly. Concern about the conditions necessary to terminate an existing policy, program or organization is too narrow a focus for policy analysis, whether theoretical or applied, descriptive or normative. What is required is a framework for analyzing the process by which an existing program or organization is replaced by, or merged into, in whole or in part, a new program or organization. In section 1.2 and Chapter 2 we attempt to provide a framework which places policy termination in the context of other forms of policy change.

For the moment, we will merely point out that we are not arguing that termination never occurs (indeed, in Chapter 4 we argue that the major study of government organizational termination (Kaufman, 1976) has understated the extent of termination in practice). One example of a policy termination which occurred in Britain in 1981 was reported in *The Times* on 4 July:

> The Government has decided to give rams the freedom of the Welsh hills for the first time in 29 years. From the end of this month they will no longer need permission from a government inspector to mingle with ewes on unfenced land. The Control of Rams Regulations (Revocation) Regulations 1981 were quietly enacted by the Ministry of Agriculture yesterday in an internal campaign against the wasteful use of Civil Service manpower.
>
> It was decided in 1952 that legal controls were needed to prevent rams from one flock associating too closely with ewes of another. Shepherds cannot tell readily when their ewes are on heat, and the Government wanted to make sure the hills would not be populated by unofficial cross-bred animals.
>
> The ministry has now consulted many organizations, including the Government's Farm Animal Welfare Council, and decided that 'the industry's husbandry skills are now such that legislative controls are no longer necessary'.

1.2 Outcomes of the policy cycle

1.2.1 *Following through the policy cycle*

The concept of the policy cycle is a popular one in the study of public policy, especially as practised by political scientists. The by now rather extensive literature on the policy cycle concentrates on the stages through which any policy must go in order to become an operative policy, and the effects of differences in process on the nature

of the outcomes of the process. Whereas the economics literature in
policy analysis stresses normative concerns of optimizing the policy
decisions taken by government, the cycle literature examines the
process more descriptively and analytically to attempt to understand
why certain policies operate as they do. In general, the policy
cycle literature begins the process with the concept of agenda-setting
and proceeds through to evaluation or even policy termination. The
steps which are usually involved in the process are:

1   *Agenda-setting*, in which problems existing in the society are
perceived as requiring some actions by government to correct them,
and those problems are moved on to some sort of official agenda for
resolution.

2   *Policy formulation*, in which the policy instruments which will
be used to attempt to alleviate the difficulties perceived in the
environment are designed.

3   *Legitimation*, in which the policy instruments are accorded the
authority of the state, through some form of official action. This
action may be legislative, regulatory, or popular, for example,
initiatives or referenda.

4   *Organization*, in which some organizational structures are
developed to administer the policy. This may, of course, simply
involve assigning the policy to an existing organization rather than
creating an entirely new structure.

5   *Implementation*, in which the administrative structures attempt
to make the policy work in practice. This will involve linking legal
authority, budgeted funds, and the organization to the environment
in an attempt to produce a series of desired outputs.

6   *Evaluation*, in which the outputs and consequences of the
outputs are analyzed and assessed according to some criteria. These
criteria may arise from the original legitimation, or from the
modifications of the original policy intentions made in the organizational structures and the implementation stage.

7   *Termination*. Various procedures have been developed to make
organizations and other policymaking bodies consider termination
of organizations and functions more often than they might otherwise.

The principle virtue of the policy cycle as a focus of analysis is that
it stresses the dynamics of making public policies. Policies are seen as
arising from a complex, sequential cycle, rather than from the *ex
cathedra* rational analyses of policy pundits. This approach also

stresses the political nature of public policy, and the numerous potential points of access within the cycle for those who seek to influence the nature of the policy.

1.2.1.1 *Developing the policy cycle model*

'Begin at the beginning', the King said, gravely, 'and go on till you come to the end; then stop.'

Lewis Carroll, *Alice in Wonderland*

Although one of the advantages of the process or cycle model of policy as an analytical framework is that it does stress the dynamics of policy, writers on policy analysis appear reluctant to follow through the implications of going all the way round the cycle, that is, explaining what happens post-evaluation and the implications of previous trips round the cycle for the next trip. There is a natural tendency, for purposes of exposition, to treat the policy process in a linear form. Thus, May and Wildavsky (1978) have edited a book which takes us from Agenda Setting through Issue Analysis, Service Delivery Systems, Implementation and Evaluation on to Termination. (It should be emphasized that in their introduction May and Wildavsky do raise some of the points we discuss here.) However, the danger with this sequence of a policy arrow ending in termination or non-termination is that it may fail to explore other possible outcomes of the policy process, or the implications of the cyclical nature of the policy process.

1.2.1.2 *Following through after evaluation*

One natural place to begin a second or successive swings around the policy cycle is at the stage of evaluation. The literature on evaluation is by now very extensive, but tends to concentrate on evaluation itself rather than on its effects or on developments after the evaluation is completed. (There are, of course, exceptions; see, for example, Wurzburg, 1979; Davis and Salesin, 1979.) A major impact of evaluation should be, and often is, a modification of existing policies. But the policy cycle literature largely ignores these effects, except when the rare termination of programs is the result. The evaluation literature has done little to make its findings more directly applicable to the needs of organizations and programs seeking to improve performance. One major exception is Wildavsky's idea of the 'self-evaluating organization', in which evaluation is an on-going organizational function, not a traumatic imposition from the outside (Wildavsky, 1979, pp. 212–37 see also 8.3.2.2). Evaluation in such a setting is assumed to lead to change, and should not be taken as a threat to the continuation of the organization.

1.2.1.3   *Inadequacies of the incrementalist literature*

Our emphasis on the extent to which much policymaking is concerned with replacing existing policies might seem similar to the incrementalist argument that new policies are (and should) be derived from a limited range of comparisons with existing policy (see Lindblom, 1959, 1979; Braybrooke and Lindblom, 1963). However, we wish to distance ourselves from the incrementalist approach in two main ways, the first concerned with the nature as well as the size of the policy change, and the second with the extent to which incremental changes shape future policy choices.

Under the incrementalist approach, all policy changes short of wars, revolutions and crises are incremental in nature, almost by definition. Yet clearly not all changes even of the same 'size' (as measured, for example, by budget or other relevant indicator) are identical in terms of the qualitative nature of the change nor of the process required to achieve them. Figure 1.1 shows four types of 'incremental' change, all of the same 'size' in terms of increased, say, expenditure, but clearly differing in the political and administrative ease of introduction and implementation. Simply increasing the level of existing benefits as in type (b) will clearly be the easiest to accomplish, since it involves continuing to give the same type of benefit to the existing clientele. Introducing a new category of clientele as in (c) will clearly be easier than either innovation as in (a) or succession as in (d).

From the illustrations that they give of liberalizing benefits, extension of coverage, and alteration of policies, Braybrooke and Lindblom (1963, pp. 72–3) are clearly aware of the range of policy changes which can occur (see also Lindblom, 1979, p. 517). However, they fail to separate out the differing implications of small-scale innovations, add-ons to existing programs and alterations to existing programs. To be fair, it has to be pointed out that the synoptic-rationality models and similarly derived models (for example, economists' optimizing models) also ignore the distinction between *de novo* and succession policies, both for process and substance. Policy analysis has to move on from a sterile confrontation between a

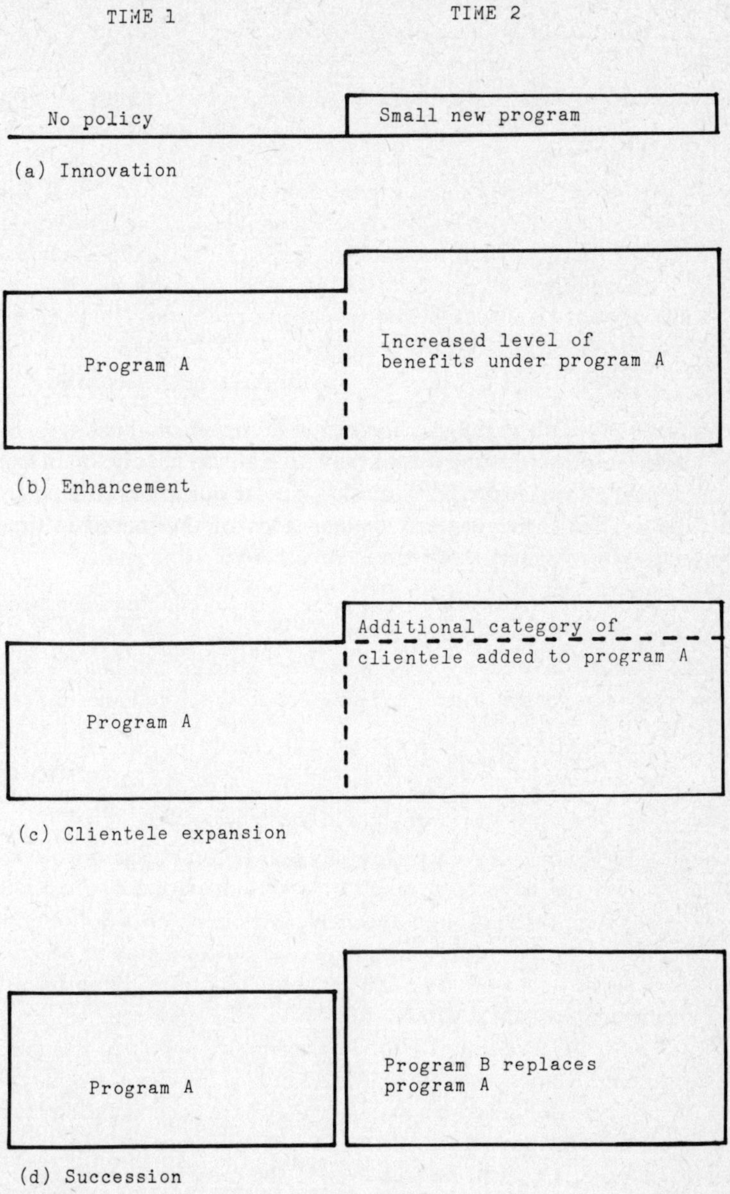

TIME 1   TIME 2

```
                              ┌──────────────────────────┐
No policy ────────────────────│   Small new program      │
                              └──────────────────────────┘
```
(a) Innovation

```
                              ┌───────────────────────────┐
┌─────────────────────────────┤                           │
│                     ┊        │                           │
│                     ┊        │   Increased level of      │
│    Program A        ┊        │   benefits under program A │
│                     ┊        │                           │
│                     ┊        │                           │
└─────────────────────┴────────┴───────────────────────────┘
```
(b) Enhancement

```
                     ┌─────────────────────────────────────┐
                     ┊ Additional category of ─ ─ ─ ─ ─ ─ ─ │
┌─────────────────────┊ clientele added to program A        │
│                     ┊                                      │
│    Program A        ┊                                      │
│                     ┊                                      │
│                     ┊                                      │
└─────────────────────┴──────────────────────────────────────┘
```
(c) Clientele expansion

```
                          ┌──────────────────────────────┐
                          │                              │
┌────────────────────┐    │                              │
│                    │    │   Program B replaces          │
│                    │    │   program A                   │
│    Program A       │    │                              │
│                    │    │                              │
└────────────────────┘    └──────────────────────────────┘
```
(d) Succession

Fig. 1.1 Four types of 'incremental' change

straw-man synoptic-rationality model and an incrementalist model which tells us little because it claims to embrace all normal policymaking. In Chapter 2, we explore the relationship between policy expansion (and decline) and various types of policy change, and in Chapter 5 we examine in detail the differences in process between policy innovation and policy succession.

In terms of description of policymaking, we share with the incrementalist writers an emphasis on the serial nature of policymaking, a view that problems are rarely completely 'solved' by policies, and a recognition of problem-shifting after the introduction of policies or even of policies themselves causing problems. However, we do not share the prescriptive complacency of Lindblom that the incrementalist strategy is the best way of meeting these problems:

> If he proceeds through a *succession* of incremental changes, he avoids serious lasting mistakes in several ways . . . he often can remedy a past error fairly quickly—more quickly than if policy proceeded through more distinct steps widely spaced in time (Braybrooke and Lindblom, 1963, p. 86).

Certainly, small steps rather than large ones do enable easier error rectification *if the error can be identified after the small step has been taken, and if there is a crude symmetry between introducing and reversing or replacing a policy*. These conditions frequently do not obtain.

The *threshold* nature of some policy effects has been noted by a number of critics of incrementalism (for example, Goodin and Waldner, 1979, pp. 5–11; Etzioni, 1976, Chapter 4). Adverse or beneficial consequences of a policy may only become apparent after a number of steps have been taken or a certain period of time has passed. In such cases, prompt and easy reversibility does not obtain.

Secondly, the reversibility argument overlooks the way in which a series of small steps over time can generate long-term commitments or entitlements which it can be difficult to reverse or replace (Rose and Peters, 1978; Behn, 1978). For example, a poorly designed income maintenance program will develop as many clients (or maybe more) as a well designed one, and once they have been made clients it will be difficult to return them to their former condition of independence. This will be true even if the proposed succession is concerned largely with adjustment of entitlements rather than cutting them back, but if cut-back or termination is an objective then it will become clear that there is an asymmetry between expansion and reduction of programs in terms of the political effort that has to go in to achieving them.

Thus, the stress of the incremental approach on the reversibility or mutability of policy if initial choices are found to be inappropriate overlooks the (variable) extent to which options exercised now will shape any future policy succession process. We are not arguing that all such long-term consequences of a policy should be taken into account when it is first proposed—we agree with Lindblom that this is merely impossible. However, the assumption in the incrementalist strategy that policies are reversible or readily adaptable can be shown to be invalid in important ways, and this suggests that at the time of design of the initial program thought should be given to the implications of alternative policy designs for future policy succession. We confront the difficulties of policy design for 'future cycle' policymaking in the concluding chapter of this book.

1.2.1.4   *The policy cycle model as a checklist*
It should be stressed that what is being argued here is not a simple hypothesis about the inevitability of inertia or difficulty of termination, but rather that the nature of the policy process involved in the transformation from one policy to another is shaped by earlier policies and the clientele, legislative and producer interests which have been built up around them. (In this book we use the term legislators to refer both to members of elected assemblies and to members of the executive who are involved in the legislative process.) Neither policy analysts nor politicial decision-makers have shown much explicit awareness of what might be the malleable variables which affect the outcome of the policy transformation process, or the extent to which their ability to affect these variables in future may be closed or widened by decisions taken now.

The process or policy cycle model is not only a useful framework within which to analyze public policy, but it is also a checklist of stages which the would-be policymaker would do well to bear in mind at the policy formulation stage if he or she is concerned to see his or her proposals result in desired outcomes rather than merely produce good ideas or score political points. Thus, writers, notably Pressman and Wildavsky (1973), have argued that potential problems of implementation must be taken into account when policies are designed. So, too, we would argue that the concept of policy succession is both a useful additional academic tool and an essential item on a policy formulator's checklist. This is true even for programs designed to be long-term, but it is even more important for policies where problems of policy succession are endemic, with the 're-entry' problem after pay control policy providing a particularly acute example.

1.2.2 *What happens at the end of the policy cycle?*

The approach adopted in this book moves away from a focus on the difficulties of policy termination or the inevitability of incrementalism towards attempting to identify the contingent features of policy succession as one of three possible outcomes of the policy cycle. Following the evaluation of an existing policy, either in a policy-analytical mode or through evaluation by clientele, producers or legislators, a policy can be terminated, replaced, or maintained. The subprocesses by which these three outcomes can be arrived at are summarized in Figure 1.2. It can be seen that there is more than one possible route to each of these outcomes.[1]

1.2.3 *Policy maintenance*

The first possible outcome of a policy cycle is *policy maintenance*, by which an existing policy, program, or organization is continued with the same task definition. (The relationship of policy maintenance to various forms of policy change will be explored further in Chapter 2.) Policy maintenance may result in a variety of manners:

1   *As a result of inertia.* In this case the existing policy is not evaluated or challenged. This does not imply contentment or quiescence, but merely a failure to make conscious choices about the policy or to have the issue of replacement placed on the political agenda.

2   *As a result of an explicit decision.* After evaluation, a dominant coalition may decide that the policy is acceptable and will legitimate the continuation of the existing policy. Again, this may not imply total contentment with the policy or organization, but merely the lack of alternative solutions offering the coalition apparently better outcomes.

3   *As a result of failed policy termination.* Here attempts at ending

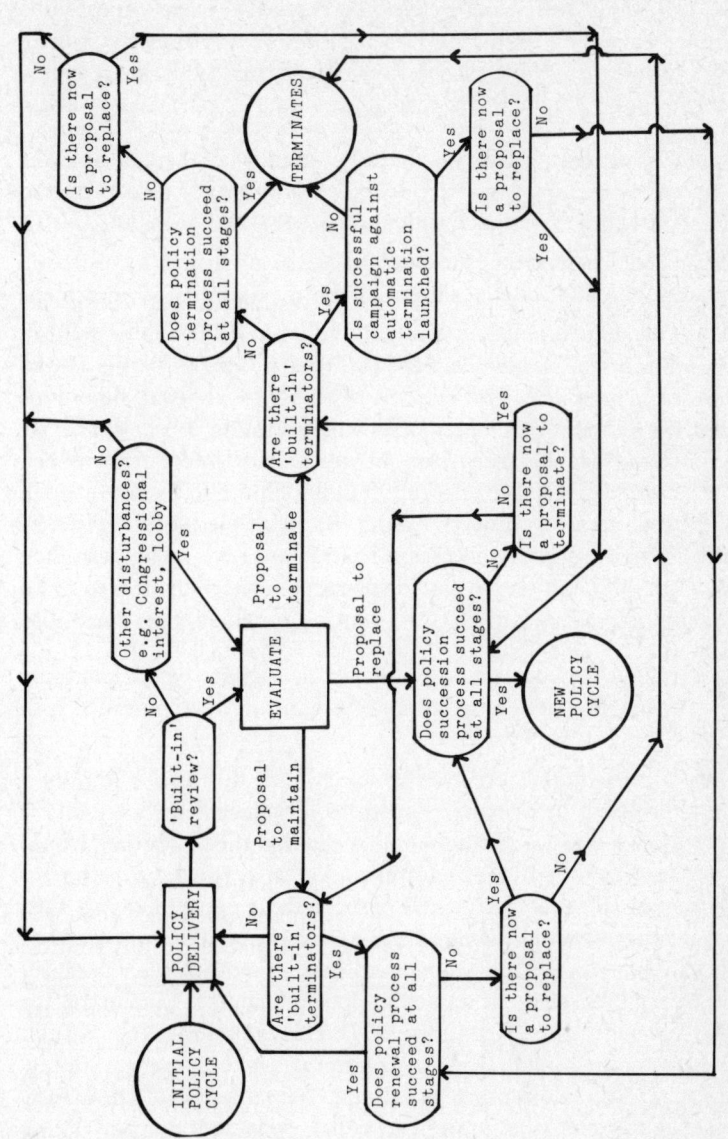

Fig. 1.2 Outcomes at the end of the policy cycle

the policy may have failed at the agenda-setting, decision-making or implementation stages. Through the lack of an authoritative termination, the policy will continue (except in cases where policy succession is proposed as an alternative when proposed policy termination seems likely to fail).

4   *As a result of failed policy succession.* Similarly, where attempts to replace the existing policy with the new policy fail then the obvious result will be the continuation of the existing policy (except in the unlikely case where policy termination is proposed as an alternative to failed policy succession).

It might be thought that we need to distinguish between policy maintenance, that is, the continuation of a program with no built-in time limitations, and policy renewal, that is, where a time-bound program is renewed. Our view is that policy renewal should be regarded as policy maintenance which results from deliberate decision. As can be seen from Figure 1.2, it differs from policy maintenance by inertia or default in that a failure to follow through the policy renewal process could, in principle, lead to policy termination (or policy succession if an alternative policy was then proposed). In practice, we would expect policy termination to be an unlikely outcome where there was strong initial support for policy renewal.

1.2.4   *Policy termination*

Policy termination, as used in this book, refers to the abolition of a policy, program or organization with no replacement being established. In most instances, this would mean that the policy area would be returned to the private sector as no longer requiring government attention or action (as in the case of the Welsh rams quoted in 1.1.4). As the policy termination literature itself has noted, terminations of policy are very rare, even where 'built-in' terminators, such as sunset laws, are in use (see the compendium of statements in Subcommittee on Intergovernmental Relations, 1977). This can reflect either the fact that no attempt is made to institute termination or a failure to follow the policy termination process to its final outcome. There are, in fact, powerful barriers that prevent a policy termination from taking place. There are many interests—clients, workers, Congressmen, etc.—so that it is difficult to form a coalition in favor of termination.

Termination can arise through several types of processes. The first is a purposive act of termination, in which a legislator or some other political actor must initiate a process to terminate a policy or program. There are relatively few programs for which the attempt to bring about a termination will be worthwhile politically. As programs serve clients and employ people to deliver those services, most attempts at termination are perceived as taking something from someone. The literature on the difficulties of organizing groups to support a 'public interest' of reducing taxation or eliminating less productive programs, as contrasted to the greater ease of organizing groups seeking certain privatized benefits, should illustrate the difficulties of organizing to bring about policy termination (Olson, 1965).

Termination can also result from 'built-in' terminators such as so-called sunset laws. The idea of these laws is that all programs would automatically be terminated unless specifically renewed by an act of the legislature. These acts have been most common in the American states, and have been tied specifically to regulatory bodies. But even with these automatic terminators, it is difficult actually to carry through a total termination. Legislatures rarely have the capacity to carry out systematic reviews of more than a few agencies, and others are likely to be allowed through by default. Even for agencies which are found to be ineffective, the same types of forces which would prevent a purposive termination will combine to attempt to have their particular policy or program renewed. The organizations which are threatened by a termination, by being existing entities, have greater political clout than would a potential organization that might come into being as a result of a new policy initiative. This may be particularly true because of the capacity for 'dynamic conservatism' in organizations, or the ability to respond to threats and to promise to do better (de Leon, 1978). Thus, while built-in terminators may serve as an opportunity to review existing organizations and to propose improvements in their policies and their administration of those programs, termination rarely results. Built-in terminators may be a more effective means of generating policy successions than policy terminations (see 8.3.2.4).

1.2.5 *Policy succession*

The final possible outcome at the end of a policy cycle is the one on which this book is focussed: *policy succession*, by which a previous

policy, program or organization is replaced by a 'new' one directed at
the same program and/or clientele. If policy succession is to be
achieved, rather than merely contemplated following an evaluation,
it will have to go through a distinctive process both of mobilizing
support to secure a decision and of devising an effective strategy to
ensure implementation of that decision. The source of the distinctive-
ness of the policy process to secure policy succession derives from the
fact that it is affected at each stage by the previous policy, with the
extent of this depending on the nature of the policy succession
attempted.

Thus, it can be seen that some form of evaluation is a necessary
condition for policy succession, but it is not by itself a sufficient
condition. Evaluation provides a trigger for decision, but can lead to
policy maintenance or policy termination. Much of the rest of the
book is concerned with analyzing the conditions under which policy
succession, rather than some other outcome, will occur at the end of
the policy cycle.

1.3   Policy, program and organizational succession

The concept of policy succession involves the idea of a policy process
with special characteristics, and it is necessary to go beyond general
reference to replacement or reform to analyze the different types of
policy succession which can occur and the likely success of each type
once initiated. Before doing so in Chapters 2 and 3, however, it is
worth discussing the relationship between policy and program
succession, and between policy succession and organizational
succession.

1.3.1   *Distinction between policy and program*

De Leon (1978, p. 279) distinguishes among functional termination,
policy termination, program termination and organizational termination. The concept of functional succession does not appear
meaningful, and in practice functional termination very rarely
occurs, except when exogenously determined. The now all but
complete termination of Britain's colonial function is an exceptional
example, as is the termination of the Panama Canal Corporation and
America's governance of the Panama Canal.

Governments may continue to be involved in a policy area and to pursue roughly the same policy goals but at the same time alter the specific programs used to attempt to deliver the policy. This would be an instance in which program succession occurred, but not policy succession. For example, placing the previous programs of Old Age Assistance, Aid to the Disabled and Aid to the Blind into the single Supplemental Security Income program in the United States reflects a continuing commitment to these categories of the needy, but alters the program structure for providing the aid. Different types of policy instruments might be used to achieve the same policy; for example, investment grants to industry might be replaced by tax reliefs of the same value directed towards the same purpose.

More rarely, governments might attempt to alter their basic policies, but still use the same programmatic structure. The Labour government in Britain in 1965 initiated a program of Office Development Permits (ODPs) designed to fulfil the policy need of reducing physical congestion in London (Wehrmann, 1978). However, even when this problem no longer existed, ODPs were retained as an instrument of regional policy.

It is often difficult to separate policy and program in practice, and changes in program normally involve some changes in policy if only at the margin. While bearing the conceptual distinction in mind, we will not always treat policy and program as requiring separate consideration. Insofar as policy and program can be distinguished, we might expect proposed replacements of policy to lead to a more highly politicized policy succession process than proposed program replacement. However, this will not be the case where service-providing interests are particularly important in the particular policy area and where they would be adversely affected by proposed program changes. For example, at least a part of the failure of negative income tax proposals in both the United States and the United Kingdom has been the resistance of employees administering social benefits. In this case, the programs would be significantly altered, while the purpose of the policy, income maintenance, would not be noticeably altered.

1.3.2 *Organizational change and policy succession*

Organizational change is more independent of both policy and program change than are program and policy change independent of each other. That is, organizations may change with the same programs existing and the same basic policies being pursued. Much of the history of the reorganization of government involves the shuffling of organizational structure with little effect on operating programs (Miles, 1977). Conversely, policies and programs may change and still be administered by the same organization. Organizations show a remarkable adaptability and persistance, although perhaps not as much as it is sometimes assumed (for example, by Kaufman, 1976), and may continue in existence in spite of remarkable changes in what they are doing. The development of the policies and programs of the Federal Trade Commission from being a trust-busting organization to being a consumer advocate may be indicative of organizational persistence in the face of pronounced policy succession. As we will show in Chapters 3 and 6, the implications of policy succession for organizational change will depend on the type of policy succession which takes place.

1.3.3 *Intergovernmental switches of responsibility*

One important area of interaction between organizational change and policy succession occurs when responsibility for administering a policy is transferred from one tier of government to another. There is a number of reasons why such a switch might be proposed, the most obvious being transfer to a level of government with a more adequate resource base and to a government whose geographical boundaries more closely conform to those appropriate for the function to be carried out, but whatever the original purpose, such switches are likely to have implications for policy succession.

One important British example of an intergovernmental transfer of responsibility was the removal in 1974 of water supply and sewage disposal from local authorities to central-government-appointed Regional Water Authorities (see Jordan, Richardson and Kimber, 1977). This involved not simply geographical consolidation into larger areas but functional consolidation of water conservation, supply, sewerage and reclamation (that is, all stages of the 'water cycle') according to a managerial concept of water management. This managerial ethos has been important in shaping the decision-making process of the new Regional Water Authorities (see Grey, 1982).

This large-scale reorganization—198 separate water supply authorities and over 1300 sewage authorities were merged into only ten Regional Water Authorities—illustrates an important difference between Britain and the United States in the ability of central government to carry out intergovernmental transfers of responsibility to secure policy succession: the water reorganization was carried out (with minor concessions) despite the opposition of the local authorities affected. In the United States, because of the existence of constitutional constraints at both federal and state level, such reorganizations, to be successful, are much more likely to require the consent or active cooperation of the governments affected. Given the characteristic of contemporary federalism that almost every policy area involves some activity by all levels of government, the shifts of functions among levels of government tend to be shifts of emphasis more than shifts of total responsibility. For example, although state and local governments retained primary responsibility for elementary and secondary education, the Federal government became more actively involved as a function of the Elementary and Secondary Education Act of 1965 (ESEA), and the formation of the cabinet level Department of Education in 1980. With the election of the Reagan administration, the emphasis is likely to return to subnational governments as education funding is reduced and the Department of Education abolished. It did make a difference that the Federal government was more involved in education: this was true not only in terms of the availability of funding but also in terms of the regulatory requirements for education for the handicapped and for bilingual education. From the perspective of the Federal (or state) government alternative methods of securing policy succession to sidestep constitutional constraints may have to be attempted in some cases, such as the establishment of quasi-nongovernmental organizations to administer social programs parallel to the existing governments.

1.4 The dynamics of policy change

When we set out to write this book, it was our intention to focus almost exclusively on policy succession. However, it seen became apparent that policy succession, and indeed the very reasons why it is such a significant and growing feature of policymaking, are best set in the context of an overview of the dynamics of public policy. One reason for doing this was that we found the previous literature on public policy did not provide adequate expositions of the types of policy change with which we wished to compare and contrast policy succession. Accordingly, while continuing to make policy succession the main analytical focus of the book, we also attempt to provide an overview of all forms of policy change.

In Chapter 2 we discuss the various forms which policy change can take and explore how far policy changes in practice conform to the 'ideal types' of policy innovation, policy succession, policy maintenance and policy termination which we have introduced in this chapter. In Chapter 3 we 'unpack' the concept of policy succession and explore the significance of different types of policy succession for the nature of the political debate surrounding policy change. In Chapter 4 we attempt to measure the extent to which various types of policy change have occurred and offer some evidence to support our assertion at the beginning of this chapter that policy succession is becoming an increasingly important feature of policymaking in Western countries. The distinctive features of the policy succession process when compared to the process involved in introducing completely new policies are examined in Chapter 5. Chapter 6 explores the implications of the truism that policy succession in the real world cannot be abstracted from the organizational setting in which changes have to be implemented. In Chapter 7 we explore the implications of policy changes which are not merely switches between programs of similar design but which involve changes in the nature of government outputs or delivery systems; in doing so we found ourselves obliged to be sidetracked into setting out a typology of variations in the form of government outputs and the implications of these for the nature of delivery systems, since we found no adequate existing classification from which we could move directly to discussing the implications of policy successions involving replacing one type of delivery system by another. In the concluding chapter, we explore one of the most important long-term implications of our argument that policy succession is of increasing significance: that decisions taken now will shape the process and form of future policy successions.

Note

1 For those who wish to take the concept of the 'policy game' literally, it can be noted that Figure 1.2 can be used as a board game. The only additions required are a die and as many counters as there are players. Each player requires to throw a six to start by moving to '"Built-in" review?'. At each yes/no decision box a throw of 1-3 determines that the player moves along

the 'yes' branch and a throw of 4-6 means a move along the 'no' branch. At the 'Evaluate' box, 1-2 requires a move along the 'Proposal to maintain' branch, 3-4 requires a move along the 'Proposal to replace' branch, and 5-6 along the 'Proposal to terminate' branch. The winner is whoever first reaches 'Terminates', 'New Policy Cycle' or 'Policy Delivery'. A variant of the game is to award extra points to Republicans who reach 'Terminates' and Democrats who reach 'New Policy Cycle'.

Chapter 2
TYPES OF POLICY CHANGE

2.1 All policy is policy change

All is flux, nothing stays still.

> Heraclitus, *Fragments of the Pre-Socratics*

THE problem for the analyst of policy change is not to distinguish between those policies which are undergoing change and those which are static in the sense of being delivered in a constant form at a constant volume. The reason for this is that few if any policies are static. All policy delivery is dynamic in the sense that it is rare indeed that in successive time periods exactly the same amount of service is delivered to exactly the same number of clients by organizations retaining the same structures and personnel. To this extent, policy is always changing, so we can never talk of one static policy being replaced by another static policy. Is it therefore possible to distinguish between policy succession and the type of 'continuous replacement' involved in developing programs and organizations? Clearly the problem is to distinguish among different kinds of policy change rather than between change and stasis.

A starting point in the classification of policy changes is that not all changes are of the same type, and that these different types of changes vary considerably in terms of the extent to which they involve purposive change, the extent to which substantial organizational change takes place, the extent to which changes in legislation are necessary, and the extent to which budgetary provision is changed. Some policy changes involve the entry of government into a new area of policy; others involve the replacement of existing policies (policy succession), minor changes to existing programs, or the termination of existing programs. Any given policy change is likely to involve elements of two or more of these types of policy change, so that it is very difficult to build up a useful simple descriptive classification of the complex mixtures of policy change which occur in practice (though for a useful attempt to develop a descriptive classification appropriate for British welfare policy, see Hall *et al.*, 1975, pp. 18–21)

Rather than abandon the attempt at analysis in the face of complex reality, we prefer to explore, initially in the form of ideal types, the different components of policy change. Our descriptive framework consists of locating individual policy changes on the dimensions between the polar ideal types. In 2.2 we will outline briefly the characteristics of each of four types of policy change; in 2.3 we will develop the distinction between types of policy change, and in 2.4 we will discuss how actual policy issues can be located in a framework consisting of these types of policy change.

This chapter accordingly spans the whole range of policy changes, but our purpose in doing so is to bring out the distinctive nature of changes involving policy succession.

2.2   Types of policy change

2.2.1   *Characteristics of types of policy change*

Any policy change in practice will contain elements of one or more of four ideal types of change: policy innovation, policy succession, policy maintenance and termination. Below we outline briefly the characteristics of each type, while Table 2.1 compares all four types in terms of organizational change and change in legislation and budgetary provision.

2.2.2   *Policy innovation*

In its ideal type form, policy innovation involves the entry of government into an activity in which it has not previously been involved. Such a change is purposive in nature, since governments normally do not enter into new fields of activity by accident. Because the area of activity is completely new, there is no previous organization, laws or budgetary provision. All these have to be established from scratch. In its pure form, policy innovation arguably rarely occurs in late-twentieth-century government. Even early-twentieth-century welfare provisions in Britain could be said to have their antecedents in Elizabethan poor law. The point in isolating policy innovation as a separate category is that the problems involved in establishing a completely new policy, with its associated organizational, legal and budgetary structures are different from those involved in the other types of policy change, all of which involve changes to already existing structures.

Table 2.1   Characteristics of innovation, succession, maintenance and termination

Policy innovation	Policy succession	Policy maintenance	Policy termination
Purposive	Purposive	Adaptive	Purposive
No existing organization	At least one organization subject to change	No purposive (that is, policy-oriented) organizational change (changes consequential in workload, for managerial reasons, etc.)	Existing organization may be terminated
No existing law	Some law superceded	No *change* in law	All relevant legislation repealed
No previous expenditure	Some existing expenditure	Continuing budgetary item	All expenditure ceases

2.2.3   *Policy succession*

Policy succession involves the purposive replacement of existing policies by others in the same area of activity. The replacement of policies may seem to contain novel elements, but, in contrast to policy innovation, policy succession in its ideal type form does not involve government engaging in a new field of activity. While, as we will be showing in subsequent chapters, the changes involved in policy succession are often complex and difficult, they are changes to existing arrangements rather than the establishment of completely new areas of policy.

2.2.4   *Policy maintenance*

Policy maintenance characterizes the 'continuous replacement' type of change referred to earlier. 'Established programs' are not fixed in the sense of being concerned with the same or the same number of clients, even where there is no change in the law (though legislative renewal may be required). Adaptive changes in the form of changes in the number of clientele eligible (for example, for unemployment benefit) or adjustments in the level of benefits to compensate for inflation or improved standards of living do not involve new purposes or the replacement of the existing policy but adjustments of program output to conform to the original policy objectives.

Policy maintenance is not necessarily a purely passive response by government: legislative and budgetary authorization may need to be adjusted consequential to other changes (for example, rules governing eligibility for a benefit which are tied to receipt of other benefits will have to be altered if the second benefit is itself replaced). The analogy is with the maintenance of a factory production line; if an active maintenance program is not conducted, production will slow or come to a halt, quality will fall, and disputes may break out. Further, such maintenance has to be conducted in the context of fluctuating demands on the production line (delivery system). Large and uncertain fluctuations in demographic or economic trends can pose acute dilemmas for governments simply concerned with the long-run maintenance of an existing program.

While in one sense policy maintenance is a less significant type of change than the new initiatives associated with innovation or the upheaval associated with succession, the adaptive changes required can involve larger changes in the volume of provision than either innovation or succession: payments under the unemployment benefit program in Britain rose (in 1980 prices) from £653m in 1979–80 to £1007m in 1980–1 without there being any innovation or succession of the program.

2.2.5 *Policy termination*

Policy termination in its ideal type form is the mirror image of policy innovation. It involves the complete winding down of the organizational structure, the cancellation of relevant laws, and the complete cessation of public expenditure on the policy. For reasons already discussed, policy termination in its ideal type form rarely occurs in practice (see 1.1.4, 1.2.4). There is, however, a steady trickle of minor terminations of obsolete legal provisions in Britain resulting from the law review process—the Civil Government (Scotland) Bill proposed the repealing of the following offences:

the discharging of a steam trumpet without the permission of the local authority; the carrying of a picture on horseback; the washing of a window by a woman whilst standing on the window sill; and the doing of its duty by a bull or stallion alfresco (letter to *The Times*, 7 December 1981).

Despite the rare occurrence of major terminations, it is useful and necessary to include termination in an overall framework, since many policy changes do involve running down programs or eliminating certain elements of them.

2.3 The dimensions of policy change

When we move from an ideal type classification to a working framework which will help us to describe policies in practice, we have to recognize that few, if any, issues or policies conform to any of these ideal types. Issues can, however, be characterized in terms of the extent to which they do have attributes of the various ideal types. Before indicating how an issue can be located in terms of all four ideal types, we will discuss how real issues vary in the extent to which they have the attributes of any given pair of ideal types. In other words, any given issue can be located on a dimension on which the ideal types form the polar extremes. In this way, we can use the ideal types not as sterile abstract categorization but as means of illuminating important differences in real issues. Policy issues range so widely in such a variety of different ways that only by using a structured framework of concepts can we impose conceptual order on the apparent chaos.

2.3.1 *Succession-innovation*

Succession and innovation have in common that both are purposive attempts to make major changes. Their major difference is that innovation seeks a change involving a new government activity, while succession seeks to replace existing activities (themselves the products of earlier innovations and successions). In practice, policy change designed to replace an existing policy will invariably embody some innovative feature (a new technique not previously employed by government, an addition to the clientele served, etc.); an apparently dramatic new initiative by government may partially overlap with previous provisions with a history of centuries behind them. The extent of innovation and succession in each case will vary, thus

enabling us to locate each on a dimension between the two ideal
types, as in Figure 2.1.

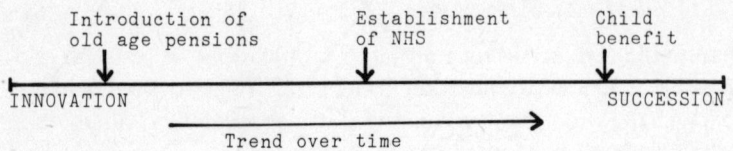

Fig. 2.1 The succession-innovation dimension

For example, the introduction of old age pensions in Britain in
1908 was not the first provision for the indigent elderly, but it was the
first systematic provision targeted at the elderly as a whole. Thus, it
lies at the innovation end of the spectrum. The formation of the
British National Health Service in 1948 was a bold initiative,
involving the nationalization of all hospitals; however, much of the
provision was already by the state through municipalities, so the
NHS lies nearer the middle of the spectrum.

This spectrum does not merely represent a static ordering on which
individual issues can be ranked, but can be used to portray a *trend
over time* whereby policies have increasingly incorporated greater
elements of succession. In other words, our argument is not that
contemporary policy issues conform to the succession ideal type and
never incorporate any innovation, nor that succession never occurred
in earlier periods, but that the *relative* distribution of policy changes
is now more heavily biased towards the succession end of the
innovation-succession spectrum, with few changes being highly
innovative; this is illustrated in Figure 2.2. Another way of looking at
the same phenomenon is to look at how many organizational changes
in different time periods are primarily innovative or largely concerned
with succession; the trend towards more changes involving succession is illustrated in Figure 2.3.

The relative distribution over time of innovation and succession
may vary, however, in different policy areas. The 1970s were years of
succession and even termination for social policies in the United
States, while for energy and environmental policy they were years of
significant innovations. Once succession has become the dominant
form of policymaking, further bursts of innovation are not pre-
cluded. The policy successions in social policy in the 1940s and 1950s

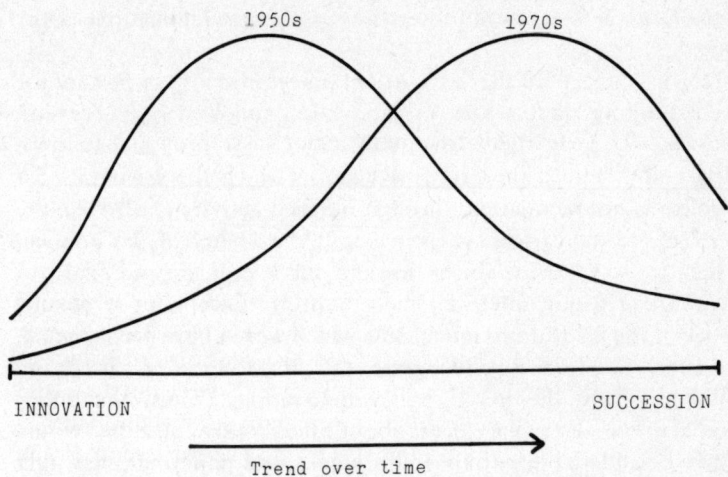

Fig. 2.2 The trend towards policy changes involving a greater element of succession

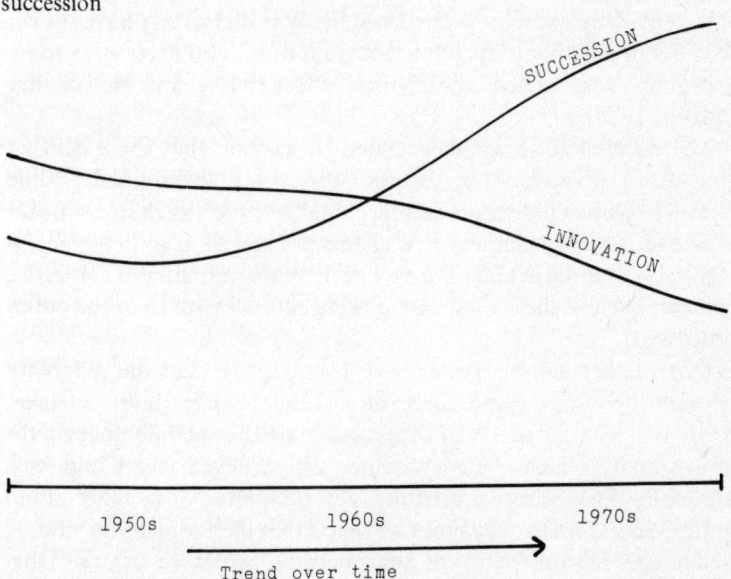

Fig. 2.3 The trend towards the greater significance of organizational succession
Note: The shape of the curves is based on the numbers of organizational initiations and successions in the United States analyzed in detail in section 4.2.1

in the United States were followed by significant innovations in the 1960s.

Downs' concept of the 'issue-attention cycle' is also important for understanding these waves of innovation followed by succession (Downs, 1972). He argues that many major social programs follow a cycle going from a pre-problem stage in which the existence of a problem is not recognized, through frenzied activity to alleviate the problem, to increasing cynicism about the ability of the political system to 'solve' the problem through public policies, and finally to government losing interest almost entirely. Except for a passing notice of the institutions and clients which would have been created, however, he does not recognize the importance of succession following from the initial policy innovations. Thus, the policy modifications and replacements about which we are concerned would not be considered important in his model, and policymaking would be assumed to have been stopped after the initial flurry of activity. We would not, of course, accept such a viewpoint, and even his example of the environmental movement and the War on Poverty have shown considerable elaboration after their initiation, and even after some questions were raised about their effectiveness and desirability (Aaron, 1978).

The discussion so far has tended to assume that the extent of innovation or succession can be objectively determined. While certain objective indicators can be employed, such as changes in size of budget and whether any new clients are served, it is important to recognize that the extent of 'innovation' is also a matter of subjective perceptions and these may vary among actors involved in the policy process.

One of the major arguments of this book is that the difference between innovation and succession is not merely about *outcomes* relative to what existed previously, but is also about differences in the *processes* by which these outcomes are achieved (see Chapter 5, especially 5.6). When presenting our preliminary thoughts about policy succession to colleagues we found that they sometimes labored under the misapprehension that because we were arguing that replacement of policies is now more important than the introduction of completely new policies we were therefore also arguing that policymaking now involved less upheaval. On the contrary, while there are difficulties facing both policy innovation and policy succession, we show in Chapter 5 that policy succession faces special difficulties because of the existence of earlier policies, organizations and clients. Indeed, it is only where there are existing policies that there is anything within government to upheave!

2.3.2 *Maintenance-succession*

2.3.2.1 *Similarities and differences between succession and maintenance*

Both succession and maintenance start from a base of existing laws, organizations and expenditures. Both may involve substantial changes from that base in terms of public policy delivered, since, as we pointed out in section 2.2.4, policy maintenance is not a static activity. However, the succession and maintenance changes differ in their policy significance. The major difference is that maintenance involves continuation of existing characteristics, perhaps on a different scale and with some consequential modifications, whereas succession involves the replacement of the characteristics by others designed to achieve the same or related purposes. To use the algebraic analogy developed more fully in the appendix to this chapter, maintenance changes involve changing values of the coefficients attached to the components (characteristics) in an equation describing a program, whereas succession involves redefining the components.

Changes involving a high degree of policy succession will normally involve legislation or an order made under legislation. Maintenance is less likely to involve legislation, apart from renewal of mandate or budgeting authorization.

2.3.2.2 *Consequential and incidental change*

Changes in the way an individual program is delivered may arise from changes which are not directed at the program concerned. Such consequential changes may arise from changes in how other programs are defined, or from changes in the general social and economic environment of the program.

Two types of consequential implications can arise when eligibility for one program is defined in terms of the characteristics of another. For example, welfare recipients in the United States are automatically eligible for assistance under Medicaid, so if the definition of those eligible for welfare is altered, the number of those benefiting under Medicaid will automatically change without any alteration to

how the program is defined. In other cases where eligibility is defined
in terms of those labelled by a different program, the alterations to the
definition of that category may necessitate the ending of the use of the
external definition of eligibility and its replacement by an internally
defined one if the program is to continue to serve its original purpose.

From the perspective of those involved in delivering a program, the
program may seem to undergo substantial change in how it is
organized without there being any change in the eligible clientele or
form of policy output. Social and technological changes not directly
related to program characteristics may have important unforeseen
implications for program deliverers. For example, developments
in computing and office technology are likely to lead to important
changes in the tasks carried out by public officials and to the number
of officials required for program delivery. Another type of change,
more directly a consequence of public policy, would be where
expansion of education led to an upsurge in the paper qualifications
obtained by school leavers. If the public service uses these paper
qualifications as a 'filtering' device to select candidates, it may
increase its minimum entry requirements to assure that entrants will
come from the same percentage band based on intelligence
rankings—or simply to ease the task of sifting candidates (see Hirsch,
1976, pp. 45–9). Although important from the perspective of policy
deliverers managing their programs, such consequential changes lie
much closer to the maintenance than the succession end of the
spectrum.

Social, economic and demographic changes may have important
consequences for the number of people eligible to benefit under a
program, and these growth or decline implications are explored in the
context of the innovation-maintenance dimension (2.3.4.7) and
maintenance-termination dimensions (2.3.5.3).

Another form of consequential impact on an existing program can
arise through incidental policy succession (examined further in 3.7),
where a new or replacement program in a related aspect of public
policy has spillover effects on the existing program—for example, by
providing an alternative program for beneficiaries of the existing
program to participate in. An example of this is the growth of various
training or work experience programs in Britain directed at those
beyond the minimum school-leaving age of sixteen. Because a
payment is made to young people undergoing such training, there is
some incentive to be enrolled in such programs rather than take

conventional routes of staying on at school or enrolling independently at further education colleges. Thus a set of programs labelled as 'manpower' programs is having important spillover effects on 'education' programs.

2.3.2.3 *The position of different types of policy succession*

In Chapter 3 we will explore in detail the implications for process and substance of different types of policy succession. Here we are simply concerned to show how they vary in terms of their position on the maintenance-succession dimension. These types of policy succession also involve varying amounts of innovation and termination.

Closest to the maintenance end of the dimension are those policy successions which are largely cosmetic, perhaps involving organizational restructuring and relabelling of the program, but essentially continuing to deliver the same type of policy output to a similarly defined target group.

Of the types of substantive policy succession, linear succession lies most clearly close to the maintenance end because the 'new' program is concerned with similar objectives and a similar clientele, though perhaps a clientele defined on a different form. Less straightforward replacements occur with policy consolidation (when one or more programs are merged), and policy splitting (when an existing program is split into two or more 'new' programs). Most replacements do not match the old programs end-to-end in a linear fashion, and non-linear successions can vary considerably in the extent to which elements of the original program are carried forward into the replacement program without alterations. Finally, policy changes in practice frequently incorporate a number of types of policy succession in a complex manner. In terms of the implications for process, explored further in Chapter 3, we would expect that changes closer to the succession end of the spectrum would be most highly politicized and most vulnerable to failures at the implementation stage.

2.3.3 *Succession-termination*

Both succession and termination policy changes start from a basis of existing laws, organizations and expenditure and have to engage in purposive action to overcome the inertia of policy maintenance—few policies self-destruct. The concept of termination emphasizes an ending to existing policy, whereas succession emphasizes change and replacement. However, from the perspective of existing clients and organizations some successions may appear to be terminations. For this reason, succession and termination may face similar problems in the policy process. Indeed, issues are in practice likely to combine elements of both. At the succession end of the spectrum, the emphasis is on the replacement in different form of features corresponding to the previous program. At the termination end, there is no replacement of any aspect of the program.

The succession-termination dimension differs from the maintenance-termination dimension discussed in 2.3.5 in that all aspects of the program are either replaced or terminated, whereas on the maintenance-termination dimension those aspects of the program which are not cut-back or terminated remain in identical form (of course, real issues may combine features of both dimensions). Thus, we would expect a change of similar size (in terms of cut-back in, say, budget or personnel) to be much more complex and controversial for issues lying on the succession-termination dimension compared to the maintenance-termination dimension.

One type of policy succession is unique in that it appears at two different points on the succession-termination spectrum. Where there is a policy 'hiatus' between a termination of a program and a subsequent replacement program being introduced, we have two points at opposite ends of the spectrum separated by time (see 3.2.5). From the perspective of policy actors, the initial termination may seem very like a complete and permanent termination, though in the case of cyclical policy hiatus, where there have been recurring cycles of terminations followed by reintroductions, historical precedent might suggest otherwise.

2.3.4   *Innovation-maintenance*

2.3.4.1   *Innovation and other forms of policy growth*
Policy changes involving the expansion of government activity can range from the establishment of a completely new program administered by a new agency to an increase in the number of standard units of output produced by a long-established agency. In between is a range of types of growth which fall short of full innovation of a completely new program, but do involve the introduction of new elements. These different kinds of policy growth are located on the

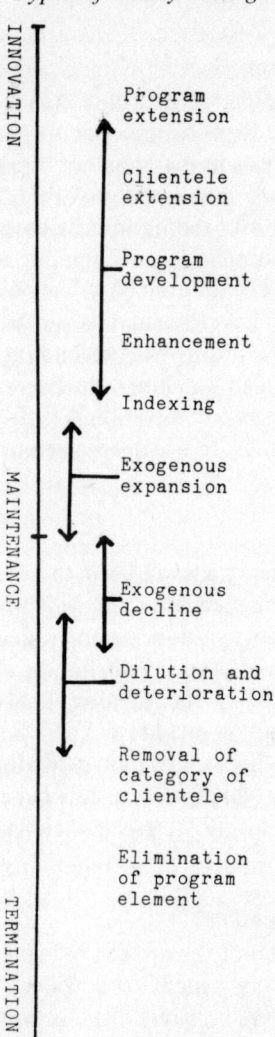

Fig. 2.4 Expansion and reduction of programs

innovation-maintenance dimension in Figure 2.4, which also illustrates the maintenance-termination dimension discussed in 2.3.5.

These different kinds of policy growth are not mutually exclusive (a policy change may incorporate a number of different aspects of growth, and it may be ambiguous which 'type' of growth is involved), nor do they rank in a neatly ordinal fashion on the innovation-maintenance dimension. Further, highly innovative changes may involve a lower volume of change in output as measured, for example, by increases in public expenditure. But the general point is clear: ranking on the innovation-maintenance dimension has practical implications for the ease of securing growth. It is clearly much easier to increase the size of an existing unit of output or the number of standard units of output than it is to enter into a new field of activity. In terms of the historical evolution of public policies, there is also the point that insofar as government has already tackled the easier policies in terms of the 'means-ends technology' required to deliver policies to secure specified outcomes, the contemporary innovations are likely to involve more complex and 'softer' policy technology than established programs to which adjustments are being made (see Rose, 1981).

2.3.4.2 *Program extension*
Program extension refers to the addition to an existing program of an additional benefit (or regulation) to be delivered to the clients of the existing program. Because it does involve a new activity, it lies close to the innovation end of the spectrum, but the new activity is likely to have close similarities to the existing provisions (for example, extending injury benefit to include sickness benefit) in terms of the techniques of policy delivery. Program extension of this sort is one of the classic methods by which welfare state benefits grew in a number of countries (see Heclo, 1974; Heidenheimer, Heclo and Adams, 1975).

2.3.4.3 *Clientele extension*
Another classic method of the growth of state provision was by the extension of an existing benefit to a wider range of clients than previously. This involves no new policy technology, simply replicating the current delivery system on a larger scale (though once size of clientele has expanded beyond a certain point this may trigger the introduction of a new policy technology more appropriate for large-scale delivery).

2.3.4.4 *Program development*
While the delivery structures of some innovatory programs, particularly those involving cash benefits, may come into operation at a

single date for all areas and all clients, other types of program, particularly those which require the establishment of a large number of specialized locally-based facilities for service delivery, may come into operation over an extended period of time, with geographical coverage gradually being increased. Insofar as the program originally envisaged gradual extension to secure complete coverage, then development of this sort could be said to involve 'maintaining' the program as already set out. However, because active effort is often required to maintain the impetus of program development, it involves more than simply policy maintenance. Universal program coverage may never be achieved because of recalcitrance by subnational governments responsible for implementation, because of reductions in planned capital expenditure, or because a replacement program is introduced before the original program achieved full coverage. These problems may be further compounded when we are concerned with the 'continuing implementation' of a program which is itself the product of a policy succession (see 5.4.5).

From the perspective of an area not previously covered by the program, its introduction may be innovatory, but the experience of public delivery elsewhere means that program development involves replication rather than pure innovation.

2.3.4.5 *Enhancement*
Enhancement refers to an explicit decision to improve the standard or intensity of an existing provision. No new clients or provisions are involved. The implications for existing delivery organizations will vary according to the nature of the program which is being improved. In the case of cash benefits, the fact that a higher benefit is being paid provides no justification for any organizational expansion, but in the case of service programs (for example, social work) or regulation enhancement may only be possible through increasing personnel.

The ambiguity of the classification of types of expansion used here can be illustrated by the raising of the minimum school leaving age in Britain in 1972. From one perspective, this involved the extension of compulsory schooling for a further one year (program extension); from another it represented the expansion of schooling for fifteen-sixteen year olds from those already receiving it to all in that age group (program development); from the perspective of individual pupils, it represented enhancement of their schooling (not necessarily recognized by all of them as a good).

2.3.4.6 *Indexing*

In an era of inflation, decisions to index benefits either by setting up
an automatic adjustment system or by a series of *ad hoc* upratings can
involve greater long-term implications for the nominal cost of a
program than all the other types of expansion so far considered.
Indexing to some measure of prices is concerned simply with
'maintaining' the real value of a benefit relative to what it can buy.
Where indexing is to the level of wages (either an average or related to
the post previously held) the intention is to allow the recipient to
benefit from general expansion in the economy (if that occurs).
Where double-indexing is introduced (that is, indexing to both
salary levels and the price level), the resulting double-counting of
inflation amounts to under-the-counter enhancement. From 1972
onwards, Social Security benefits in the United States have been
increased both as average wages increased through inflation, and as
inflation affected the benefits for those already retired (Munnell,
1977, pp. 33–6); this resulted in a real improvement in the position of
the retired and future retirees, and created a substantial drain on the
already threatened Social Security Trust Fund (see 4.3.2). In Britain
in the 1970s, some cash benefits were indexed to wages or prices,
whichever rose the faster in any given year, thus ensuring that in the
medium term benefits rose faster than either; this situation was ended
in 1979, when future indexation was confined to increases in prices.

The reciprocal device of indexation of benefits is the indexation of
taxation levels based on nominal amounts, of which the most
politically sensitive are income tax allowances. From the perspective
of the taxpayer, failure to index is undercover enhancement of the
government's extractive role. From the perspective of the government, indexation, particularly at a time of high inflation combined
with economic decline, represents an erosion of its taxable base.

2.3.4.7 *Exogenous expansion*

Each of the previous types of expansion referred to explicit decisions
by government to expand the scope of an existing provision or, in the
case of indexing, at least to maintain it in real terms. However,
program expansion can be triggered by changes outside the immediate control of government, such as an increase in the size of a
problem, particularly an exogenous increase in the size of the
potential clientele. In such cases, expansion of the program is needed
simply to maintain the level of output delivered to each client. As the

increase in those relying on income-maintenance programs illustrates, such exogenously generated increases in clientele can be far
larger in scale than those arising from explicit decisions to expand the
eligible clientele. Such increases can cause very serious problems for
managers of universal or entitlement programs, since the element of
discretion involved in the types of expansion is absent (though where
there is no automatic indexation, declines in the real value of a benefit
can be allowed to compensate). This task is made more difficult by the
coincidence of increased claimants for cash benefits and social work
with a reduction in economic growth to fund them.

Exogenous fluctuations in demand may arise from other factors,
such as demographic profiles. Demographic fluctuations can cause
particular problems, since expansion of a program to meet perhaps
temporary and uncertain changes in potential clientele imposes
accelerator effects in terms of training delivery personnel and
building capital facilities, perhaps to see a reverse accelerator effect
occurring in a few years. In a period of expansion in the 1960s and
early 1970s claims for increased budgetary allocations to cope with
exogenous growth even for non-entitlement programs were likely to
be treated with sympathy, since even if a future down-turn was
anticipated, slack resources could be used to allow enhancement of
the unit level of output. In the atmosphere of retrenchment of the
early 1980s, the first thought may be of how to make compensating
adjustments: exogenous growth may trigger the difficult quest to
institute the types of cut-backs and termination discussed in the next
section.

2.3.5   *Maintenance-termination*

2.3.5.1   *The asymmetry between expansion and contraction*
In one sense, the spectrum between maintenance and termination is
the mirror image of the spectrum between innovation and maintenance, with purposive wholesale change (in this case complete
elimination of policy) at one end, and inertial policy maintenance at
the other (see Figure 2.4). However, the maintenance-termination
spectrum differs from the innovation-maintenance spectrum in one
important feature which makes the process of securing policy
changes involving a high degree of termination quite different from
that required to produce innovation. Both maintenance and termination start with the pre-existence of a set of organizations, law and

budgetary allocations, which have associated with them a set of producer and clientele interests which are likely to be major actors in the policy process. These interests, themselves the product of existing policy, are not in existence, or structured in the same way, in the case of innovation. Furthermore, in the case of anything except pure maintenance, the benefits available to either producers or consumers, or both, are under threat to an even greater extent than in the case of policy succession. Typically, decision-makers wishing to secure a cut-back in a program will have to devote substantially more political resources to securing a cut-back of a given size than to secure an increase of the same size, though the likelihood of their succeeding in either case will depend on the general budgetary climate at the time.

2.3.5.2 *Cut-back and termination*

The distinction between the maintenance and termination ends of the maintenance-termination spectrum is that at the maintenance end the response to perceived inadequacies of existing policy is by marginal *adjustments to the program*; termination seeks to deal with in-adequacies by *ending the policy*.

There is a range of different types of cut-backs and termination, and the position of a given proposal or outcome on the maintenance-termination dimension varies both between and within types. In general, we reserve the term cut-back to refer to reductions in scale, for example, reduction in numbers of a given category of client or level of benefit; and termination to refer to the elimination of complete programs or program elements. Of course, the distinction may often be difficult to maintain, and will be partly dependent on the level of aggregation at which a program is observed. What is merely a cut-back in school enrolment at county level may entail the complete closure of a school in a small community. Thus cut-backs in programs delivered through a large number of community-based facilities will typically generate more widespread political controversy and have 'termination' features, contrasted with programs delivered through large-scale units with only indirect contact with clients.

In such cases, the scale of reduction in provision actually achieved will depend on the location of responsibility for deciding which facilities will be closed: the more locally based the decision about the fate of individual facilities, particularly when any budgetary allocations from above are related to volume of provision rather than level of demand, then the less chance of the total number of closures corresponding to the overall decline. On the other hand, a more centralized decision-making structure may become overwhelmed with the volume of representations relating to individual facilities. Astute central bodies seeking to implement cuts will therefore seek to delegate responsibility for decisions about closure of individual facilities to a lower level, but will seek to set budgetary constraints which will make termination decisions inevitable.

2.3.5.3 *Exogenous decline*

The type of decremental change closest to the maintenance end of the spectrum is that triggered by *exogenous decline*, though of course, the scale of decline both of clients and of the program may vary considerably. Where an exogenous increase in demand for a particular policy occurs (for example, increase in school population; increase in unemployed claiming benefit) the government agency responsible for the delivery program will obviously take the initiative in putting in a bid for increased finance, and in some cases (especially cash benefits) the government may be under a legal obligation to provide the increased outlay. However, in the case of a decline in exogenous demand, there are both practical and political considerations which tend to ensure that reductions in the program corresponding to reductions in demand are not realized.

In terms of practical considerations, many programs are delivered through units which either cannot logically be reduced through subdivision (you cannot sack half a man, or sell off half a fire engine) or which are best delivered through units of a minimum optimum size. This is the phenomenon labelled by Levine (1978) as 'the paradox of irreducible wholes': some units either have to be maintained fully in operation or closed down completely; it may not be feasible simply to reduce provision even or especially by a small proportion, even when there is a reduction in demand. This paradox will apply particularly in the short term (in the longer term, for example, catchment areas can be redrawn) and particularly to programs delivered through a large number of relatively small locally based facilities with internal specialization of skills or equipment.

When an exogenous increase in demand occurs, the agency responsible for delivering the program will draw attention to the need to inject additional resources. However, in the case of a exogenous decline in demand, the agency cannot be relied on to point out the full scope of potential savings, especially in staff costs. Where a service facing exogenous decline is delivered through a local authority or other grant-aided agency, some aspects of the adjustment entailed between centre and locality may be dealt with automatically; for example, where the number of school-age children is reflected in the formula for grant distribution. Other aspects of the adjustment, such as closures of colleges engaged in teacher training, may require negotiation and discussion. This further illustrates the point that what is exogenous decline at macro-level may entail complete termination at the level of the facility.

Where adjustment to decline in exogenous demand is not automatic the initiative for pointing out the full scope of potential savings will be more likely to rest with the central budget agency, such as OMB or HM Treasury than with the agency or authority actually delivering the service. In the words of a report from the British government's 'think tank', the Central Policy Review Staff:

> It will require special vigilance, for example through adequate and in depth policy analysis or through monitoring of standards to ensure that
> (i) the scope for adjustment, after making allowance for the genuine constraints, is not understated;
> (ii) advantage is taken of worthwhile opportunities for temporary redeployment, and that, when necessary and prudent, steps are taken as early as possible to achieve long-term redeployment of assets and personnel;
> (iii) resources are not misallocated by default, i.e. they should not 'automatically' accrue to the improvement of a particular service as a result of the accident of its having fewer clients unless this is consistent with overall priorities (CPRS, 1977, p. 52).

Thus, even where there is a decrease in 'demand' for a particular output, there will be far more resistance to a corresponding decrease in expenditure or, particularly, public employment, than would be the case for expansion. When there is a fall in eligible clientele, producer interests in particular will argue that the existing budgeting allocation should be largely maintained to allow an enhanced provision for the remaining clientele. Alternatively they may argue for elements of succession in the form of a replacement program to absorb 'surplus' resources (for example, teachers switching from teaching children to adult education). This is especially likely to be true of service delivery rather than transfer programs, which are more easy to define in terms of desired unit of output, and are likely to be delivered by less-skilled public employees, with a low degree of professionalization (and thus claims to define 'service' delivery criteria) and a higher degree of staff turnover, reducing the need for compulsory redundancies. In service-delivery programs, personnel costs are also a much higher proportion of the total so that no substantial cuts in budget can be achieved without reducing staff. Hence, greater mobilization by service-delivery personnel compared to transfer program personnel to campaign against cuts in total budget allocation reflects both an accurate perception of the threat and also a greater claim to involvement in defining the criteria for service delivery.

The CPRS report already referred to neatly sets out in the context of demographic change why cuts in resources when the size of eligible clientele falls are not proportionate to the increases which occurred when clientele expanded:

(i) Long life assets—in particular buildings and trained manpower—cannot be quickly shed or easily redeployed.

(ii) It may not be prudent to shed resources if a demographic upturn is likely in the foreseeable future, and opportunities for temporary redeployment may be limited.

(iii) Every service has its own priorities for improvement and those responsible for a service understandably tend to argue that resources released by demographic easement should at least in part be made available for improved provision with the same service, particularly if that service currently falls short of the desired standard or fails to meet demand.

(iv) There can be considerable practical problems in monitoring the effects at a local level of even quite substantial reductions in numbers at a national level, particularly if central control mechanisms over local resource allocation are loose or indirect (as they often are) (CPRS, 1977, p. 51).

Anyone on either side of the Atlantic who has observed the resistance to school closures or teacher layoffs in response to massive decline in children of school age will be familiar with the way in which these points enter into political debate.

It will be particularly difficult to reduce the resources devoted to a program in response to demographic or other exogenous decline where the program is currently partial or selective in its coverage (such as day-care for the under-fives) compared to universal programs such as compulsory education (CPRS, 1977, p. 51). Where existing coverage is only partial it is easier for producer and client groups to argue that the same resources should continue to be provided to enable a more extensive coverage, even if in other circumstances the particular program would not have been considered a priority for more extensive coverage. Where the government has offered a long-term, if vaguely specified, commitment to provide more extensive coverage, it will find it particularly difficult to ensure a cut-back proportionate to the exogenous decline.

2.3.5.4 *Dilution and deterioration*

Exogenous decline implies a reduction in the number of clients in a target group, and where this is not proportionately matched by a reduction in resources, there will actually be an increase in the value of resources devoted to each client. In contrast, dilution or deterioration, which still does not imply the elimination of any program element or category of eligible clientele, occurs when the volume of output delivered to individual clients or targets is reduced.

Such dilution can occur in a range of types of programs, and may vary in the extent to which it is the result of inertia or an explicit short- or long-term decision. Dilution of transfer payments may occur as a result of an explicit cut in the level of benefit, or a failure to maintain the real value of the benefit to compensate for inflation; for example, in Britain unemployment benefit, sickness benefit, maternity allowances, industrial injury benefit and invalidity benefits were raised by 4 percentage points less than was needed to compensate for inflation in November 1980.

Dilution of programs involving service delivery can occur when there is a sudden upsurge in clients, or when there is a reduction in personnel, either as a result of temporary freezing of replacement staff or a long-term decision to reduce staffing levels. This can pose a dilemma for social care personnel, who normally have considerable ability to allocate their own time: either they reduce the care they provide to all clients (perhaps below a threshold where care is effective) or they have to concentrate on cases considered most deserving and effectively neglect other clients (see Parker, 1967).

Dilution does not apply only to programs involving the delivery of benefits or services; it can also apply to regulatory and enforcement activities. Where the staffing of a regulatory agency is reduced, it has to decide whether to concentrate on particular regulations or on particular firms (for example, chosen on basis of size or considered likelihood of breaches of regulation), or whether to lengthen the time between regulatory inspections. The Reagan administration appears to be engaged in a process of diluting the impact of a wide range of regulatory programs by reducing the number of personnel available to enforce the regulations. The 1982 Budget calls for a reduction of 4400 positions from twenty-eight regulatory agencies. These cuts are not distributed equally, however, and a 6 per cent cut for the twenty-eight agencies includes an 82 per cent cut for the Economic Regulatory Administration, 27 per cent cuts for the Consumer Products Safety Commission and the National Highway Safety Administration, a 17 per cent cut for the Federal Trade Commission, and a 16 per cent cut for the Occupational Safety and Health Administration (*Regulation*, 1981).

Dilution can also occur in government activities which involve the use of capital assets. Maintenance (for example, of roads) may be reduced, or the replacement rate of capital assets may be lowered or even frozen. This will lead to a deterioration (in some cases irreversible) of the capital stock, and often to perceptible loss of quality of the service available to citizens. Deterioration of this type is a standard short-term response of governments to what are normally hoped to be short-term fiscal problems, but the long-run cost of deterioration may in some cases outweigh the value of the short-run savings (see National Council of State Planning Bodies, 1980).

2.3.5.5 *Removal of a category of clientele*
In contrast to terminations defined in terms of program elements (which may or may not have a differential effect on recipients) are terminations involving the removal of coverage of the program completely from a specific category of previous clients, with the program continuing to apply in the same way as before to the remaining clients. For example, from 1980 school leavers in Britain who are unable to find a job are no longer eligible to receive supplementary benefit (a non-contributory cash income maintenance payment) in the vacation following their last term at school. If this category of potential recipients had not been eliminated, the total

costs of supplementary benefits would have risen even higher because
of the sharp increase in unemployment among school leavers.
Similarly, in the United States benefits for social security dependents
over eighteen in higher education institutions have been eliminated,
although the program as a whole continues.

2.3.5.6   *Elimination of a program element*

Moving away from cut-back as we have defined it to reductions
involving termination, it is possible to abolish a specific element of a
program while still allowing the remainder of the program to
continue. The distinction between this and dilution is perhaps best
made by example, again from income maintenance policy in Britain :
in 1981–82 earnings-related supplements to unemployment benefit,
sickness benefit, maternity allowance, industrial injury benefit and
widow's allowance were phased out, leaving the standard rate for
these benefits payable to all. Thus, in the period November 1980 to
January 1982 a number of benefits suffered both dilution (a lower real
rate for all) and the elimination of one element of such programs
(which in these paticular cases happened to have a differential impact
on recipients).

It is also worth noting that 'deregulation' may often mean not the
complete termination of all relevant regulations applying to an
industry, but the elimination of only some or their replacement by
less strict regulations. For example, the Staggers Act of 1980, which
was hailed as a major deregulation of the railways actually affects
only a small portion of the total number of Interstate Commerce
Commission regulations affecting the railroads (Caves, Christensen,
and Swanson, 1981). Likewise, the much lauded deregulation of the
banking industry by the Depository Institutions Regulation and
Monetary Control Act of 1980 leaves most of the 'intricate mass of
bank regulation quite untouched' (Scott, 1981, p. 40).

2.3.5.7   *Elimination of program*

The various types of cut-back and partial termination discussed
above are not uncommon in the context of fiscal stress. Faced with a
rising potential clientele and/or a reduced budget, government
agencies will be obliged to reduce benefit (or scrutiny) to some or all
of the clientele for which they are responsible. For as long as possible,
the agency will seek to avoid losing clients or functions, but, if

necessary, it will sacrifice 'fringe' elements or 'fringe' clients in order to protect what it regards as the core program elements and the core target group.

Much less frequent, as we have already argued in Chapter 1, is the extreme end of the maintenance-termination spectrum, where an entire program is completely eliminated (at least not without being replaced). A government department responsible for a range of programs will normally prefer dilution and trimming the fringes of a number of programs, rather than eliminating their programs to preserve the remainder intact. That is not to say that such elimination never occurs: the abolition, in 1977, of the Regional Employment Premium (a labor-related subsidy to manufacturing industry in depressed British regions) released a large sum of money.

Fiscal stress may not be the only source of program termination: the disappearance of a problem and changing fashions in regulation are also possible sources of program elimination, though in the first case this is likely to be preceded by a long period of exogenously determined decline, and in the second is more likely to involve elimination of some program elements, rather than the complete abolition of the relevant agency.

2.4   Analyzing issues in terms of types of policy change

The variety of forms of policy change which we have identified along single dimensions provides our justification for building up the discussion by starting from ideal types and then moving through dimensions of change before attempting to confront the even greater complexity of all aspects of policy issues in practice. Policy issues will rarely fit neatly on to a single dimension, but will concern proposals involving varying elements of succession, maintenance, termination and innovation. The introduction of child benefit in Britain is an example of a policy change which scores zero on policy maintenance, modestly on policy innovation, modestly on termination (some families would received less than before) and very high on policy succession.

The discussion of types of policy change which we present in this chapter is accordingly a framework which can be applied to understand individual policy issues rather a set of categories or dimensions into which individual issues will necessarily fit. Indeed such is the complexity of the change involved in some issues that we have enough of a problem *describing* in a succinct form what has occurred, let alone seeking to understand why these particular changes have occurred. In the appendix to this chapter, we present a means of attempting to summarize in algebraic form the major characteristics of policy changes, and to go beyond that to provide a means of representing the 'genealogy' of programs.

However, our concern in this book is to go beyond a framework for analyzing policy change in terms of changes in outputs to exploring the implications for the political processes associated with proposing and achieving such changes. In the next chapter we relate different types of policy succession to the policy processes necessary to achieve them.

Appendix: The algebra of policy change

The purpose of this appendix is to outline a means of representing complex policy changes in a quantified and concise format. As we have seen in Chapter 2, policies can change in a wide variety of ways, and any given policy change may incorporate a number of different types of change. With verbal descriptions of complex change it is often difficult to get behind the necessarily lengthy detailed accounts to assess in a quantified way the significance of the change in the sense of how much is new, how much has been terminated, how much has changed, and how much remains more or less the same.

Further, it would be useful to have a means of tracing the 'genealogy' of a program, so that we can see which elements of previous programs remain as 'residues' either in original or modified form, perhaps following a chain of policy successions (see 3.9). This would also enable us to trace back through past consolidations and splittings of programs to find the grandparents of the existing program, and to see how far the traits of these predecessor programs live on in their offspring.

This appendix presents a means of representing policy change in the form of algebraic expressions. Any program can be summarized in terms of its component parts, and changes to that program can be represented in the form of functions of different kinds (maintaining, terminating, replacing, innovating) which act on each of these components. The algebraic representation is not a substitute for verbal descriptions, which continue to provide a useful interpretive accompaniment.

In stripping away the verbal descriptions of change, there is a requirement for precise specification of program components, preferably in measurable form, since this will enable us to assess the relative significance of different types of change. As anyone who has tried to measure 'policy' will know, this can be a frustrating task (we discuss the use of indicators of policy succession in Chapter 4). Obvious candidates to use in breaking a program into its component parts are organizational units, budget entries and categories of clientele. Which of these is used will depend on availability of information and suitability for any specific focus of analysis which is desired. For some programs it will be desirable to break the components down further; for example, to separate out an indexing component from a component which has a coefficient varying with eligible population.

The usefulness of such an approach can be developed further if it is possible to provide weightings in the form of coefficients for each component of a program. No single suitable basis for measurement for all types of program can be devised, and there will be particular difficulty in weighting regulatory elements of programs, but obvious candidates for weighting include budgetary cost, manpower, and number of clients. Where such weightings can meaningfully be devised, they can be used to measure the relative significance of maintenance, succession, termination and innovation in policy changes and the average 'age' and 'generation' of individual programs.

Representing policy maintenance

Viewing policy maintenance in algebraic terms, we can see that while the value of the coefficients may vary (for example, as a result of demographic change) the specification of the components remains constant. If we assign subscripts to each variable, we will be able to identify whether any given component is the product of an innovation or has subsequently been modified by a policy succession. Subscripts can also be used to date each component.

In the following hypothetical program (P_j), component x was established in that form by the original policy innovation in 1948 (indicated by a subscript i), while y is a component which has undergone a single succession in 1956 (indicated by a subscript s), and

z has been modified by two successions (indicated by a subscript $s2$), the second of which occurred in 1972. a, b, c are coefficients representing, for example, the amount of expenditure on each component.

$$P_j = ax_{i, 1948} + by_{s, 1956} + cz_{s2, 1972}$$

Where a program is delivered through a number of similar agencies, such as local governments, each component can be represented by a vector. This is a particularly useful way to conceptualize program development (see 2.3.4.4).

A slightly different presentation can be used to represent programs in which there is an indexing component, for example, where the level of a social security benefit is linked to increases in prices or wages. In the example below the original benefit introduced in 1950 has subsequently been modified by the introduction of an indexing component (u) in 1965, replacing previous provision for *ad hoc* upratings. The indexing component is multiplied with rather then added to the other component. The coefficient d would represent the number of eligible persons in any given period, and the coefficient e would be the value of the index employed.

$$P_k = dr_{i, 1950} \times eu_{s, 1965}$$

While the primary purpose of the algebraic presentation offered here is to assist description of a program at any given time, if the expression is well specified and there is a good understanding of the factors determining the size of the coefficients, equations of the kinds illustrated above could be used to model the program and generate forecasts of, for example, future expenditure on the program.

Representing policy transformations

Algebraic expressions can also be used to represent the process of transformation from one policy state to another. Innovation involves the introduction of a new component, succession involves the redefinition of one or more components, and termination involves the removal of a component from the equation. The hypothetical example below illustrates how a highly complex policy change can be summarized in a compressed form.

$$P_m \rightarrow P_n = m(v_i) + s(w_i, x_s) + t(y_i) + i(z)$$

where

v, w, x, y and z are program components,

subscripts i and s indicate which components are the result of previous innovation or succession respectively,

m is a function representing the maintenance of an existing component,

s is a function representing the replacement of one or more components (in this example a joint replacement of two components by one consolidated component),

t is a function representing the termination of a policy component,

i is a function representing the introduction of a new innovative component.

The successful outcome of such a transformation might be:

$$P_n = v_i + q_{s2} + z_i$$

where q is the component which has replaced w and x.

Establishing genealogies of public policy

So far, our concern in this appendix has been with describing policy changes or the state of a program at any given time. The use of this approach can be extended to provide succinct but detailed histories of programs, giving both a record of all transformation changes and indications of how the scale of the program has varied during 'maintenance' phases.

Wherever possible, we should attempt to separate out the values of the coefficient and the numerical value of the benefit (or whatever) contained in each component, since this enables us to assess which changes in total volume are due largely to changes in the coefficient (for example, the number of people eligible) and which to changes in the specification of the benefit.

The hypothetical example in Figure 2.5 shows the history of two benefit programs, one (P_1) initiated in 1950 and the other (P_2) in 1953, and their subsequent consolidation in 1958 into a third program (P_3), which also introduced a new benefit (u). If the value of benefit q was \$1000, benefit r \$1250, benefit v \$1500, and benefit u \$500 then:

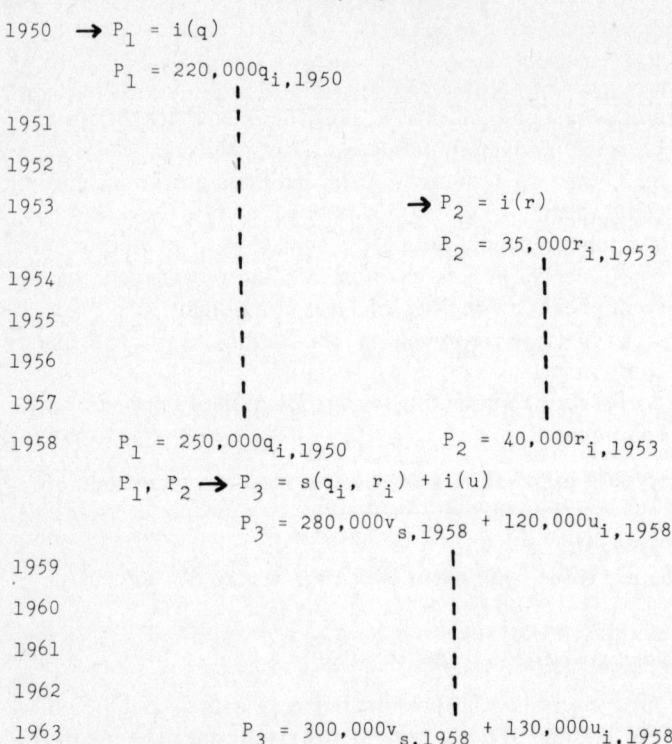

$1950 \rightarrow P_1 = i(q)$

$P_1 = 220,000q_{i,1950}$

1951

1952

$1953 \qquad\qquad\qquad\qquad \rightarrow P_2 = i(r)$

$\qquad\qquad\qquad\qquad\qquad P_2 = 35,000r_{i,1953}$

1954

1955

1956

1957

$1958 \qquad P_1 = 250,000q_{i,1950} \qquad P_2 = 40,000r_{i,1953}$

$P_1, P_2 \rightarrow P_3 = s(q_i, r_i) + i(u)$

$P_3 = 280,000v_{s,1958} + 120,000u_{i,1958}$

1959

1960

1961

1962

$1963 \qquad\qquad P_3 = 300,000v_{s,1958} + 130,000u_{i,1958}$

Fig. 2.5 Hypothetical example of history of social benefit programs

in 1950 expenditure in the first year of
$P_i = 220,000 \times \$1000 = \$220\,m$;
In 1953 expenditure in the first year of
$P_2 = 35,000 \times \$1250 = \$43.75\,m$;
by 1958 expenditure on $P_1 = 250,000 \times \$1000 = \$250\,m$
$P_2 = 40,000 \times \$1250 = \$50\,m$
Total $P_1 + P_2 = \$300\,m$.
following succession in 1958
$P_3 = 280,000 \times \$1500 + 120,000 \times \$500 =$
$\$420 + \$60\,m = \$480\,m$.
by 1963 expenditure on
$P_3 = 300,000 \times \$1500 + 130,000 \times \$500 = \$450\,m + \$65\,m$
$= \$515\,m$.

In this particular example we can see that while some increase in total expenditure arose from the increase in the numbers eligible for any given benefit and from the introduction of an additional new benefit in 1958, the bulk of the increase over the ten-year period up to 1963 came from the uprating of benefit when the two former separate benefits q and r were replaced by v (despite the reduction in overlap which occurred as a result of the consolidation).

An illustration: the history of Federal housing programs in the United States

We can use the algebra described above to demonstrate the development of low-rent public housing in the United States (see Figure 2.6). Although certainly not as significant in the provision of shelter to citizens as the council housing programs in the United Kingdom, some 1.3 million American families live in low-rent public housing. Further, it is also important to remember that public housing is a relatively minor component of the total support of housing in the United States, with the majority of that support coming through tax expenditures for mortage interest and state and local property taxation (Headey, 1978).

The involvement of the American government in low-rent public housing began with the Housing Act of 1937, funded in the amount of $7.6m, with the money being used as loans to local governments for the construction of rental units. After this initial allocation of loan money, a revolving fund was established which recycled the money as interest and principal were repaid to the federal government. But the repayment of previous loans did not provide sufficient capital for the growing demand for public housing, and Congress continued to increase obligational authority, at least before and after the end of World War II.

The rather modest beginnings of the Housing Act of 1937 were expanded greatly by the Housing Act of 1949 which authorized an additional $308m in loans to be spread over a five-year period ($P_{HA1} \rightarrow P_{HA2}$). In addition to the basic public housing program, Congress authorized the Defense Housing Act of 1951 (P_{HDA}), with an additional $100m in loans for local governments which were heavily impacted by growing military employment. This program was wound down throughout the 1950s, and was terminated in 1958 ($t(d_{1,1951})$).

Year		Total expenditures ($million)
1937	→ $P_{HA1} = i(h)$	
1938	$P_{HA1} = 7.6h_{1,1937}$	7.6
1939		
1940		
1941		
1942		
1943		
1944		
1945		
1946		
1947		
1948	$P_{HA1} = 0.3h_{1,1937}$	0.3
1949	$P_{HA1} → P_{HA2} = s(h_{1,1937})$	
1950	$P_{HA2} = 0.3j_{s,1949}$	0.3
1951		
1952	$P_{HA2} = 0.8j_{s,1949}$	
1953	$P_{HA2} → P_{HA3} = m(j_{s,1949}) + i(k)$	0.9
1954		
1955	$P_{HA3} = 1.2j_{s,1949} + 0.1k_{1,1954}$	1.3
1956	$P_{HA3} → P_{HA4} = m(j_{s,1949}) + s(k_{1,1954})$	
1957	$P_{HA4} = 2.3j_{s,1949} + 0.07f_{s,1956}$	2.5
1958		
1959	$P_{HA4} = 5.7j_{s,1949} + 0.16f_{s,1956}$	
	$P_{HA4} → P_{HA5} = m(j_{s,1949}) + s(f_{s,1956}) + i(e)$	

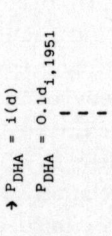

→ $P_{DHA} = i(d)$
$P_{DHA} = 0.1d_{1,1951}$

$P_{DHA} = 0.14d_{1,1951}$
→ $t(d_{1,1951})$

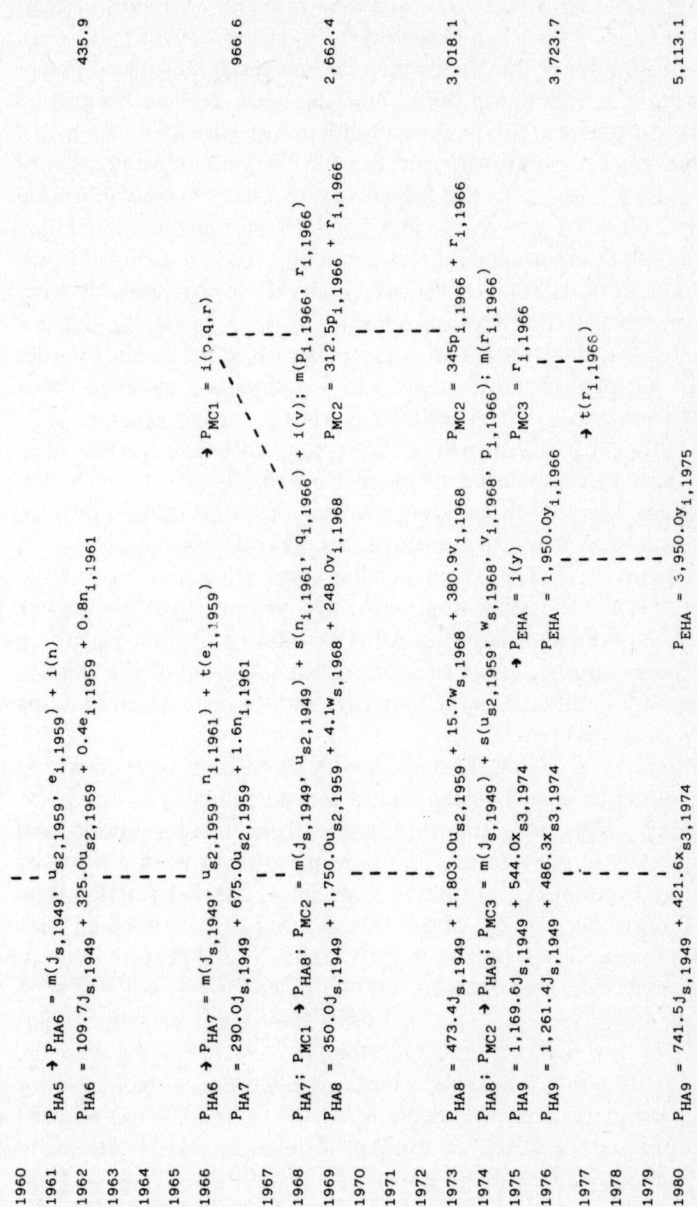

Fig. 2.6 The genealogy of Federal housing programs

The Housing Act of 1954 constituted a major policy succession by placing public housing in the broader social and economic context ($P_{HA2} \rightarrow P_{HA3}$). This Act allowed up to 10 per cent of the total grant authorization for housing to be used for non-residential development (Foard and Fefferman, 1966). This allowed local authorities to prepare programs of urban renewal with money which was ostensibly housing money. Following from the 1954 Act, the Housing Act of 1956 placed housing in the framework of General Neighborhood Renewal plans ($P_{HA3} \rightarrow P_{HA4}$), and the 1959 Housing Act expanded the concept of urban renewal to 'community renewal' ($P_{HA4} \rightarrow P_{HA5}$). The majority of the funds authorized under these programs still went to the construction of low-rent housing for the poor ($j_{s,1949}$), but this had become to some extent an intermediate objective for the broader goal of urban revitalization and was accompanied by some funds directed towards urban renewal ($k_{i,1954}$; $1_{s,1956}$; $v_{s2,1959}$).

The Model Cities Program of 1966 (P_{MC1}), although broader in its goals than just a housing program, to some degree reversed the movement away from building low-rent housing units, and also undertook to reinvigorate the provisions in earlier housing acts which allowed some of the funds from housing appropriations to be used for rehabilitation of existing housing owned or rented by low-income families. The Federal Housing Administration's 'Project Rehab' in 1967–9 was another effort to promote the retention of the existing housing stock rather than the bulldozer and the subsequent building of new housing units.

At the same time that the above policy successions were occurring in the direction of urban renewal, a second policy succession was happening. This was the shift away from relying upon local governments to provide low-rent housing in favor of non-profit or even profit-making corporations. The Below Market Interest Rate provisions of Section 202 of the Housing Act of 1959 allowed non-profit corporations to borrow money, originally at 3 per cent interest, to construct low-rent housing for the elderly who required such housing housing ($e_{i,1959}$). The 1961 Housing Act had similar provisions for building units for families which fell between the eligibility for public housing and the economic wherewithall to buy or rent in the private market; Section 221 (d) (3) of that Act allowed non-profit, cooperative, or even profit-making organizations to borrow money under these low-interest provisions.

The Housing Act of 1968 consolidated the latter provision in a single act (Section 236) which also included some similar provisions which had been a part of the Model Cities program. This Act also provided assistance for the potential home buyer who could not afford market rates of down-payment or interest (Section 235). A number of difficulties and apparent inequities arose under the Housing Act of 1968 and with the election of the Nixon administration it came under increasing attack. As a part of the Housing and Community Development Act of 1974 the majority of housing programs were consolidated into a single block grant to local governments, with the local governments given the opportunity to decide how the money would be spent. Also covered by this block grant was a rent supplement program which would maintain rents for low-income families at no more than 25 per cent of their adjusted incomes. (At the Federal level with which we are concerned here, the block grant constitutes a single component; allocation at the local level between the programs covered by the block grant could be represented by vectors.) These provisions were supplemented by the Emergency Housing Act of 1975 which provided \$10 billion in mortgages at slightly below market interest rates both to supplement a depressed housing market and to make it easier for moderate-income families to purchase their own homes (P_{EHA}).

The written description of the generalogy of low-income housing policy in the United States should be seen as a supplement to Figure 2.6. Once the symbolism of the algebraic statements contained in that figure is understood, it can serve as a means of representing and comparing patterns of policy succession and policy change more generally. The example of housing policy in the United States illustrates rather well the utility of this approach in documenting the policy initiations, terminations and successions which have occurred over the four decades. The algebraic representation cannot replace detailed histories of programs for understanding processes of change, but it can be used for a general understanding when attempting to develop theoretical propositions concerning policy succession and reveals in concise form patterns of information not readily presentable in verbal form.

Chapter 3
TYPES OF POLICY SUCCESSION

3.1 Distinguishing types of policy succession

So far, we have been talking about policy succession as a single concept to distinguish it from policy innovation, policy maintenance and policy termination. However, policy succession can take many forms, and the form which finally emerges may not be the same as that proposed when the policy succession was first initiated. Policy successions vary in the extent to which they produce a one-for-one replacement of existing policy. This occurs in two main ways:

(a) The 'coverage' (for example, in terms of clientele) of the replacement policies may not match that of the old. The replacement program may not cover all of the clients of the old, but may provide for previously uncovered clients. Likewise, even if the coverage of the replacement policy is identical to that of the old, the objectives of the policy may vary.
(b) Policy succession may result in the same number of programs, fewer or greater.

Figure 3.1 illustrates a variety of possible types of policy succession which capture key distinctions in terms of the above variations. This is not intended to be an exhaustive or mutually exclusive set of categories; as we show below, real world issues frequently exhibit complex patterns of change, with two or more types operating simultaneously and interactively. On other occasions one type of change may follow on the heels of another so that the effects of each may be difficult to isolate.

The two dimensions of types of succession mentioned above—coverage and number of programs—have implications for the process of changing policy, or, to be more accurate, we must discuss policy succession in terms of a *variety* of processes. When a policy succession involves a reduction in the number of clients or organizations, or a shifting of the objectives of programs, the process is likely to be more conflictual and actors more defensive. These types of changes are 'minus-sum games', in which there will be more losses

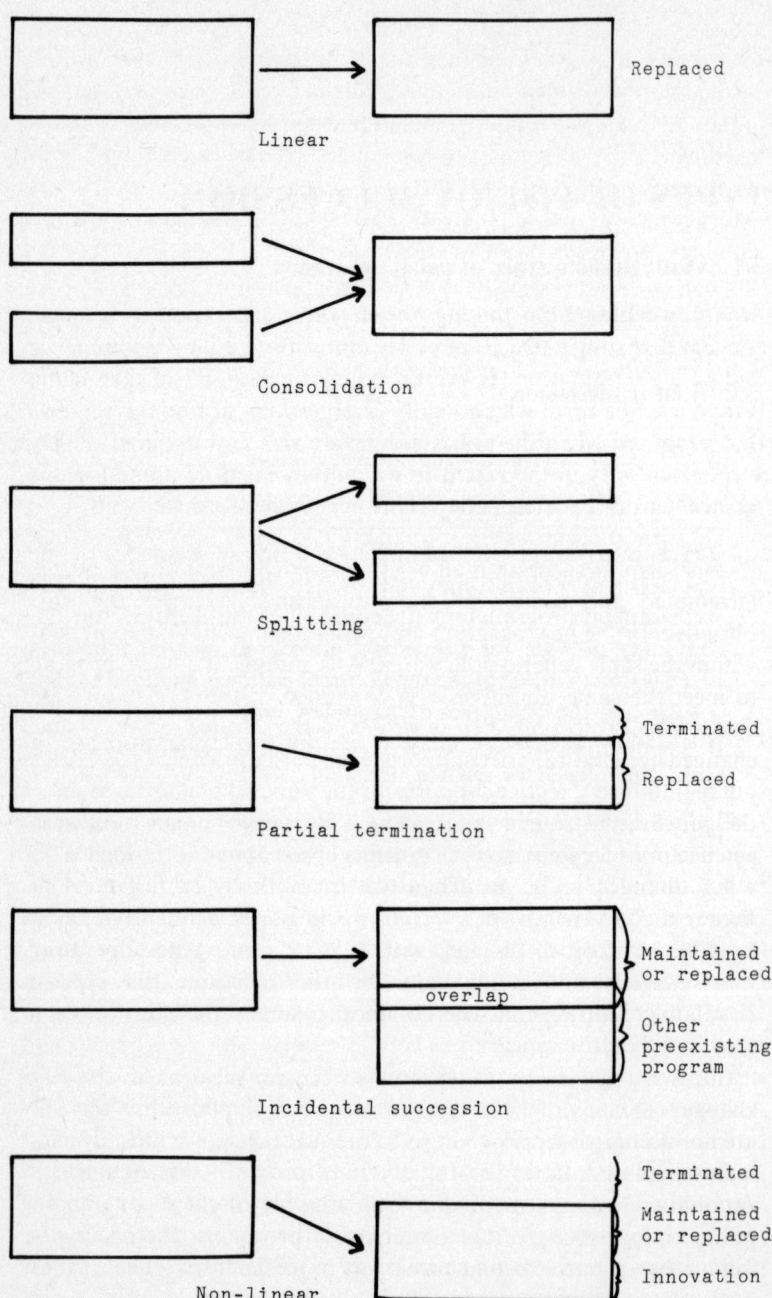

Fig. 3.1 Types of policy succession

than gains. In general, the intensity of involvement of actors will be related not only to the magnitude of change but also to its direction: potential losers will tend to fight harder than potential gainers. Thus, even where overall gains and losses balance out, there would be an asymmetry in the intensity of involvement of gainers and losers. More complex types of policy succession will be associated with more complex processes, with a greater number of policy actors, and greater variations in perceptions, interests, and opportunities for coalition-building.

3.2 Linear succession

3.2.1 *Direct replacement of policy or program*

Of the forms of succession, the 'purest' and the one which we would suggest occurs rather infrequently, is 'linear' policy succession. In this form of succession an existing policy or program is entirely terminated and a new program established to meet the same objective, or the new program may pursue somewhat different goals within the same general policy area. An example of a 'new' program to meet the same objectives was contained in the Agriculture and Consumer Protection Act of 1973 in the United States, which changed agricultural price supports from parity prices to target prices but maintained the price supports for the same commodities as under the previous acts, and also retained provisions for setting aside acreage in order to qualify for benefits. The impact of the legislation was to change from a system in which prices for agricultural products were related to changes in other products to one in which they were established target prices, for example, $2.05 per bushel for wheat.

It is especially interesting that these linear policy changes appear to be relatively infrequent, whereas linear changes in organizations in the United States appear to be common (see 4.2.1). This reflects two features of the relationship between organizational and policy change: (1) many reorganizations are cosmetic in the sense that they are not accompanied by changes in the substance of policy, which is maintained in more or less the previous form; (2) although organizational change may involve a simple replacement, accompanying policy changes may be more complex in the sense that they involve innovative or termination elements or have 'spillover' effects on the operations of other organizations (see 3.5–3.7).

3.2.2   *Implications of contraction or expansion*

The degree of political contention in the policy process associated
with proposals for linear succession will depend on the extent to
which the new proposals benefit existing clientele to a greater or less
extent that the existing program, and on whether the organization
responsible for administering the existing program is also given
responsibility for the new. The acrimony will be least in cases where
the interests of those most immediately affected appear to benefit
from the change. Thus the replacement of a pay freeze administered
by a small regulatory body by more relaxed guidelines administered
by an expanded bureaucracy would meet less resistance from those
directly affected than the reverse substitution.

3.2.3   *Implications of changes of allocative mechanisms*

One obvious type of linear succession is to replace one way of
delivering a policy by another. For example, a program of direct
housing subsidies may be replaced by a system of subsidy through the
tax system; alternatively a system of rent control in the private
housing sector might be replaced by overt subsidies from government
to tenant. Because the process of policy delivery and types of
organizational structure vary, the transition associated with such
policy successions will typically be more complex and involve greater
upheaval. These implications, which vary widely for different types of
transition, are the subject of detailed analysis in Chapter 7.

3.2.4   *Policy reversal*

Some changes reverse the thrust of previous policy, for example,
where labor laws making closed shops binding are changed into ones
which enable closed shops to be challenged. More generally, we can
conceive of policy successions having directionality—expanding
forwards the existing type of provision, 'sideways' into a different
type of provision, or reversing the thrust of previous policy. These
policy directions can be related to the dimensions of policy change
discussed in Chapter 2.

Many imagined 'policy reversals', including some supposedly
stemming from adversary party politics, are not reversals but
'sideways' policy successions. For example, decisions about second

pensions schemes were switched when parties changed office in Britain in 1970 and 1974, but these were about the appropriate design of a scheme, not about whether or not there should be one. Other apparent reversals (for example, over incomes policies) turn out to be temporary policy hiatuses (discussed in 3.2.5).

There are, however, plenty of examples of policy reversals. In 1974 and 1979 in Britain the governments coming into office not only undid some aspects of their predecessor's labor legislation but introduced legislation which took the law in the opposite direction. The 1950s and 1960s in Britain were notorious for 'stop-go' economic policies involving alternating expansionary and contractionary policy stances (see Brittan, 1970). In the United States there has been some success in the campaign to reverse the thrust of previous regulatory policies.

Policy reversals are clearly much more dramatic and disruptive than other forms of linear succession which merely involve substituting one program for another with similar objectives. It may, indeed, be difficult to get an existing organization to be vigorous in implementing a change involving elements of reversal (see 6.4.5). Where there are identifiable clients or beneficiaries of the existing program (true of labor legislation, but not necessarily of general economic policies) we would expect policy reversals to be fiercely contested, since not only may previous gains be eliminated, but further losses may be sustained. Those campaigning against policy successions will naturally attempt to characterize them as reversals in an attempt to mobilize political support, even if the successions do not have the objective characteristics of reversals.

3.2.5 *Policy hiatus*

In general, linear succession will relate to occasions when the termination of the old policy or program and the introduction of the new coincide. However, there are some policies (for example, prices and incomes policies, commitments to align currencies) where the initial policy may be terminated only for a more or less similar policy to be reintroduced after a relatively short space of time. We would term this a policy hiatus, and the process involved, a disjointed succession.

A policy hiatus can occur in one of at least two ways. One is a cyclical policy hiatus, where the problems of disjointed policy succession are endemic. Incomes policy is an excellent example of this phenomenon, where one policy follows another, although usually after a period in which the question of wage and price determination is left to the market. After an incomes policy has been in place for some period of time, pressures from more productive or more politically powerful groups, combined with administrative difficulties, lead to a return to less constrained wage bargaining. But unless there is a fundamentally sound economy there may soon be a need to return to the administrative determination of wages. Government may appear to accept a functional termination, but in effect it is only a short-term retreat from an on-going concern with major economic conditions.

The organizational manifestation of this can be termed the 'comet phenomenon', to denote bodies that are set up on a more or less regular cycle, blaze into activity for a period and then disappear, only to reappear after a policy hiatus (Hogwood, quoted in Hood, 1981, p. 105). Thus, associated with the cyclical return to incomes policies described above, there has been the intermittent appearance of *ad hoc* machinery for determining pay issues in Britain from the National Incomes Commission in the early 1960s to the Standing Commission on Pay Comparability in the late 1970s, now in its turn abolished, predictably to be replaced by another similar body when the comet of incomes policy makes its next dramatic appearance.

The second type of policy hiatus is the one-off policy hiatus in which there is a temporary absence of a policy which will soon be replaced by another policy or program. Policy hiatuses of this sort tend to result from exogenous forces. One common source is the action of courts, which may rule invalid or unconstitutional the programs adopted by a government. Anti-pornography policy in the United States has frequently been subject to these absences as the courts rule a particular set of criteria for deciding on obscenity invalid.

3.3   Policy consolidation

3.3.1   *The complexity of consolidation*

A more complex form of policy succession occurs when two or more programs are wholly or partly terminated and a single new one instituted to pursue similar policy objectives which replace those of the original programs. The new program may represent a greater or less commitment of resources than the programs it replaces. We would term this type of policy succession 'policy consolidation'. The complexity of policy consolidation has important implications for the process of gaining political support and for subsequent reorganization.

3.3.2 *Process implications of consolidation*

An example from Britain can serve to illustrate policy consolidation, both the policy outcomes and some of the process-related issues. In 1975 the Labour government (with Opposition support) passed a Child Benefit Act. This provided for the replacement of both family allowances (a cash benefit payable in respect of all except the first child, which was partly clawed back for those on higher income) and income tax allowances in respect of children by a non-taxable 'child benefit', a cash payment made in respect of all children. Although there were some innovatory features of this 'new' benefit (cash payments for first children, and special treatment for single parents), this change was largely a new form of delivery in the well-established field of income maintenance relating to children. The amount of 'new' money for child benefits was also relatively small. In financial year 1976–77, the expenditure (at 1979 prices) on family allowances was £746m and the expenditure equivalent on child tax allowances was £1700m (total £2446m); in addition there was expenditure of £27m on child interim benefit, introduced in 1976 as an interim benefit for the first child of single parents as a transitional stage to child benefit. When child benefits had been completely phased in by 1979/80, total expenditure (again in 1979 prices) was £2820m (figures calculated from Cmnd 6393, 1976; Cmnd 7841, 1980). Thus the amount of new money was about 15 per cent.

The distribution of net benefits among different family types altered, but overall child support was increased. However, child benefit was to be collected by *mothers*, and the take-home pay of *fathers* would be reduced by the removal of tax allowances for children at a time when the Labour government was seeking the cooperation of trade unions in pay restraint. As a result of concern felt by some Labour politicians about the repercussions of this, the original plan to introduce the benefit in April 1977 was abandoned, and its introduction was phased in over three years (see *New Society*, 1976).

3.3.3   *Coalitions for and against consolidation*

Problems can arise in attempting to follow through policy consolidation because of the possibility that the two or more groups of
existing clients or service providers may form a coalition in an
attempt to thwart the change. Resistance from service providers may
be reduced (and may be turned into active support) if one or more of
the existing groups of service providers is given responsibility for
administering the new program. Resistance from an organization to
removal of an activity will be greatest where that activity is central to
the organization's functions or even its survival. Where a program is
peripheral the removal of the program may have minimal effect on
the organization and may even increase its focus on its core functions.
As Holden (1966) and Downs (1967, pp. 198–9) point out, organizations attempt to preserve their 'heartlands' and are willing to
concede functions that dilute their purposes.

Policy consolidation may raise special problems of policy transition. Even where the replacement program provides a greater net
benefit than the previous two or more programs combined, there may
be individuals who lose out, either temporarily or permanently. This
is quite a likely occurrence, since the purpose of policy consolidation
may be to remove existing anomalies or inequities arising from the
interaction of existing programs, as in the case of the introduction of
child benefit in the United Kingdom referred to above.

Clearly, while clientele, service providers and legislators associated
with an existing program may all be in the same coalition during a
battle over policy succession, this may not necessarily be so. Consider
the situation where a replacement program larger than existing
programs A and B combined is to be administered by the organization currently administering program A but will be of greatest
benefit to the current clientele of program B. Which program the
legislators associated with programs A and B will support will depend
on whether they identify more with service providers than clientele.
Thus a coalition of interests might form as follows:

Pro-consolidation coalition	*Anti-consolidation coalition*
Clientele B	Clientele A
Service providers A	Service providers B
Legislators B	Legislators A

The outcome of the policy succession process in this case would depend on the relative political strengths of the participants in the coalitions.

3.3.4 *The implications of policy consolidation for organizational integration*

The implementation of policy consolidation may involve difficult and extended problems of organizational adjustment if two previous organizations are combined into one. This is particularly likely to be the case if the nature of the tasks of the previously separate organizations was different, even where the two organizations were working within the same policy field and shared the same general aims. Such problems can be illustrated by the establishment of the Commission for Racial Equality (CRE) in Britain, the subject of a highly critical House of Commons Committee report in 1981. The CRE had been formed in 1977 from the merger of the Race Relations Board, established in 1965, and the Community Relations Commission, established in 1968. The Race Relations Board had previously a law-enforcing role concerning anti-discrimination law, whereas the Community Relations Commission was concerned with promoting racial harmony. Following the merger, staff and unions refused to accept any new structure which departed too radically from what they had known, and management was not prepared to force the issue (*The Times*, 26 May 1981). Following an internal inquiry into management at the CRE in 1980–81, two of the three directors, plus the principal research officer, left the CRE. The CRE has been criticized from all sides: from blacks for being ineffective and from Conservatives concerned about interference from a non-elected 'quango' into the affairs of firms and other organizations. The Conservative government tried unsuccessfully to block the CRE investigation into the government's immigration service. While many of these problems do not stem directly from the establishment of the CRE, its inability to carry out full organizational integration led to the CRE being vulnerable to internal disputes and external criticism, all of which detracted from its ability to pursue its agreed objectives.

3.3.5 *Cosmetic policy consolidations*

Finally, we must draw attention to the possibility of a purely cosmetic policy consolidation, which results in previous programs continuing to be executed in much the same way. This may be associated with organizational mergers which do not lead to any effective integration of the previous structures or activities. Such largely symbolic mergers may, however, be sufficient to defuse pressure for more substantive policy consolidation. Such cosmetic consolidation may also be the unplanned outcome of a policy consolidation decision intended to have substantive effects, but which fails to follow through success- fully in the implementation stage by overcoming problems of organizational integration. The history of many efforts at govern- ment reorganization in the United States could be taken to indicate that policy and organizational consolidations frequently produce only different names on the letterhead rather than significant policy changes.

3.4 Policy splitting

3.4.1 *The visibility of organizational splitting*

The reverse of policy consolidation is policy splitting, meaning that existing programs or organizations are divided into two or more parts. Such splitting occurs in its most visible form when an existing organization is divided into two or more parts, as when the Department of Energy was carved out of the Department of Trade and Industry in the United Kingdom at the end of 1973, or in the separation of the Department of Education out of the Department of Health, Education and Welfare in 1980 in the United States.

Organizational change is the most manifest indicator of splitting, but may at times indicate more fundamental changes in policy. For example, when the Atomic Energy Commission in the United States was split into the Nuclear Regulatory Commission and the Energy Research and Development Administration in 1974, this signalled a shift from the production and regulatory aspects of atomic energy policy being conducted by the same individuals to a division of these tasks. This tended to provide a greater opportunity for stronger regulation than when regulatory decisions were made by a group which was manifestly pro-nuclear.

3.4.2 *Substantive implications of policy splitting*

However, there also may be more substantive, if more complex, relationships between organizational and policy splitting and policy succession. The establishment of a new, separate organization may be intended to give a new focus to policy formulation, which may in time lead to policy succession. For example, removing the Department of Education from the Department of Health, Education and Welfare would have, in all likelihood, resulted in a more active proponent of change in educational policy if the Department had not subsequently been slated for 'termination' (or, rather, reallocation of its functions). Also, this splitting would have protected the education budget from being the scapegoat when budgets needed cutting and both health and social welfare had large entitlement programs which could not be cut readily (Miles, 1977, p. 157).

Splitting also gives clients a more visible target towards which to direct their political activities and may facilitate the 'capture' of the organization by its clients (Wilcox, 1968). Such a capture would, in turn, tend to produce policies more favorable to the interests of the client group. In a somewhat related fashion, splitting may also prevent an organization from being overcome by the interests of the majority of a larger organization. For example, removing responsibility for arms control and disarmament from the Department of Defense prevented this more pacific policy area from being overcome by the rest of the Pentagon.

Finally, organizational splitting can be used as a means of changing committee assignments for programs which are unpopular with one legislative committee or another. Such a change may not only improve the budgetary outlook for an organization, but it would also be likely to alter the programmatic priorities of the organization as well. The new oversight or budgetary committee would, then, produce policy changes as the organization attempts to adapt to this change in its relevant environment.

3.4.3 *Implementing policy splitting*

Organizational splitting with the intention of providing a new focus may not necessarily be followed through successfully to the implementation of policy succession. For example, in 1964, the incoming Labour government in Britain established a Department of Economic Affairs (DEA) with general responsibility for economic coordination, the preparation of a five-year plan, and the drawing up of an industrial policy, a regional policy and an incomes policy (see Brittan, 1970, pp. 310–20; Leruez, 1975, pp. 131–41, 183). The DEA took over responsibility for overall medium-term economic policy from the Treasury, which retained responsibility for short-term economic policy. However, the DEA had few direct managerial or executive responsibilities; its main task was to coordinate the work of the other economic departments, including the Treasury, which until the split had the economic coordinating role. 'The danger of friction or even outright conflict between the two departments was only too obvious, unless they reached some sort of *modus vivendi* providing for constant close cooperation' (Leruez, 1975, p. 131).

There are two important ingredients in any such *modus vivendi*: political cooperation, including the role of the Prime Minister in adjudicating between the two departments, and agreement about the allocation of tasks. Political cooperation failed to develop, and Brittan (1970, p. 312) characterized the establishment of the DEA as 'the catastrophic experiment of two rival economic ministers locked together in uncreative tension, with the Prime Minister swinging sometimes one way and sometimes the other on no known principle'. The designation of George Brown, the minister in charge of the DEA, as the most senior minister under the Prime Minister did not in practice provide him with an effective power base from which to exercise the political aspects of the DEA's coordinating role.

The agreed allocation of tasks between the Treasury and the DEA was that the DEA would concentrate on the long term and the Treasury on the short term, and that DEA would concentrate on physical resources and the Treasury on finance. However, in Britain (and in most Western countries) the policy instruments by which production is influenced are budgets, monetary policy, exchange rate policy and some financial controls. Thus, 'if the Treasury remains responsible for the balance of payments, for taxation, for the Bank Rate, and for the use of devices like the Regulator, it is likely to remain the effective economic ministry, whatever nominal changes are made' (Brittan, 1970, p. 313).

It was this, reinforced by a series of short-term crises concerned with the balance of payments and the exchange rate, which helped to determine the fate of the DEA. A series of short terms very quickly becomes the medium term. Thus, the projections of the 1965 National Plan, drawn up by the DEA, were almost immediately contradicted by measures taken by the Treasury in response to the crises. The DEA's responsibilities were gradually whittled away from 1967, and the DEA was eventually abolished in October 1969, with the Treasury taking back the responsibilities which had been handed over to the DEA.

3.4.4 *Cosmetic policy splitting*

As with policy consolidation, organizational splitting may turn out to be largely cosmetic. In the United Kingdom the Department of Transport was separated out from the Department of Environment in 1976. However, the two departments continue to have joint common services, and have combined offices in the regions. Further, in the case of splitting of large departments, the direct impact on programs may be minimal, since departments are typically responsible for a large number of programs, and the organizational split is unlikely to cross-cut programs.

3.5 Partial termination

3.5.1 *Partial termination as qualitative and quantitative change*

In referring to partial termination as a form of policy succession, we are distinguishing it from simple rundowns or cut-backs of programs. Here we are concerned with transformations of policy or programs which involve a reduction in the resources committed to the program or in final policy outputs; in other words, a qualitative change combined with a quantitative one. In terms of the dimensions of policy change introduced in Chapter 2, we are concerned here with changes that lie on the succession-termination dimension (2.3.3) rather than on the maintenance-termination dimension (2.3.5).

An example which illustrates the combination of qualitative and quantitative aspects of change involved in partial termination is the reshaping of regional investment incentives by the incoming Conservative government in Britain in 1970. The investment grants system established by the preceding Labour government, including a differential for depressed regions, was abolished, and a system of tax allowances for investment introduced. Higher tax allowances for the depressed regions were available, but the effective differential for the regions was lower than in the program which had been abolished. This example also provides a cautionary note when attempting to use indicators of policy succession (as we do in chapter 4), since looking only at the public expenditure side of the budget would suggest that a functional termination had taken place (see 1.3.1), since no expenditure program for regional incentives replaced the one that was abolished (apart from the residue of past commitments under the previous program; see 3.9). In fact, the incentives had not been abolished but had been switched (albeit at a reduced level) to the form of tax expenditures which, particularly in Britain, are much more difficult to identify and quantify than expenditure programs (see 7.2.8).

3.5.2　*Partial termination as outcome of failed termination*

Partial termination can be a possible outcome of failed termination as well as a type of policy succession which may be deliberately sought by decision-makers. Many Conservatives in Britain in 1979 would have liked to see the abolition of the National Enterprise Board set up under the previous Labour government. The Conservative government confined itself to running down the shareholding role of the NEB, firing much of the top leadership when it opposed government policy, and changing its emphasis to promotion of new technology, eventually merging it with the National Research Development Corporation to form the British Technology Group.

3.5.3　*The intergovernmental aspects of partial termination*

Partial termination may result from an attempt by one level of government to reduce the volume of resources handed over to another, normally smaller-area, level. Where this involves program redefinition or reworking of the criteria of eligibility this involves succession rather than simply cut-backs. An example is the British Conservative government's removal of the obligation on local education authorities to provide subsidized school meals of specified kinds for all school pupils at prices fixed by central government. The aim here was not the complete termination of the school meal program, but a reduction of the total commitment of public resources to it as a result of local authorities exercising their discretion to raise charges or alter service provision. In calculating the block grant it hands over to the local authorities, the government has assumed that local authorities will alter their policies so as to reduce public expenditure on this program. Local authorities are exercising this discretion to varying degrees, so the degree of partial termination varies among local authorities, and central government will not be able to determine the overall degree of implementation of the partial termination. This particular strategy of reducing both obligations and block grants will be effective if the primary aim of the center is to secure specified global levels of cuts in resource inputs. It is not a very effective mechanism for targetting cuts on specific programs which are disliked for political reasons.

In the United States, the reduction in subsidy to the school lunch program by the Reagan administration produced a reduction in the nutritional requirements of the meal (from one-third to one-fourth of daily needs), lowered the income levels at which reduced-price and free school meals would be available, and led to such silliness as having ketchup classified as a vegetable. Again, the intent was ostensibly not to eliminate the program entirely, but only to reduce the amount of money expended on it.

3.5.4 *Resistance to partial termination*

In general, we would expect there to be fairly strong opposition to partial termination from clients, service providers and legislators associated with the original program, since, unlike other forms of policy succession, the replacement program does not fully fill the gap left by the rundown of the old. Indeed, it may be because of such anticipated opposition that partial rather than complete termination is proposed in the first place, or is adopted in response to failure to push through a proposal for complete termination. In the case of the Conservative government's consideration of the school means program, this was undoubtedly an influence, as is the handing of the 'poisoned chalice' of responsibility for implementing partial termination to the local authorities.

3.5.5 *Partial termination as precursor to total termination*

Clients and service providers may have reason to fear a partial termination as a precursor to total termination. There may not be a sufficient coalition available to terminate a program at once, but it may be possible to terminate it in a piecemeal fashion. Lambright and Sapolsky (1976) quote the example of the decision by President Johnson in 1967 to terminate the Supporting Universities Program sponsored by NASA. The NASA administrator fought the decision and succeeded in preventing an immediate termination, but the program was phased out over three years through successive budget reductions. Bardach (1976, p. 125) argues that 'this sort of moderately paced and deliberately implemented phasing out of a policy seems a quite infrequent termination scenario'. Biller (1976) emphasizes the desirability of introducing mechanisms which would ensure smooth rundown rather than abrupt termination, and explicitly sets such termination in the context of the replacement policies. However, there is a danger in using partial termination as a strategy to secure eventual total termination or succession that the process of change may be subverted before it is complete: anti-termination coalitions do not necessarily disperse after losing the first round of a budget battle.

3.5.6 *'Paradox of irreducible wholes'*

Relatedly, proposals for a partial termination may result in a total termination for programs for managerial reasons. Partial termination may mean that clients have to go elsewhere, and the organization and its program be dismantled as ineffective. Such an implication may not be realized at the time when the initial partial termination is proposed. Levine (1980, pp. 306–7) speaks of this as the 'Paradox of Irreducible Wholes'.

In Britain following the abolition of the statutory requirement on local authorities to provide school meals of a specified kind at a fixed price (see 3.5.4) at least one authority which increased prices found that the resulting reduction in demand increased costs-per-head so much that it had to contemplate ceasing provision altogether (except for the statutory requirement to provide free school meals to certain categories). Another example from Britain is the decision which faced Strathclyde Regional Council in Scotland in the mid 1970s about the future of Strathclyde Educational Television: because a whole team was needed it was not possible to cut only some members, so the whole service was abandoned.

3.6 Non-linear succession

In our discussion of partial termination we have started to move away from the idea of succeeding policies matching those they replaced which was implied in the discussion of linear succession and, to a lesser extent, splitting and consolidation. If we envisage at one extreme linear succession by which a new program more or less replaces an old one, and at the other extreme policy innovation which in no way replaces any policy termination with which it may coincide in time, we can characterize intermediate positions as non-linear policy succession.

3.6.1 *Terminated, overlapping and innovative characteristics*

Specifically, we are using the term non-linear succession to character-ize circumstances where the new program is closely related in some way to the policy underlying the old program but has significantly different policy objectives, program characteristics and/or organi-zational form. Thus, where a progam which defined clientele in terms of age or employment status is terminated and a new one instituted which defined clients in terms of income, it would be characterized as a non-linear rather than a linear change, since we would expect a combination of terminated, overlapping, and innovative characteris-tics in comparing the two programs.

Non-linear succession can be considered in terms of the dimensions of change discussed in Chapter 2. The succession-termination, succession-innovation and succession-maintenance dimensions form a three dimensional space within which all non-linear changes can be represented. Using the algebraic presentation developed in the appendix to Chapter 2, we can present the general form of non-linear succession as follows:

$$P_1 = a_i + b_i + c_i$$
$$P_1 \rightarrow P_2 = m(a_i) + s(b_i) + t(c_i) + i(d)$$
$$P_2 = a_i + b_s + d_i$$

where a is the element of the previous program carried over to the new one,

b is an element replaced in the new program,

c is the element of the previous program which is terminated,

d is an innovatory element introduced for the first time in the re-placement program.

The history of American housing policy described in the appendix to Chapter 2 provides a number of examples of non-linear succession.

Both the 1954 and 1961 Housing Acts involved maintaining the provisions of previous Acts but added a new provision. Both the 1956 and 1959 Acts involved maintaining some provisions of previous legislation but the replacement of others.

3.6.2 *Program change and organizational change are not isomorphic*

One of the most common forms of non-linear change may be the result of program change and organizational changes not being conducted in synchronization. In general, organizations are more permanent than the policies which they administer (see Chapter 6). As a result some organizations may be left with the vestigial elements of policies to administer, while others will be given a range of types of policies to try to combine into a meaningful array. It may also be that the organization would change its basic structure without commensurate changes in the policies being administered. This occurs most frequently as organizations go through cycles of decentralization and centralization, with the locus of decision-making and the locus of service delivery at times becoming more or less separated. In short, although form and function should be related in theory, the differential rates of change of organizations and their policies, and the consequent discontinuities, may produce the type of non-linear changes described above.

3.7 Incidental policy succession

3.7.1 *Consequential changes to existing programs*

From the perspective of those who perceive themselves as initiating policy innovation, the occurrence of any policy succession relating to .their 'new' program may appear incidental and peripheral and the associated politics as an intrusion. Such 'incidental policy succession' arises from consequential change to existing programs, the replacement or alteration of which is not the purpose of the policy proposal. If our earlier argument that there will be few, if any, completely new policy innovations in Western societies is correct, such incidental policy succession will be an intrinsic feature of apparently dramatic policy changes. Although such consequential adjustments to the existing programs may seem peripheral from the perspective of the proponents of change, they would be foolish to ignore their implications for the chances of successfully implementing the proposed change. Skilled politicians will seek the active support or at least the passive assent of those involved in programs which may be peripheral from their immediate perspective but which may be central to the perspective of powerful potential allies, or political enemies with the power to contribute to the thwarting of their broader proposal. In seeking such support advocates of change may have to modify their existing proposals to meet the objectives of those already involved in the existing programs which would be affected.

3.7.2 *New programs as actual or potential rivals to established programs*

Even where a proposed policy does not appear to have any direct effect on existing programs, as indicated, for example, by amendments to authorizing legislation, there may still be incidental policy succession in the sense that the proposed new program may constitute an actual or potential rival to established programs. It will not be surprising if such suspicions are engendered, since the purpose of the establishment of new programs and agencies is often to sidestep existing agencies whose philosophy does not conform to the purposes of the new policy. For example, locating the Office of Economic Opportunity outside of the Department of Health, Education and Welfare during the War on Poverty was an explicit attempt to prevent a more innovative approach to problems of poverty from being swallowed up in the large existing organization. Even where there appears to be no immediate threat to the existing program itself, its supporters may fear that the establishment of a new program may lead to a diversion of resources which would otherwise have gone to the existing program and may even pose a long-term threat to its survival. One example may be the War on Cancer in the United States, started in 1971, which constituted a rival to established programs in the National Institutes of Health.

3.7.3 *Uninvited policy actors*

Thus, incidental policy succession, whether actual or hypothetical, may lead to 'uninvited' policy actors presenting themselves at parties to launch 'new' programs. We have already described one example of this in 3.3.2, where introduction of child benefit was primarily an income maintenance matter, but, because it had an impact on take-home pay at a time of attempted pay restraint, politicians concerned with incomes policy participated in Cabinet discussions and helped to postpone its introduction.

Attempts to push through a policy succession which would create a neater, more self-contained organizational structure might have to be modified to meet the claims of an 'outsider'. In 1.3.3 we described the establishment of Regional Water Authorities in England and Wales from a multiplicity of separate water supply and sewerage authorities. The initiative came from the Department of Environment and the major existing delivery agencies were the local authorities. However, the Ministry of Agriculture, Fisheries and Food (MAFF) became involved because of the concern of farming groups that their interest in land drainage would be harmed by being lost in an organization with many other water responsibilities (see Richardson and Jordan, 1979, pp. 48, 145–6). In the end, the MAFF retained departmental responsibility for land drainage, and separate land drainage committees were established within each Regional Water Authority.

3.8   Complex patterns of policy succession

The various types of policy succession so far discussed have mostly been 'ideal types', relatively simple categories which may bear close resemblance to the examples used to illustrate them, but which by no means embrace the entire range of combinations of characteristics which policy succession may take in the real world. Frequently, the forms which policy succession takes will be more complex, but will nevertheless contain elements of the ideal types discussed above.

One such complex type of policy succession, normally associated with organizational changes of equal complexity, is a combination of splitting and consolidation. An obvious example is the formation of the Department of Energy in the United States from elements split off from other departments as well as from free-standing organizations. In Britain, the splitting off of local authority health functions in 1974 from reorganized local authorities and their reallocation to the also reorganized health authorities illustrates the same pattern of change.

Another type of complex pattern involves splitting or consolidation combined with partial termination of some policy elements. The demise of the Office of Economic Opportunity (OEO) illustrates this type of change. In 1973, all but three of the programs administered by OEO were transferred to the Departments of Health, Education and Welfare (HEW), Labor, and Housing and Urban Development (HUD) for the purposes of termination in most instances. The three remaining programs were transferred to the Community Services Administration in 1975. These three programs are almost certainly to be terminated during the Reagan administration. The complex history of the Reconstruction Finance Corporation, beginning in 1938, involved several consolidations and terminations, each involving terminations of some portion of the powers accumulated by the organization. This ended in 1957 when the organization was split among the Housing and Home Finance Agency, the General Service Administration, the Small Business Administration, and the Department of the Treasury.

3.9 Policy residues

... it vanished quite slowly, beginning with the end of the tail, and ending with the grin, which remained some time after the rest of it had gone.

Lewis Carroll, *Allice in Wonderland*

Although policy residues are not themselves a type of policy succession, they are worth mentioning here as an important consequence of many policy successions. By policy residues we mean recognizable organizational or program elements from the 'replaced' policy which continue to exist.

Policy succession of whatever type rarely involves a complete break with previous programs. The 'new' program may incorporate a substantial number of features from the old. This has both advantages and problems for success in implementing succession. The advantages lie in the ability to make use of existing skills and accumulated knowledge about the policy area; the disadvantages lie in the possible subversion of the succession, particularly because of barriers to policy succession thrown up within existing organizations (see Chapter 6).

The form which a succession will take will to a large extent be determined by the form of the existing program, for two related reasons. In many cases, the 'limited comparisons' aspect of the incremental model will be an accurate description of how policymakers examine succession options; that is in terms of changes from existing programs rather than a completely fresh consideration of a wider range of alternatives (see Lindblom, 1959). Considerations of resistance to dramatic change will also tend to favor successions which incorporate substantial elements of existing programs. However, to argue that succession was merely incremental would miss the point that succession differs in terms of process and substance from other types of policy change (see 1.2.1.3).

The method of algebraic representation described in the appendix to Chapter 2 provides a means of tracking the residue elements of a succession, since it distinguishes between those components which are simply carried over (maintained) from the previous program, those which involve replacement of similar components, and those which are innovations.

Even when a replacement program does not incorporate features of the previous program, commitments entered into under previous programs may continue to entail financial outlays and the employment of administrators for years after the program has been replaced. For example, there continued to be a section of the British Department of Industry in the late 1970s responsible for administering a program of industrial investment grants which had been replaced by the Conservatives in 1970 (in the meantime there had been several further policy changes). This continuation related to projects planned at the time of the change which were therefore eligible for assistance under the program.

A rather different form of policy residue, again from the United Kingdom, relates to the earnings-related supplement to basic state pension: the introduction of second pensions under a 1975 Act effectively replaced this provision, but because contributions have been made towards it, this residue of the previous program will be around for decades. In the United States, it took until 1979 to terminate the Renegotiation Board, established to renegotiate defense contracts from World War II. It had some functions relative to the Korean conflict, but after that was largely a vestigial organization.

In the United States, the 'grandfathering' of the clients of a program after the program is scheduled for termination or replacement results in significant policy residues. (The term 'grandfathering' comes from the post-bellum South where, to prevent illiterate whites from being disenfranchised by literacy laws, persons were given the right to vote if their grandfathers had had the right to vote. The term has now been extended to include any retention of rights or entitlements.) For example, dependents of Social Security recipients are no longer eligible for benefits for higher education—unless they began their education before 1 July 1982. Students who have begun are eligible for reduced benefits for up to four years.

'Grandfathering' appears to be more common in the United States than in Britain, but one literal example of 'grandfathering' was a clause in the Labour government's Commonwealth Immigration Act of 1968 designed to enable the descendents of white settlers, colonial officials, etc., to escape from immigration restrictions imposed on largely Asian UK passport holders resident abroad (Ashford, 1981, pp. 240–4). This 'grandfathering' or 'patrial' route to discrimination was reinforced in the Conservative government's Immigration Act of 1971 following the introduction of an amendment to remedy the 'problem' that tougher immigration controls planned for Asians and Africans would also apply to whites.

If our contention about the increasing future significance of policy succession is correct, we should expect such policy residues to become a substantial, if esoteric, aspect of public administration. This also points to the importance of designing programs for termination so that residual clients and functions do not require the continuation of outdated programs (see 8.3).

By contrast, some policy residues may either by design or the turn of events or political fashion serve as a base for reactivating the original policy (see Biller, 1976, p. 147). An example of a residue deliberately maintained to meet a contingency is the retention of Selective Service Boards in the United States after the introduction of the policy of an all-volunteer army in 1972; these were able to participate in registration of potential conscripts when a policy of registration was reintroduced by President Carter in 1980. An alternative way of characterizing such episodes is as a special type of 'policy hiatus' discussed in 3.2.5.

3.10 Using the classification of policy succession types

Although the types of policy succession outlined in this chapter do not provide categories into which we can neatly fit all the occurrences (past and future) of policy succession in practice, we feel that the discussion of them has been valuable in that it has enabled us to isolate relevant features of the policy succession processes and outcomes associated with each type. This analysis can be applied to policy succession in practice (by retrospective analysts or would-be policy transformers) by identifying the extent to which the characteristics of an individual attempt at policy succession conform to one or more of the types.

At a basic level, the classification emphasizes the importance of paying attention to which kind of succession is being undertaken since this will determine how many enemies and friends the proponent of succession is likely to have, and the extent to which these will already be structured into organizations or groups. Related to this is the variation in complexity between different types of succession. In general, greater complexity will be related to greater uncertainty about the outcomes of the succession, because of the greater opportunities for alternative coalitions, for bargaining, for the arrival of uninvited policy actors (3.7.3), and for unanticipated interaction effects following implementation.

Different types of policy succession will have different problems associated with them which it would be sensible to take into account in considering alternative strategies for securing policy change. For example, consolidation poses important *intra*-organizational problems at the implementation stage, while splitting may pose *inter*-organizational difficulties (for a discussion of these organizational problems see Chapter 6).

Care must be taken in generalizing about types of policy succession since different political systems will have different balances of types of succession. For example, because of the structuring of British government into departments there will be a greater proportion of complex successions combining splitting and consolidation than is the case in the US Federal government with its more agency-oriented structure. Some evidence about these differences will be presented in Chapter 4. The important point to note here is that these differences (quite apart from other systems-related variations) will have implications for the process of securing succession, since the politics of the process varies according to succession type.

Chapter 4
INDICATORS OF POLICY CHANGE

4.1 Measurement

Measurement in policy analysis is difficult in the best of circumstances. The world of policymaking is complicated, complex and confusing. The problems of measuring change which are inherently involved in analyzing policy succession are perhaps especially significant. We are attempting to assess at times rather slight differences from the original policy to the successor policy and even when there are noticeable changes the categorization of those changes may be difficult. The categories of the types of policy change (Chapter 2) and the types of policy succession (Chapter 3) are intellectually distinct, but the real world frequently does not attempt to conform to our intellectual standards. The measurement of policy succession requires the application of good judgement as much as it does the application of rigorous research methodologies.

Even given the difficulties associated with the measurement of policy succession, such measurement must be undertaken. We have presented a number of hypotheses about policy succession, and we will present more in subsequent chapters, and we need some method of making at least preliminary judgements about the accuracy of those hypotheses. At the most basic level, we need to know if our hypothesis of the increasing importance of policy succession as compared to other forms of policy change is correct or not.

We can approach the measurement of policy succession, or other forms of policy change, in several ways. One is to use an organizational unit of analysis, and assume that a change in an organization will be indicative of a change in the policies administered by the organization (see 4.2). Further, it assumes that a change in policy will necessarily have organizational ramifications. This, of course, is not necessarily true and many major policy changes may be conducted without any concomitant change in organizations. However, organizations do have the virtue of being highly visible and well-documented entities, and changes in organizations are indeed frequently associated with changes in policy.

Another approach to measurement of policy succession is to examine changes in the legal framework of policy delivery (see 4.3). This indicator has the advantage that almost any change in the legal structure of the policy area will involve a policy succession, or some other form of policy change. However, unless we monitor not only the activity of legislative bodies, but also the making of secondary legislation (regulations, executive orders, statutory instruments, etc.), then we may miss a great deal of the policy succession and even policy termination and initiation. Once a basic law has been enacted, major changes may occur in the policy without any activity by the legislature. Many of the changes resulting from secondary legislation will be technical and involve only administrative change, but many are substantive and may have a great effect on the policy as implemented (Freedman, 1978). Thus, using law as an indicator of policy succession involves a monitoring of a huge amount of legislative and executive activity.

Finally, although closely related to both organizational structure and legislative activity, the budget may be used as a means of measuring policy succession. This approach is in some ways particularly attractive because it may allow measurement of the *degree* of change, as well as the simple occurrence of that change. This is, to some degree, illustrated in the appendix to Chapter 2. The budget does have the major disadvantage that the changes in monetary amounts involved within a policy area may be a function of so many factors that it is frequently difficult to estimate how much change is due to policy succession, and how much to the influences of maintenance as documented in 2.3.2 and 2.3.4.

Each of these approaches to the measurement of policy succession enables us to gain one portion of the total picture of the changes which are occurring in a policy area. Each has its weaknesses, and its strengths, and the utilization of one or the other may depend upon the particular circumstances of a particular investigation. For example, as we will show below, the organizational basis of American government makes the use of this type of indicator particularly applicable to the United States, and also makes it somewhat easier to gather the relevant data. But we do not claim to have definitive answers to any of the questions we have raised. We can only hope that we can catch some glimpse of the dimensions of the problems we have identified.

4.2 Organizations as indicators

Policies are abstractions which only achieve substance once they are delivered (Davis, 1979). As we saw in Chapter 2, all but the most insubstantial forms of policy output, such as exhortation, require the establishment and maintenance of one or more organizations through which the policy is delivered. Because of procedures for budgetary allocations and financial and political accountability these organizations are normally formally defined and delimited—though ambiguities about classification of just what type of organization may still remain, particularly in Britain (see Hood and Dunsire, 1981; Moe, 1979). Thus the existence of organizations is relatively well documented. The researcher into American federal government organizations will also find terminations and replacements of organizations systematically recorded over time (4.2.1), though the researcher into British government may have to engage in some considerable detective work to track down an elusive organization whose initiation but not termination is mentioned in a source (4.2.2).

Organizations are reasonably reliable as units of analysis across time, though the researcher always has to be aware of the possible implications for his analysis of changes in the political fashion for particular forms of organization, such as the rise and partial fall of 'giant departments' in Britain in the 1960s and 1970s, for example, the formation of the Department of Trade and Industry following a succession of mergers, and its subsequent splitting into the Departments of Industry, Trade, and Energy.

Unfortunately, organizations are not reliable units for direct comparisons between different countries because of different constitutional and administrative structures: in the United States the main organizational unit is the agency with a relatively specific task; in Britain the main unit is a widely embracing department, and in addition we may have to look at nationalized industries and other appointed bodies. However, the fact that the organizational units are not directly comparable and that this has implications for their use as indicators of policy succession does not rule out the possibility of comparison. It merely means that crude numerical comparisons are not possible and that explorations of the significance of the differences in organizational units have to be introduced into the analysis.

Using organizations as indicators of policy change may suffer from two further contrasting flaws: they may record too much change, and (at the same time) they may record too little. Organizational changes may record too much change where they are what we have called cosmetic changes (3.3.4, 3.4.4), involving the relabelling, splitting or consolidation of existing organizations with little impact on processes or outputs. Too little change may be recorded because some significant policy changes may occur within existing organizations which continue under the same title; this is a particular problem in analyzing policy succession in Britain and indicates a need to explore changes below the level of the organization as a whole. An example of this type of 'microsuccession' analysis is conducted in 4.2.2.2.

These difficulties do not mean that we should abandon the attempt to use organizations to provide quantitative indicators of change. They simply mean that we cannot use organizational changes as the sole measure of change and that we should use the findings of organizational analysis with interpretative care and preferably in conjunction with other indicators of change.

4.2.1 *Organizational succession in the United States*

Research into organizational succession in the United States is facilitated by the listing of these changes provided in the *US Government Organization Manual*. Appendix C in this document for the year 1980–81 lists all changes and terminations of organizations from 1933 to the time of publication. This listing does not include (necessarily) all new organizations which are formed, and as a consequence budgets and *Government Organization Manuals* for the intervening years were examined in order to gain a complete enumeration of new organizations being formed. The results of coding all these organizational changes are presented in Table 4.1.

The most significant finding in Table 4.1 is that in the postwar period our underlying hypothesis that succession is becoming a more common type of policymaking than innovation in industrialized societies is supported. In absolute terms, the number of organizational initiations has been declining steadily over the past fifty years, with the exception of a slight rise in initiations in the 1940s associated with World War II (see Figure 4.1).

The level of organizational successions in the 1930s was higher than our expectations when compared with both initiations in the 1930s and organizational successions in the postwar decades. It was

Table 4.1 Patterns of organizational change in the United States, 1933–79 (percentages)

	1930s	*1940s*	*1950s*	*1960s*	*1970s*
Initiation	41.6	29.9	47.3	40.9	26.0
Termination	11.6	13.7	17.7	18.5	21.9
Succession					
of which:	46.8	56.2	35.0	40.6	52.1
Linear	34.7	38.4	25.4	28.7	34.1
Consolidation	9.5	12.2	6.9	6.3	11.4
Splitting	0.6	2.4	1.2	3.5	4.5
Other	2.0	3.2	1.5	2.1	2.1
Total	100.0	100.0	100.0	100.0	100.0
N =	346	531	260	286	334

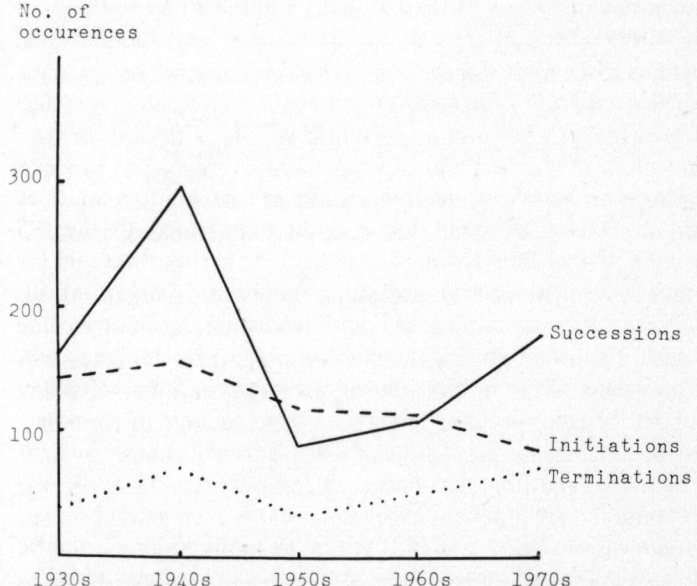

Fig. 4.1 Trends of organizational initiation, succession and termination

only by the 1970s that the absolute level of successions rose above that of the 1930s. This finding emphasizes the need to avoid positing a simplistic inevitable steady rise in succession and decline in innovation for all decades in all countries. Attention also needs to be

paid to the public policy history of each country to explain short- or
medium-term fluctuations from the long-run pattern of the increasing relative importance of succession compared to innovation. In the
absence of comparative data, it is not possible to provide a definitive
explanation of the relatively high total volume of organizational
activity and particularly of succession in the 1930s in the United
States, but from our knowledge of American history and some
limited comparative evidence from Britain we can suggest that these
features are consequences of special features of the New Deal period
in the United States which we should not expect to find repeated in
other countries. Chester and Willson (1968, appendix), using indicators which are not directly comparable to those used for the
United States, found that there was a substantially higher level of
changes in ministerial responsibility for functions and other reorganizations in Britain in the 1950s than in the 1930s.

The 1940s saw a sharp rise in the number of organizational
successions in the United States, which was more than reversed in the
1950s. This temporary rise is readily explicable as a result of the huge
number of reorganizations during World War II, with some organizations going though a chain of successions during a few years or
even a few months. We would expect a similar pattern of a temporary
rise in successions in other nonoccupied industrialized countries
involved in World War II.

Within the total number of successions occurring during the period
1933–79, the majority were linear, with one organization assuming
the duties of another. During the postwar period, linear successions
have increased as a proportion of all organizational changes,
although they have declined slightly as a percentage of all policy
successions. More complex forms of organizational change, such as
consolidations, splitting, non-linear successions, etc., have become
more common as the 'policy space' has become even more crowded
with organizations (see 1.1.1). But even in the 1970s the proportion of
these more complex changes did not surpass that of the 1940s as
government sought to adjust its organizational capacities to cope
with the pressures of war. In the 1930s, as the New Deal programs
produced massive growth and change in government, there was a
very high proportion of consolidations of organizations.

Another finding of interest is the somewhat larger number of
organizational terminations which occurred than might have been
anticipated from the conventional wisdom. This wisdom, as charac-

terized by Herbert Kaufman's *Are Government Organizations Immortal?* (1976), is that very few governmental organizations ever go out of business. However, in this enumeration of organizational changes, some 285 terminations were recorded. A large number of these terminations, as well as a large number of the initiations, were of special commissions, presidential advisory bodies and the like, whereas Kaufman's sample of organizations came entirely from the executive departments. But if the conventional idea that once initiated a government program will survive and have a dynamic of its own were to be correct, then even these organizations should not be terminated as frequently as they are. It is interesting that if these special organizations are removed from the enumeration there were still 144 terminations and 451 initiations. It is also interesting to note the extent to which the organizations that did cease existence tended to have automatic terminators built into their legislation. This would appear to support the arguments of those advocating 'sunset' laws that such laws would be effective in bringing about the demise of agencies and programs which may have outlived their usefulness. However, this may to a considerable extent simply reflect the intrinsically temporary nature of the functions the organizations were asked to perform in the first place.

Despite this number of organizational terminations, there have been many fewer functional terminations (de Leon, 1979). While organizations may come and go, the vast majority of the functional activities of government have remained untroubled. In terms of the trend across time in organizational terminations, the absolute level has shown a steady upward trend over the past fifty years, apart from a temporary rise in the 1940s (see Figure 4.1).

Apart from a similar temporary rise in the 1940s, the absolute level of organizational terminations has shown a steady upward trend over the past fifty years. As a proportion of all organizational changes, there has been a smoother upward trend (reflecting the temporary rise in all forms of organizational change during the war). It should be noted that this long-run trend cannot have been affected by the recent academic and political interest in terminations, which only developed in the second half of the 1970s.

Despite all the necessary caveats, we feel that this analysis of organizational changes has shown that available indicators can be used to provide insights into the changing pattern of policy dynamics in particular countries. The explanation for the pattern cannot, of course, be derived solely from the numbers themselves but has to be related to the history of public policy developments of that country.

4.2.2 *Organizational succession in Britain*

The researcher wishing to conduct an analysis of policy change in the United Kingdom on a comparable basis to that for the United States in 4.2.1 is faced with two major problems. The first problem is the lack of an official publication giving systematic historical data comparable to that available in the *US Government Organization Manual*. The researcher accordingly has to compile his own data set from a wide variety of government and non-government publications (of which the most useful are Rodgers, 1980, and Chester and Willson, 1968). The second problem is the unit of analysis: the concept of the 'agency' as a basic, relatively clearly defined unit of policy delivery does not apply to Britain, while Britain at the same time has a concept of 'sponsoring' departments which exercise oversight over non-departmental bodies and private firms in an industry which has no direct parallel in the United States. Many British departments, especially the modern 'giant departments', are far larger than is ideal for use as indicators of policy change, since substantial internal reorganization may be concealed; however (with the exception of some 'hived in' organizations like the Property Services Agency within the Department of the Environment), there is no self-contained organizational unit which is comparable across departments or across time. It is important and revealing to examine subdepartmental changes (as in 4.2.2.2 below) but these problems cause great difficulties in using 'organizations' as a whole as indicators of policy change. There are difficulties enough in devising strategies to measure British government organizations at one point in time (see Hood and Dunsire, 1981) let alone across five decades. The problems are not insurmountable, but their resolution provides the agenda for a major research project rather than part of a chapter in this book. Accordingly, no attempt is made here to carry out an analysis of the universe of organizations comparable to that for the United States in 4.2.1. Instead, two more narrowly focussed analyses of organizational change are presented as illustrations, one of changes at the level of organizations in a single policy area (energy), and the other of changes in responsibility for a specific function (involvement in shipbuilding), many of which occurred *within* the same organization.

4.2.2.1   *Organizational succession in energy in Britain*
Table 4.2 presents the results of an analysis of changes in all
government organizations involved in energy policy between 1930
and 1979. (Government organizations are here defined as government departments, nationalized industries, other executive bodies
appointed by government, and consultative committees to which the
government makes paid appointments.) The pattern of change shows
that succession has been relatively (though not absolutely) more
important in energy policy organizations in the 1970s compared to
the 1940s (but see note to Table 4.2). We are not arguing that the
profile of this particular illustrative policy area can be generalized to
all fields of British public policy. Indeed, the pattern revealed in Table
4.2 shows up certain distinctive features of energy as a policy area.
    Prior to World War II there was a Mines Department established
in 1920 and a Central Electricity Board established in 1926, with the
Ministry of Transport being the department responsible for electricity; the Board of Trade had some responsibilities relating to fuel. All

Table 4.2   Patterns of change in energy organizations in Great Britain,
1930–79

	1930s	*1940s*	*1950s*	*1960s*	*1970s*	*Total*
Initiation	1	9			2	12
Termination		1			1	2
Succession						
of which:	2	11	8	3	6	30
Linear	1				1	2
Consolidation		3		2	3	8
Splitting			2		1	3
Other	1	8	6	1	1	17
Total	3	21	8	3	9	44

Notes: Northern Ireland is excluded because of lack of available information. To avoid distortion of the figures systems of regional boards are
counted as single units; if each regional board had been counted a separate
unit, the effect would have been greatly to increase the amount of initiation
recorded for the 1940s and the amount of succession (consolidation)
recorded for the 1970s. Where responsibility for individual non-
departmental bodies is switched, this is counted as an organizational change;
where changes in ministerial responsibility result solely from departmental
reorganizations, only the department changes are counted. It proved
impracticable to obtain the date of origin of the Electricity Consultative
Committee, and it is therefore excluded.

these responsibilities continued through the 1930s, and there were few organizational changes during this decade.

The 1940s saw two major developments. One was a series of splittings and consolidations of departmental responsibility for energy functions during the wartime period, culminating in the formation of the Ministry of Fuel and Power in 1942. Many of the organizational changes lasted only for very brief periods, echoing the pattern for all US organizations during World War II found in 4.2.1. The other development was the nationalization of the coal, gas and electricity industries, accounting for the peak of organizational initiations in the 1940s. In the case of gas and electricity, much of the supply had already been provided by the state through municipalities, illustrating the dangers of using organizational initiations as crude indicators without qualification. It is also worth noting that because new functions are less likely to be accompanied by organizational initiations in Britain than in the United States, new functions may not be picked up by organizational indicators. An example is responsibility for nuclear power, which was initially undertaken by the Department of Scientific and Industrial Research; subsequent organizational successions concerning nuclear power are, however, recorded in Table 4.2.

After the burst of initiation in the 1940s, the 1950s were a period of organizational successions of organizations established in the previous decade, most noticeably in the reorganization of electricity generation. The 1960s were a period of organizational calm before a resurgence of activity in the 1970s; the one development which did take place is worth noting, however: responsibility for all energy functions (except for Scotland and Northern Ireland) was united in one department when the Ministry of Power was absorbed into the Ministry of Technology, which also took over responsibility for nuclear power.

It is not surprising, in a decade which saw the emergence of Britain as a major oil producer, the traumatic coalminer's dispute of 1973–74 and the 'energy crisis' following the oil price rise of 1973, that there should be an upsurge in both organizational initiation and succession. What is perhaps surprising is how little organizational adjustment was necessary. The only departmental change was the separation of the Department of Energy from the Department of Trade and Industry; because responsibility for almost all energy functions was already in one department, no consolidation was necessary, in contrast to the United States. The discovery and exploitation of North Sea oil was followed by the establishment of the British National Oil Corporation (though even this was not pure initiation, since it took over the North Sea oil interests of the National Coal Board). Otherwise, the bulk of the organizational changes recorded in Table 4.2 were associated with the reorganization of the gas industry in 1972 (a proposed reorganization of the electricity industry was abandoned).

One noticeable difference between the types of succession shown in Tables 4.1 and 4.2 is that the majority of successions in the United States are linear, whereas in Britain almost all changes are complex, involving the splitting off of part of one organization and its merger with another. This reflects the different structure of the executive in the two countries, with individual agencies being responsible for relatively specific programs in the United States and departments with widely embracing responsibilities in Britain.

Because the British government has not published (or, it would seem, even collected) information about advisory committees over the period we are interested in, these are not included in the analysis reported in Table 4.2 (which is therefore not comparable to Table 4.1 for the United States). Similarly, Royal Commissions and Committees of Inquiry are not included, (Examples of such committees are Coal Derivatives 1959–60, Generation and Distribution of Electricity in Scotland 1961–62, Delays in Commissioning Power Stations 1968–69). At the end of the 1970s, the following advisory bodies came under the Department of Energy: Advisory Committee on Fixed Offshore Installations, Advisory Council on Energy Conservation, Advisory Council on Research and Development for Fuel and Power, Energy Commission, Offshore Energy Technology Board, Offshore Industry Liaison Committee, Offshore Safety Enquiry, Severn Barrage Committee (Pliatzky, 1980). Most, if not all of these, relate to new concerns of the 1970s associated with North Sea oil and the energy crisis.

We would not see energy policy as being typical in terms of organizational change, because of the relative upsurge of change in the 1970s following a drop in activity in the 1960s. The pattern of an initial burst of initiation followed by succession and/or quiescence is, however, one we would expect to find in other policy areas.

4.2.2.2   *Microsuccession: shipbuilding as a case study*

Study of organizational changes below the level of whole organizations is important for a number of reasons: minor transfers of responsibility which do not affect the basic structure of either organization frequently occur, particularly in Britain. The study of how such transferred functions are allocated within organizations can show us how expressed reasons for a transfer may not be followed through in practice. Functions may also be transferred between sections within an organization and these may reflect or have implications for substantive policy succession.

The example chosen to illustrate 'microsuccession' is changes in responsibility for the British shipbuilding industry since World War II (see Hogwood, 1979a). Other lessons can be drawn from reallocation of responsibilities for this industry during the two World Wars (see 8.4.2). The main changes in responsibility for shipbuilding are shown in Table 4.3.

Table 4.3   Changes in responsibility for British shipbuilding, 1959–77

Year	Change
1959	Transferred from Admiralty to Ministry of Transport (MOT); comes under Shipbuilding and Repair Group
1960	Transferred within MOT to Shipbuilding, Ports and Shipping Group
1961	Transferred within MOT to Shipbuilding and General Group
1963	Transferred within MOT to Shipping Policy and Shipbuilding Group
1964	Transferred to Board of Trade (BOT); comes under Engineering Industries Division
1965/66	Transferred within BOT to Division 4
1966	Transferred to Ministry of Technology; comes under Shipbuilding, Electrical Engineering and Chemical Plant Division
1967	Shipbuilding Industry Board (SIB) formally established
1970	Ministry of Technology merged into Department of Trade and Industry (DTI)
1971	Within DTI Shipbuilding Policy Division is set up; takes over residual functions of SIB
1972	Formation of Industrial Development Executive (covering shipbuilding) within DTI
1974	DTI split up; shipbuilding comes under Department of Industry
1977	Nationalized British Shipbuilders set up

Source: Hogwood (1979a, p. 240).

From 1940 to 1959, responsibility for shipbuilding lay with the Admiralty (on the 'customer as sponsoring department' principle). In 1959 shipbuilding, along with shiprepairing and marine engineering, was transferred to the Ministry of Transport (already responsible for shipping) as part of a general reallocation of functions that followed the abolition of the Ministry of Supply and the creation of a Ministry of Aviation. Mr Marples, the Minister of Transport, justified the transfer of shipbuilding on the grounds that 'shipping, shipbuilding and shiprepairing in any sensible concern would be brought under the same management because they are now closely related' (*House of Commons Debates*, 25 November 1959, col. 510).

However, during its period of sponsorship by the Ministry of Transport shipbuilding came under various groupings of functions. Initially shipbuilding was placed under a small section of its own under a Deputy Secretary (the civil service rank immediately below the top rank of Permanent Secretary). In 1960, this section became part of a Shipbuilding, Ports and Shipping Group. The following year, shipbuilding became part of a Shipbuilding and General group, which also included an International Inland Transport Branch, a Statistics Division, a General Division, and later the United Kingdom Railway Advisory Service! Shipbuilding spent its final year or so at the Ministry of Transport in a Shipping Policy and Shipbuilding Group, which also included two Foreign Shipping Relations Divisions and a General Shipping Policy Division. (These various sections, groups and divisions were all integral parts of the Ministry rather than separate agencies as would normally be the case for corresponding functions in the United States.)

The way in which shipbuilding was transferred between these various groups suggests that they were the result of conveniently sized groupings for managerial reasons rather than to find the grouping which would be most effective for bringing shipping and shipbuilding 'under the same management' as desired by Mr Marples. However, the effect of these frequent internal changes should not be exaggerated. The same civil servant was in charge of the Shipbuilding and Ship Repair Division for most of its stay at the Ministry of Transport, and because the industry was of special concern to the Permanent Secretary, the Under-Secretary in charge of whatever group shipbuilding happened to be under could be 'short-circuited'.

In the list of ministerial appointments following the Labour victory at the October 1964 General Election it was announced that Mr

Wilson, the new Prime Minister, was creating a new transport department at the Board of Trade which would be responsible for shipping and shipbuilding. (The use of 'department' in this context illustrates the confusion which bedevils the organizational terminology of British administration.) However, according to his subsequent statements, it was always Mr Wilson's intention to transfer shipbuilding together with machine engineering to the Ministry of Technology when that was properly established. The reason for the transfer of shipbuilding to the Board of Trade when it was already intended to transfer it to the Ministry of Technology appears to lie in its relationship with the shipping industry. Many shipowners had thought that the Board of Trade was a more appropriate sponsoring department than the Ministry of Transport because of the international aspects of the shipping industry.

Although the original announcement had stated that shipping and shipbuilding would be together in a transport department at the Board of Trade, during its stay at the Board of Trade shipbuilding was in the Industries and Manufactures Department and was separated from shipping. Within the Industries and Manufactures Department shipbuilding was first of all in the Engineering Industries Division, which was responsible for plant and machinery, shipbuilding, shiprepairing, metals except iron and steel, timber, woodpulp, paper and paper products, and most metal durable goods, and then in a reorganized Division 4, which looked after matters concerning shipbuilding, shiprepairing, metals except iron and steel, timber, woodpulp, paper and paper products and miscellaneous consumer goods. The latter grouping in particular suggests that shipbuilding was put in with other industries simply to make up a division of a suitable size and that organization to assist coordination of policy was not the main concern.

When shipbuilding was actually transferred to the Ministry of Technology in 1966, it occurred at a crucial time for policy for the industry, following the publication of a government-sponsored report calling for restructuring of the industry with government help and the establishment of a government appointed and funded Shipbuilding Industry Board, which was formally established in March 1967.

When this latest transfer was debated in the House of Commons on 16 July 1966 the Prime Minister indicated that the government preferred the principle of horizontal organization of shipbuilding with other metal-using industries to vertical organization with shipping. However, as was shown above, shipbuilding was not arranged 'vertically' with shipping within the Board of Trade, but was lumped in with a variety of other industries, including some metal-using ones.

Within the Ministry of Technology shipbuilding was organized, initially in one branch and later in two, within a Shipbuilding, Electrical and Chemical Plant Division. When the Ministry of Technology was merged into the Department of Trade and Industry (DTI), shipbuilding remained in this division. However, in late 1971 a Shipbuilding Policy Division with three branches was created (the number of civil servants administering shipbuilding has varied inversely with Britain's share of world production). This change coincided with the termination of the Shipbuilding Industry Board at the end of 1971 and the assumption of its residual functions by the DTI. In 1974, the incoming Labour government split up the DTI and shipbuilding came under the Department of Industry. 1977 saw the nationalization of all major British shipyards—though some of the firms 'nationalized' were already 100 per cent government owned. The Department of Industry continued to be the sponsoring department for the now-nationalized industry.

Between 1959 and 1972 divisions or groups which have covered shipbuilding have also covered such a diverse list of other functions that it is difficult to discern any pattern or trend in the criteria used for changes in responsibility within departments. In terms of change between departments, we can see a long-term change from grouping with the users of the industry's product (or rather with the users of some product of the UK shipbuilding industry and its rivals) to grouping with producers of other goods. In this sense, the changes can be explained as a regrouping in terms of major purposes or functions. However, it is difficult to see why so many reallocations were necessary to bring about this change, especially given that the justifications for some of the transfers were not reflected in the allocation of responsibility for shipbuilding within the new department. It seems more plausible to explain some of the changes in terms of the political fashions of the time. Shipbuilding is by no means the only example in Britain of promiscuous transferring of responsibilities in this way: civil aviation was treated even more dramatically in the same period. These transfers of individual industries must also be seen in the context of the riot of institutional tinkering during the period, with the setting up and disappearance of departments like the Department of Economic Affairs, and the evolution and dismember- ment of the DTI as a giant department to deal with all aspects of industry (see Clarke, 1975).

4.3   Laws as indicators

4.3.1   *Laws as pervasive indicators of policy change*

In addition to organizational changes, changes in the legal frame- work of policy may be used to indicate the occurrence of a policy succession. This is, in one way, the most definitive indicator of policy succession, as little can be done to change policy in most in- dustrialized societies without a legal change of some form or another. However, there are important problems in utilizing law as an indicator of policy succession.

The first is that given the number of ways in which a law, or law- like statement, can be made, it may be difficult to capture in any detail the changes which are occurring. A great deal of the legal change surrounding particular policy issues does not appear in compendia of statutes, but rather in the compendia of secondary legislation or regulations which are made in pursuance of statutes. The locus of a great deal of lawmaking has moved from constitutionally designated legislative bodies to the public bureaucracy. This is indicated in the United States by the rapid growth of the *Federal Register* as compared to the *Statutes in Force*. The regulations emerging from the bureaucracy have the force of law if made according to designated procedures. In addition, as they are generally easier to modify, there should be more policy succession occurring in this manner. But the multiplicity of regulations, and the difficulty of understanding their real impacts on policy, makes the use of law as an indicator more difficult than might be imagined.

A second problem is that there is no readily defined unit of analysis such as exists with the organization. An act or a statute is too large a unit, as it may contain a wide range of provisions. Some of these may be initiations, some successions, and some terminations, and it is consequently impossible to capture the meaning of the act as a single unit. In addition, an act or statute cannot be equated to an executive order or a regulation, and no means of weighting the differences between them appears available or even justifiable.

If the statute is too large a unit it is not clear what smaller unit could be used instead. Again, sections or paragraphs may contain different types of provisions, and different types of legislation may contain differing degrees of detail and of delegation to the public bureaucracy for elaboration.

Also, it is difficult to assess the significance of a legislative change. The number of words sometimes is used to try to measure legislative activity, but is actually quite unsuitable for such an effort. This is in part because of the differences in detail mentioned above. However, it may also be a function of changes in procedures. Conservative critics of the growth of government in the United States frequently pointed to the rapidly increasing size of the *Federal Register*, while failing to understand that changes in legal requirements forced each proposed regulation to be published once more than it had been previously, thus automatically increasing the volume of words printed.

The above problems with the use of law as an indicator of policy succession would appear to indicate that *qualitative* assessment should be at least as prominent as quantitative assessment at this stage of development. As a consequence, much of our initial analysis of laws as indicators will concentrate on individual legislative histories, rather than the more quantitative type of analysis presented for organizations.

More sophisticated analysis of legal indicators of policy succession is possible when legislative indicators are combined with budgets. When this is presented, as in the appendix to Chapter 2, this enables relatively complex changes to be presented in a quantified and compressed form which will allow comparisons across policy areas and types of activity (initiation, succession, etc.). For example. in the United States housing example presented in that appendix, if we begin with the Housing Act of 1937, $0.7 billion in spending could be taken to be the result of successions to that original act, while $4.3 billion in spending could be taken to be the result of policy initiations in the housing area.

4.3.2   *The Social Security program in the United States as an example*

> one trait has characterized the Social Security Administration from its inception: a belief that all social security legislation is only a prelude to more such legislation
>
> (Stevens, 1970, p. 389)

The evolution of the legal structure of Social Security in the United States is illustrative of the utility, and difficulties, of law as an indicator of policy succession. The Social Security program was enacted in 1935, but almost from the time that President Roosevelt signed the Act there were attempts to modify the program (Altmeyer, 1968; Stevens, 1970). The major policy successions which occurred came as the result of legislative actions. For example, the Social Security Amendments of 1939 had a very significant impact on the program. They converted what would have been primarily an annuity program for workers, with benefits calculated on the basis of total contributions during the individual's working lifetime, to a system of social insurance which would begin to pay benefits to retired workers who had made only minimal contributions. In addition, these amendments extended coverage from the insured worker to widows and orphans of insured workers who had previously been offered no protection under the program. Likewise, the Amendments of 1950 and 1952 had the effect of increasing the level of benefits for all insured, especially those who had made very low levels of contributions, and increased the ability of those receiving Social Security to earn money in employment. Arguably, these amendments almost completely changed the Social Security system from its original rather restrictive definition to a more broad-scale social insurance program, but did not go so far as to break the connection between having made contributions and receiving benefits, although small programs for the elderly were developed as a part of the Old Age Assistance Program.

A similar pattern of development of the Social Security program continued with the Social Security Amendments of 1954, 1956, 1958 and 1960. The general impact of each of these sets of changes was to increase benefits, expand the income base covered under Social Security (from $3600 prior to 1954 to $4800 in 1960) and to increase the amount of money which retirees could earn without losing Social Security benefits (from $900 prior to the amendments in 1954 to $1800 by 1960). But there were several more significant policy successions involved in these amendments. One was to consolidate the disability insurance system into the old age and survivors insurance system. This began with the 1954 amendments which recognized disability as a problem limiting the ability of workers to qualify for benefits under the program. In the 1956 amendments disability benefits for workers over fifty were made equivalent to social security benefits, and the Old Age and Survivors Insurarce (OASI) system became the Old Age, Survivors and Disability Insurance (OASDI) system and the administration of two programs was merged.

The second development was a liberalization of the definition of a 'fully insured worker'. Prior to the first reform in 1960, a worker had to make the legally established minimum contribution in one-half of all quarters from the age of twenty-one until the time of retirement. In 1960 this was reduced to one-quarter in three, and later to one in four (1961). All these changes made it that much easier for any worker to become eligible for Social Security benefits upon retirement, and the system became increasingly a general system of social insurance rather than the more restrictive system envisaged at its inception.

During the mid-1960s the Social Security system went through significant expansion. In particular, the health insurance program for the elderly—Medicare—was added to the system by the Social Security Amendments of 1965. In addition to that very significant change, the 1965 amendments further increased the benefits (at least 6 per cent), increased the income covered by the program to $6600 and increased the income available to pensioners to $2400. Also of interest in the 1965 amendments was the extension of benefits to a wife who was divorced from her husband after at least twenty years of marriage. While this criterion was further modified to ten years in the 1977 amendments, it is still regarded as sexist by many women although at the time it was adopted it was considered quite progressive. In 1967 further amendments increased benefits by at least 13 per cent and increased the income base of the program to $7800.

The Nixon administration, in addition to the attempts to modify the existing system of public assistance into a negative income tax system, had several significant policy successions in relation to social security. One of these, the Supplemental Security Income program was an outgrowth of the attempts to create the negative income tax program through the Family Assistance Program. The second was the indexation of the benefits of social security by linking the value of those benefits to the Consumer Price Index and to changes in wages by means of the Social Security Amendments of 1972. The linking of benefits to *both* of these variables resulted in an over-indexing of benefits, with consequent fiscal drains upon the financial basis of the system (Munnell, 1977, pp. 25–6).

Much of the policy change in the Carter and the early portion of the Reagan administrations has been directed at the financial problems of the Social Security system. This has meant the elimination of some minor benefits, for example, the burial benefit and the exclusion of children over eighteen who are attending college as beneficiaries, and the threats during the Reagan administration to eliminate the minimum benefit provisions of the program which aid those with low earnings during their working lifetimes, or widows, divorcees and others who have returned to work late in their lifetime. The elimination of this benefit would return the program to something more like that conceived when it was initiated—with earnings more strictly reflected in benefits—but would place a great burden on a group of people who have few other financial resources.

The above discussion has demonstrated the importance of legal changes in producing policy successions. Many of the changes produced by these amendments were elaborations of the existing program, or mere extensions of the benefits, but the legal change was essential to produce the benefits. These legal changes certainly do not tell everything about the development of the Social Security program, but they do provide milestones of that development.

The majority of activities with respect to Social Security over the period of 1935 to 1981 was succession. The majority of the amendments described above involved changes in the definitions of eligibility, changes in benefit levels, or consolidation of various program elements, such as the change from OASI to OASDI. The major exception to that generalization was the addition of the Medicare Programs to Social Security in 1965. Also, several minor terminations have been occurring, with small elements of the program such as the burial benefit and the support of survivors and dependents in college until the age of twenty-one being abolished. But our hypothesis of the increasing use of succession as contrasted to initiation does appear to be supported in the history of this program.

4.4 Using indicators of policy change

The methodological approaches and findings we have presented in this chapter constitute contributions to a research agenda rather than definitive measurements of types of policy change over the past fifty years. We have presented evidence which suggests that there has been a long-run decline in the volume of changes involving policy innovation and that, in the United States at least, policy succession constituted a higher proportion of policy change compared to innovation in the 1970s than at any other period over the past fifty years. However, this is a very broad-brush conclusion, and there are other aspects of attempting to measure policy change which will need to be explored further than has been possible in this chapter.

1   How far do organizations, laws and perhaps budgetary allocations move 'in step' as indicators of policy change over time?

2   Do these different indicators give the same measurements of the relative significance of innovation and succession?

3   How far do the 'profiles' of changing relative significance of innovation and succession differ between policy areas? Is the overall trend much more than the sum of perhaps differing trends for different policy areas? Our hypothesis, based partly on the overwhelming direction of the overall trend and partly on our interpretation of developments in a number of individual policy areas, is that while the slope of the profiles will vary, and the dispersion of the total volume of change over time may differ, the overall trend in almost all policy areas will show a higher proportion of succession changes relative to innovation in the 1970s than in the 1950s and 1960s.

4   Granted the problems of finding cross-nationally reliable indicators, is it possible to say anything about the differences between industrialized countries in the timing of their profiles of succession and innovation changes? In particular, is there any relationship, as we would expect, between the relative size and relative rate of growth of the public sector and the ratio of succession to innovation changes?

Given the problems of methodology and sources which we have identified in this chapter, it will be difficult to devise research strategies to tackle these questions and in some cases it may be impossible to provide definitive answers. However, it is more important to provide tentative, partial or qualified answers to important questions like these than to provide precisely quantified answers to deeply uninteresting questions.

Chapter 5
THE POLICY SUCCESSION PROCESS

5.1 Policy succession as process

IN this chapter we will be referring to policy succession in its ideal type form, rather than discussing separately each of the types of policy succession outlined in Chapter 3 (though these will be drawn on to provide illustrations). Our objective in this is to focus on the distinctive implications for the nature of the policy process associated with policy succession as contrasted with policy innovation. This is done to highlight the major differences between policy succession and policy innovation, rather than provide an all-embracing description of policymaking, since, as we have stressed earlier (2.3.1), individual issues span the whole spectrum between the polar ideal types of succession and innovation.

In other words, the generalizations which can be drawn from the analysis in this chapter are not in the form of an attempt at universal description but in terms of the relative mix of succession and innovation embodied in individual issues. Issues involving a relatively high degree of replacement of existing policies will go through a process with the characteristics described in sections 5.2–5.5, unlike those involving substantial new elements, which will exhibit characteristics of the innovation process as described in section 5.6. We would also stress that the process applicable in individual cases will reflect the type of policy succession involved, the issue characteristics and context, and the resources and attitudes of the policy actors. Thus, the generalizations in this chapter have to be applied appropriately, but as we hope to make clear, these generalizations are by no means trivial.

Rather than seeking to provide statements only about the policy succession process as a whole, we would argue that at each stage of the policy process there are important implications arising from the fact that policy succession is concerned with replacing existing policies rather than starting from scratch. Certainly both the processes of policy innovation and policy succession can be described in terms of the same stages: agenda-setting, mobilizing support to secure an authoritative decision, implementation, and impact. However, the nature of the activities carried out at each of these stages differs substantially depending on whether policy innovation or policy succession is being considered. We will first provide a detailed analysis of the stages of the policy succession process in sections 5.2 to 5.5, before providing a comparative overview of both innovation and succession in terms of these stages in section 5.6.

5.2   Agenda-setting for policy succession

> We accept the verdict of the past until the need for change
> cries out loudly enough to force upon us a choice between
> the comforts of further inertia and the irksomeness of action.
>
> Learned Hand, address, Supreme Judicial Court of
> Massachusetts, 21 November 1942

As with genuinely new policy initiatives, proposals for policy succession must go through processes of agenda-setting, mobilization of political support leading to an authoritative decision, and effective implementation. Before any proposal involving changes in existing government policy can be adopted, it must first gain a place on the agenda of the political system. As with a new policy initiative, a proposal for policy succession will have to gain a place on two agendas. The first is the general discussion, or 'systemic', agenda of the political system, and the second is one or more 'institutional' agendas; that is, the list of issues which are given active and serious consideration by the authoritative decision-makers (see Cobb and Elder, 1972, p. 14).

5.2.1   *Overcoming the hurdle of legitimacy*

In the case of the systemic agenda, which can be seen as consisting of 'all issues that are commonly perceived by members of the political community as meriting public attention and as involving matters within the legitimate jurisdiction of existing government authority' (Cobb and Elder, 1972, p. 85), policy succession issues have already passed a crucial hurdle. Because issues of policy succession are concerned with activities in which government is already involved, the legitimacy of the issue as a proper concern of government has already been established. A caveat must be made insofar as many members of the political community may not regard the existence of an established program as legitimating proposals for consolidation or expansion. For example, the existence of Medicare in the United States would not be universally accepted as implying that the issue of a broader national health insurance program is a legitimate one for active government consideration. However, the very fact that there is a debate over whether such health insurance is appropriately within the sphere of government activity indicates that the issue is currently on the discussion agenda of the American political system.

Proponents of policy succession faced with challenges to the legitimacy of their proposals have to show that the logic of state involvement underlying the proposal is the same as for the existing government policy, and at the same time show that the existing policy is unsatisfactory in some respect. Of course, it is not sufficient to establish the legitimacy of the proposal; sufficient interest must be generated to stimulate discussion. Here some policy succession proposals may face an additional hurdle. As there is, by definition, already a policy to 'solve' the problem in question, it may be more difficult to obtain agreement for active consideration among members of the political community in the same way as when there is a complete gap in government provision, even when it is accepted that the existing policy is not totally satisfactory. Here proponents of policy succession must show that the existing policy is sufficiently unsatisfactory for replacement policies to deserve serious consideration.

5.2.2 *Institutions as consequence and cause of agenda-setting*

Again, it is not sufficient to generate general political debate about an issue. For any change to take place, the issue must be taken seriously by the relevant political institutions. Thus, we must consider how and why issues which have already been processed at least once by authoritative institutions return to the agenda for additional consideration. Here, because there are established programs, an issue being considered for policy succession has the additional advantage of being taken seriously by active and attentive publics, and/or organizations concerned with the issue. One thing which an existing program will do is to create a consortium of interests, even where one had not existed previously. This consortium will certainly have producers in it: politicians and bureaucrats who gain votes and/or employment from the continuation or transformation of the program. The consortium may also include the consumers of the policy, for example, welfare recipients or aircraft manufacturers. Both producers and consumers will be attentive to any proposed changes in the existing programs. While this may not assist in bringing about the policy succession—more probably it will impede it—it does assist in placing the issue on an institutional agenda. The existence of these groups will mean that the issue is almost sure to become politicized rapidly; much more rapidly than for issues which had not previously been considered by the institution(s). One of the primary factors affecting this prompt consideration may be uncertainty on the part of providers who want the issue resolved so that they can make plans about service delivery.

5.2.3   *Routes to institutional agendas*

There are various ways in which issues relating to policy succession may achieve a place on institutional agendas. It will be rare for any one of these ways in isolation to be sufficient to ensure that an issue is taken up, but they frequently occur in combination and interact to overcome the 'gatekeepers' guarding institutional agendas (see Easton, 1979, pp. 86–96).

5.2.3.1   *Routinized recurrence of issues*
The simplest explanation for an issue returning to the institutional agenda is that some policies are authorized repetitively; they require frequent or annual reconsideration. Resource allocation issues such as budget allocations, debt ceilings and review of accounts of past expenditure require annual action by government. The issue here is generally how much for existing programs, rather than altering in any substantial way the basic policy involved, and therefore deliberations fall outside policy succession as we have defined it. However, such reviews, though normally treated as entirely routine, do provide opportunities for drawing attention to the defects of existing policy and thus provide possible triggers for the initiation of the policy succession process not available in the case of policy innovation. Potentially, this is especially true of more comprehensive budgeting procedures such as PPBS or ZBB which at least attempt to ask questions about program effectiveness, as well as the more mundane question of how money will be spent (see Wildavsky, 1978).

5.2.3.2 *Dissatisfaction*

Perhaps the most important source of policy succession proposals coming to the institutional agenda is dissatisfaction with existing policy. This dissatisfaction may be felt by the producers of the policy, or by politicians and the broader public. We can make certain assumptions about the types of dissatisfactions which each of these categories of actors may express. We can assume that in most instances the dissatisfaction of clients will be with specific programs rather than with broad policy. Very few clients will want to have their policy concerns removed from the political agenda, but more typically will want to have their programs expanded or improved.

One major exception to this generalization is that the putative clients of many regulatory policies have sought to have their industries deregulated, although even here we find that frequently some of the strongest advocates of regulation are the regulated industries themselves. (This is, of course, a feature of the traditional 'capture' theory; see Salamon and Walmsley, 1976.)

Policy succession may be more subject to influence by client groups than would be initial policy formation, if for no other reason than that the existence of policies and programs tends to engender the formation of client groups. In fact, for some policies and programs in both the United States and the United Kingdom, the formation of such groups is a part of the legislation creating the program, and consultation with these groups is likewise mandated (see Advisory Commission on Intergovernmental Relations 1979, table 1). For example, urban renewal programs and the Model Cities program in the United States required citizen participation. Clearly client or potential client groups may influence the initial formation of policy, but we would expect significantly greater influence when issues of policy succession are being raised.

Likewise, we would expect producer dissatisfactions to be directed towards specific programmatic features rather than towards the policy as a whole. These dissatisfactions will likely be concentrated on the administrative aspects of the program rather than on its substance. Any attempt to make major alterations in its substance may be seens as threatening the entire existence of the policy, and hence the jobs of the producers. As with client groups, there will be much greater influence of producers at the policy succession stage than at the initial formulation stage. There is now a specific group of producers charged with the administration of the program, where previously the producers who might have been involved were tangential to the management of the new policy—or perhaps actively hostile to a policy which would threaten their 'turf'.

Legislative actors may seek to return an issue to their institutional agenda as a result of dissatisfaction with potentially one of two purposes in mind. One would be the preservation of the basic policy in effect, but the replacement of the existing program, while the other would be the termination of the policy as a whole. Whereas prior to many of the concerns voiced in the 1970s about 'big government' legislators scored political points by advocating new policies and programs, increasingly legislators have been able to score points by advocating the termination of policies. Placing an issue of policy termination on the agenda may, however, not produce the intended result and may actually lead to policy or program succession. The types of dissatisfaction voiced by legislators will depend upon a number of factors such as their own ideologies, their perception of the politically most profitable stance, and the nature of their party's position on the issue. Perhaps of special concern would be their constituencies, as the tendency of Congressmen in the United States is to become more the servant of a constituency rather than a policymaker in a broader sense (see Fiorina, 1978). These dissatisfactions will also depend upon their connections to other actors involved in the policy area, especially consumer and producer interests who may actively place pressure for policy succession on the legislator.

As much of the formal decision-making concerning a policy—either its termination or its succession—must be performed by holders of political office, it is rather obvious that they will be crucial to policy succession. But, compared to other actors, we would hypothesize that they would be relatively less involved in the policy succession process than they are in policy innovation. As noted above, the creation or activation of both clientele and producer groups involved with the policy will tend to increase the influence of these actors relative to legislators in policy succession. However, the dissatisfaction of the political office holders with the progress—or lack of it—in a policy area may be crucial for determining the placing of a policy succession issue on the formal institutional agenda.

5.2.3.3 *Cross-fertilization*
Another means of placing an issue of policy succession on the agenda is through cross-fertilization. That is, through the importation of

ideas about how a policy or program could be improved from other governments or possibly even from the private sector. As governments have developed extensive networks for the diffusion of information and advice on policies, the policy succession process has been increasingly influenced by programs of other governments. Cross-fertilization is also important in policy innovation, but the important difference with policy succession is the existence of service-provider organizations as receptors or active searchers for ideas about policy improvement.

There are three types of cross-fertilization important for the study of policy succession: intra-level, inter-level and cross-sector. These are fancy names for very simple ideas. Intra-level policy diffusion is the importation of an idea from another government of the same type, as when one local government learns the experience of another. This type of cross-fertilization could be important at the stage of policy initiation, but appears especially important for policy succession. Governments of the same level tend to have relatively similar 'portfolios' of policies, especially subnational governments within a single national system. Thus the question involved in diffusion may not be 'what to do', but 'how to do it'. Also, as functional networks are important for the diffusion of policy ideas, it is less likely that a government would be tied into a network unless they had already initiated a policy in the area. In general, we would expect the policy successions resulting from these types of diffusions would be rather modest in scope, involving largely technical modifications of existing programs.

Inter-level cross-fertilization occurs when policy ideas are diffused across levels of government, and policy succession occurs as a result. Thus, a policy or program at the Federal level in the United States may be used as a model for a state or local policy, or vice versa. For example, the reform of the civil service during the Carter administration has become a model for some similar reforms being attempted in state civil service systems. These states had merit systems for public employees previously, but have been modifying them in order to try to build in the incentives used at the Federal level. As the functional and program obligations of the different levels of government are commonly different, we would expect many of the diffusions which occur across levels of government to be managerial or technical in nature.

Finally, cross-fertilization resulting in policy succession may occur

between the private and public sectors. For example, Zero Based
Budgeting as a successor to previous policies concerning the formation of the Federal budget came as a diffusion from private
industry to the public sector through state government and then to
the Federal level (see, for example Phyrr, 1975). As with cross-level
fertilization, this type of diffusion is more likely to produce managerial or technical succession rather than major changes in on-going
service programs.

5.2.3.4   *External pressures*
A special case of policy diffusion across levels of government occurs
when one level of government can place pressure on another to alter
its existing policies. This can be done either through direct legal
mandate or through the use of incentives that encourage a government to alter its operating programs. In unitary governments this
diffusion is (relatively) straightforward, with the central government
having the formal power to command local authorities to make
policy changes; in practice, this sort of direct command may not be
used, with a bargaining style of interaction being adopted (Rhodes,
1981; Thoenig, 1978). In federal systems the ability of the central
government to command behavior of the subnational government is
limited, and hence the use of incentives, such as grants, tends to be the
more common mechanism for reaching goals of policy succession.
Central governments in federal regimes do, however, at times force
direct policy succession (see Lovell and Tobin, 1980). Examples are
Federal mandating of education for the handicapped and clear
drinking water standards in the United States.
   A special case of external pressures is the formation of the
European Communities government affecting the internal policies of
the ten constituent governments. This has brought about a number of
changes in policies of the member nations, perhaps most notably in
agriculture.

5.2.3.5   *Opportunities*
Finally, some policy succession occurs because unique opportunities
present themselves, or because of the serendipitous effects of the
interactions of a number of factors. Given the declining availability
of economic resources and policy space in most Western nations,
these opportunities are likely to be less prevalent than they might
have been at one time. They may still, however, exist. These

opportunities may be more in deregulation or contracting out services than in direct service provision.

One example of a recent policy succession or change resulting from the availability of an opportunity is the development of the Food Stamp Program in the US Department of Agriculture. This provided agriculture the opportunity to become involved in urban problems—then an issue area very much in vogue. The shift from the distribution of food via surplus commodity programs to the more personalized Food Stamp Program has proven to be a big boost not only to the budget of the Department of Agriculture, but also to the visibility of that department among the non-farm portion of the American population.

5.3   Making policy choices

> The innovator makes enemies of all those who prospered
> under the old order, and only lukewarm support is
> forthcoming from those who would prosper under the new.
>
> N. Machiavelli, *The Prince*

5.3.1   *The conflictual nature of the policy process*

Once an issue comes onto the agenda, perhaps the easiest portion of the policy succession process has been concluded. It then becomes necessary for those interested in policy succession to develop a coalition to push the proposed policy through the decision-making systems of government. To do this will require generating political support among a number of interests, some of which may be satisfied with their situations under the status quo. These conflicts will be primarily of four types: organizational, clientele-based, producer-group based and ideological.

5.3.2   *Organizational conflicts*

Altering any existing program or policy obviously has implications for existing organizations. In some instances, the policy succession may be merely the replacement of one program for another, involving only changes in administrative procedures with the same personnel and with organizational 'turf' intact. In other circumstances organizations may, quite rightly, feel threatened by a proposed policy or program change which either advocates the termination of their program or even their organization, or which opens up their turf to more poaching. Thus, types of policy succession such as consolidation, or even splitting, may make organizations resist proposed changes. Also, as these organizations, as existing political actors, may have political connections which would not have been possible prior to the adoption of the original policy now being replaced, policy succession is not so easy organizationally as forming new policies or organizations.

There may, however, be types of organizations or organizational actors which would welcome, or at a minimum not resist, possible changes. One conventional image of the bureau chief in the public bureaucracy is of an extremely conservative administrator seeking to avoid risks and hence attempting to hold onto whatever power and programs he or she may have. However, there may be individuals and situations in which organizations may actively attempt to promote policy succession rather than opposing such changes. These would include:

1   Many policy successions, rather than being externally generated, actually emanate from within the affected organizations. Many policy initiatives are bureaucratic in their origin, and represent attempts at policy succession by the organizations which would be affected. Obviously most of these changes would tend to enhance the power and budget of the agency in question. Defence department policy successions involving newer and more sophisticated weapons systems would be an obvious example of this organizational pressure for change. Both the United States, with the MX missile system, and Britain, with the Trident submarines, are currently undergoing the pressures.

2   Risk-takers would attempt to win big in budgetary or policy terms by accepting a gamble on a proposed policy succession rather than adopting a more conservative role and averting risks and defending the status quo.

3   There may well be situations in which opposition to a proposed policy succession would itself be risky, as when there is a developing consensus that change is necessary and desirable.

4   Some organizations may welcome consolidation or splitting because they may wish to reduce the size of their operations or their number of functions in order to serve better the organizational 'heartland'. While this runs counter to a great deal of the con-

temporary analysis of the aggrandizing characteristics of bureaucracy, there are certainly examples of organizational behavior of this type (see, for example, Goodin, 1975). Also, this may allow an organization to split off some of its less popular activities and retain the more popular ones for itself.

Thus, we should not be so sure that existing organizations will invariably resist policy succession, and they may actually encourage certain types of succession.

We would expect organizational conflicts over policy succession to be most pronounced in the cases of partial termination or consolidation of programs. In these cases, there will be fewer earmarked resources to work with after succession than before. We would also expect relatively less resistance to linear policy succession, or to policy splitting. Witness the support of the British Post Office Corporation for its own splitting into two separate organizations—one responsible for the posts, the other for telecommunications. In the United States the conflict over the division of the Atomic Energy Commission into separate production and regulatory agencies was muted at best. Likewise, the organizational opposition to partial termination, and especially to consolidation, is likely to be particularly intense when programs or policies to be joined cut across broad organizational and functional boundaries. For example, opposition to the negative income tax has been explained in any number of ways, but one of the most important explanations must be the organizational resistance to consolidating tax and benefit programs into a single program, and thereby impacting a number of tax and social service programs.

One of the most interesting phenomena in the study of policy termination and succession might be termed the 'musk-ox phenomenon', or the willingness of agencies to form a circle to defend their weaker counterparts. Although they may have something to gain from the termination of other programs, agencies appear to have developed something of an ethos of not attacking other agencies threatened with termination. Of course, there is a distinct logic to this behavior. It both normalizes competition among agencies to competition for more—rather than for survival—and it lessens the probability of future attacks on one's own program. Those who are strong now may be weak later, and a mutual defence pact, be it tacit or explicit, prevents excessive internecine warfare. In policy succession terms, this means that forming a coalition among existing agencies to expedite a policy succession involving major changes in the structure and functions of an existing agency may be difficult, as there may be few takers to join in a coalition perceived as threatening the interests of another agency. The mere persistence of public organizations, as well as a number of less quantifiable indicators, lend credence to the argument that organizations may tend to conflict at the margin, but not over the continued existence of an organization.

5.3.3   *Clientele conflicts*

If the conflicts among organizations in policy succession may be restrained by real or presumed threats to the existence of an organization, the threats to clientele groups involved in succession are perhaps more real and immediate. Changes in policy may be directed at serving the same clientele group, but the manner in which a group is served may be as important as the actual level of services. For example, in our earlier example of the change in family benefits and tax allowances in the United Kingdom, the policy which emerged involved a change from one in which the husband and wife shared the benefits to one in which the wife received all the benefit (see 3.3.2). The total benefit was slightly improved, but the manner in which the benefit was delivered has significant implications for family structure in the United Kingdom.

Likewise, a program or organizational change which consolidates one program with another program will tend to dilute the influence of an existing clientele group. Whereas with a singular organization the clientele group would have its own spokesman in government, a policy succession may make an organization the spokesman for any number of clientele groups. Many groups would be able to maintain their political clout in such a situation, but many would not. But, to run the scenario in the other direction, policy splitting as in the case of the formation of a Cabinet-level Department of Education in the United States places the clientele group in a much more favorable position (Miles, 1977).

5.3.4   *Producer-group conflicts*

We tend to think of the clients of public programs as citizens who are receiving personal benefits from the program. However, in a very real sense, some of the major 'clients' of public programs are producers rather than consumers. That is, the major affected groups are the public employees working in the program, or various professional groups oriented towards public sector support and financing (see, for example, Staaf, 1977). The implications of policy succession for these groups are perhaps even more significant than for the recipients of the program benefits. Not only do provider groups depend upon public employment for their livelihood, but they also tend to be involved in the design of programs on a professional basis. That is, they tend to believe not only in the continued existence of their program, but also in the continued delivery of the services in a particular way. Any proposed policy succession might therefore challenge not only their continued employment in the program but also their professional right to deliver services in their preferred manner.

When the profession changes its own conceptualization of the proper manner of delivering a service, as with major changes in social work and even some aspects of medical practice, the public sector manager may have a difficult time in adjusting agency norms to professional practice. In essence, this may be another means of obtaining a policy succession through the back door. This appears to be particularly common when a profession is not employed entirely by government, and continuing interchanges and interactions take place with the private sector.

5.3.5   *Ideological conflicts*

> Most of the change we think we see in life
> Is due to truths being in and out of favor.
>   Robert Frost, 'The Black Cottage', *North of Boston* (1914)

Related to the above discussion of policy change occurring within a profession is a broader concern with ideological changes which may produce conflicts, but which may also accelerate and ease policy succession. The ideologies involved may be at a broad societal level, for example, socialism or democratic liberalism. However, more important are the types of ideologies propounded at lower levels of generalization. In some instances these are propounded in terms of efficiency or effectiveness of government, and have a decided emphasis on managerial techniques, or more recently on reducing the size of the public sector and forcing policy succession through 'cutback management' (Levine, 1978, 1980). In other instances ideologies are developed both by professionals and by citizens concerning how certain policy areas should be programmed. For example, much recent concern by citizens over the 'permissive' treatment of offenders has tended to conflict with emerging professional ideas about reducing recidivism. Also, popular concern over basic education in the United States has tended to conflict with the more 'progressive' ideas of many educators. Many contemporary ideas about the treatment of the mentally ill in the community or at home have tended to conflict both with established institutions such as state mental hospitals and with communities which fear, or simply dislike, the presence of the mentally ill (see Foley, 1975; Cameron, 1978).

In each of the above examples, changes in policy ideologies, or less grandiosely, changes in the accepted manner of delivering certain types of public services, have produced conflicts over policy succession. The resolution of these conflicts is likely to depend upon a number of factors, including the relative strength of existing interest groups and those advocating succession, the level of popular mobilization, and the structure of decision-making institutions. Obviously, entrenched interests will tend to have an advantage over those seeking the policy succession, but when those advocating the succession are of high prestige, such as members of the medical profession advocating community health, the actual balance of power may favor succession. Similarly, we would assume that the majority of the mass public would favor the status quo on most issues, but the existence of a highly vocal and effective interest group may counter-balance mere numbers. Those advocating a policy succession may actually have an advantage, as they would be forced to develop a more consistent 'policy ideology' to counteract the inertia inherent in most policymaking systems.

Finally, the institutional rules for decision-making tend to lessen the probability of a policy succession, and enhance the inertial characteristics of public policies. This is especially true when there is a strong professional or interest group role in decision-making, and the affected profession has a particular dogma concerning the manner of service delivery—as most do. For example, the medical profession is generally involved in all changes in health policies—through the local health agencies if through no other means—and hence has a legitimate institutional, as well as an interest group, impact upon health policy choices (for an overview, see Durham and Marmor, 1978; see also Crossman, 1978).

5.3.6 *Pushing policy succession through the legislature*

As well as forming a coalition of affected interests (service providers and clients), a policy succession will normally involve obtaining a majority in the legislature to legitimate that policy change. The legislative stage may not be necessary for a large and increasing number of policy choices, however, as these are made through regulatory and administrative mechanisms (see Freedman, 1978).

Assembling a majority in a legislature is a common problem, but the necessary solutions differ between political systems. First, political systems may differ in the location of that necessary majority (or, in some cases, consensus). For example, in the United States, majorities must be stitched together in each House of Congress after having been stitched together in committees. In Britain, by contrast, the key locations lie within the Cabinet system, where ministers *in their role as legislators* decide on the content and allocation of legislative time for a bill (see Walkland, 1968). Except in cases where the British government is in a minority in the House of Commons or faces an unusually strong backbench revolt, the majority in the House of Commons is automatically available.

Secondly, the strategies employed in obtaining majorities may differ markedly between political systems. For example, in the United States allocational and support-trading strategies, to use Arnold's terminology, are likely to be more important than in Britain (Arnold, 1979). That is, 'pork barrel' and 'log-rolling' are used in Congress to form majorities of legislators lacking strong partisan ties but with strong regional power bases. In Britain, general support strategies related to political parties tend to fix policy preferences for their members.

In Britain, once a bill has actually been introduced, the process by which the bill passes through its Parliamentary stages is normally similar to that for a genuinely innovatory piece of legislation. In more fragmented legislatures such as Congress, on the other hand, the legislative processing of policy succession is likely to be more difficult than the passage of the initial innovation. For legislators, there may be little to be gained by modifying and improving existing legislation: legislators make a name for themselves by advocating new programs and policies. Policy entrepreneurship by legislators has, for example, been cited as the major source of policy innovation at Federal level in the United States (Advisory Commission on Intergovernmental Relations, 1980). Once a program is in operation, a legislator would have to contend with provider and client groups which have vested interests in the program and would tend to oppose all but clearly linear policy successions.

The choice of the strategy to form a winning coalition to legitimate a policy succession in the legislature involves the manipulation of a number of different incentives, but the wide variation in the roles of different legislatures means that the selection of the appropriate strategy is more systems-related relative to issues or specific circumstances than at other stages of the policy succession process, where a striking similarity of problems and strategies across systems obtains. (For a general discussion of systems-related differences in policy succession, see 8.2.2.3.1.)

In the process of assembling a majority to push through a proposed policy change, it is likely that the promoters of the policy succession—in addition to bargaining about the distribution of policy benefits and trading support in a log-rolling fashion—will be obliged to make concessions to critics of specific aspects of the proposed change. This is true even in Britain with its government domination of the legislature; in Britain the concessions are normally negotiated directly between government and interest groups and presented to Parliament in the form of government amendments to its own bill (Griffith, 1974; Richardson and Jordan, 1979). Almost invariably, concessions at the legislative stage of policy succession will involve reducing the degree to which the proposed policy succession would differ from the policies it is designed to replace. Particularly where there are threshold effects or concessions involving exploitable loopholes, such concessions may undermine the policy theory implied in the original formulation of the proposed succession (see also 8.2.2.2).

Attempts at policy succession may, in fact, be counter-productive. They may re-open issues which had previously been settled, and in the process the legislature may accept more special interest concessions than existed previously. The failure of tax reform at Federal level in the United States provides an important illustration of this point. Failure to make concessions at all, on the other hand (even where these are not actually forced), may lead to failure to get any version of the proposal through the legislature or to interest group recalcitrance at the implementation stage.

5.3.7 *Pinning resources to policy succession*

Legislatures make two types of decisions about a policy succession. One of these is on the substantive change in the policy, while the other is on making resources available to implement the policy succession after it has been adopted. In the United States, with the separation of functional and appropriations committees and their associated subcommittees, this distinction can be quite important. A policy succession may be accepted by the substantive committee and then by the entire legislature, but the implementing organization may not be given sufficient funding to do its job adequately. This lack of adequate resources may be a function either of real policy differences between the substantive committee and the relevant subcommittee in an appropriations committee, or it may be a way in which Congress may please both sides of a conflict.

The first type of failure to pin resources to a policy succession can be illustrated in the area of coal mine inspection. The Federal Mine Safety and Health Amendments of 1977 consolidated and strengthened existing laws and implementing organizations. But due to inadequate funding—about 750 inspectors to monitor 5000 coal mines and that number to be reduced in the Reagan administration—very little effective enforcement can be done and miners continue to die in record numbers in American coal mines (Handler, 1978, p. 180).

The second type of failure to pin resources to a policy succession may be illustrated by the implementation of civil rights legislation during the 1960s. With the expansion of the civil rights movement in the 1960s, Congress was in the position of trying to balance the demands of blacks for stricter laws against discrimination and the resistance of Southern and other conservative legislators. One means of striking that balance was to pass relatively more stringent laws (although related to previous laws and court decisions) but not providing adequate enforcement personnel that might upset those opposed to desegregation (Radin, 1977; Rodgers and Bullock, 1972).

Clearly the issue of pinning resources to policy succession lies on the borderline between policymaking and implementation, especially when we move from consideration of the initial appropriation to longer-run allocations. The initial intent of the legislation may be subverted, or the scope of the program expanded greatly, as it is implemented and funded year after year.

5.3.8   *The significance of the choice-making stage*

The conflicts which develop as a result of attempted policy succession, then, are not only over turf and organizational interests, but may also be over policy ideas. There may be a number of situations in which it is impossible to distinguish the two types of conflict over policy succession. Institutions embody policy ideas, and ideas about policy frequently arise from a particular institutional setting. However, it may be important for political analysis to be able to distinguish the two sources of conflict. Conflicts over organizational turf and policy influence can be resolved by budgetary allocations and by ambiguous allocations of jurisdictions. As we have noted, a general means of conflict resolution has been log-rolling among institutions and interests. This becomes less possible as a period of serious resource constraint appears probable (see Thurow, 1980).

Conflicts over ideas and values may be more difficult to resolve, although competent policy analysis may help in highlighting the probable consequences of each alternative. In either case, however, producing a decision to proceed with a change in policy involves forming some type of dominant coalition with either the muscle or the brains to push the idea through the relevant chain of decision-making institutions.

5.4   Implementing policy succession

If individuals or organizations interested in policy succession are able to pass the multiple clearance points in the agenda-setting and coalition-formation processes, they still have to implement the policy succession. There is an extensive body of theoretical work on the process of organizational change, although very little of this work is directly linked to associated changes in the policies and programs of the organizations (see Leemans, 1976; Warwick, 1975). The organizational change literature does, on the other hand, provide some guidance as to the type of factors which should be considered important for an understanding of policy succession, and the consequent interaction with organizational change. Some of the principles derived from the organizational change literature specifically relevant to implementation will be outlined here, while Chapter 6 will review all aspects of the organizational setting of policy succession.

5.4.1 *The internal dynamics of implementing policy succession in organizations*

The first lesson from the organizational change literature is that the implementor of a policy succession must understand that organizations exist at places other than their headquarters. Likewise, organizations are composed of actors other than the top leadership. Thus, it is necessary to understand the internal dynamics of the organization, and especially the relationship of the field staff to the rest of the organization, to be able to implement a policy succession successfully (Theonig, 1978; Theonig and Friedberg, 1976; Kaufman, 1960; Hood, 1976, p. 27). The field staffs must actually put the new policy into effect on the ground and it is therefore crucial to coopt the field staffs into the acceptance—if not support—of a new policy. It is perhaps more important to influence the field staff than the top leadership (Peters, 1978, pp. 10–12). It is at that level that real decisions about clients will be reached, and perhaps as importantly it is at that level of the organization that the new programs will have to be 'sold' to clients who may be skeptical or outright hostile to the changes in their program.

The control of field staffs is important even in centralized political systems, but is even more important when, as in both the United States and the United Kingdom, local governments are given a great deal of responsibility for the implementation of central government policy. In the United States even the agencies of the Federal government are given so much latitude that it may be difficult to provide much central direction to implementation by field staff (Rourke, 1979). In short, an effective policy succession will in all probability be accompanied by aggressive efforts on the part of those responsible for the succession to train and to convince workers of the desirability of the changes.

5.4.2 *Personal and organizational goals*

Secondly, individuals have personal as well as organizational goals, and the goals propounded in the policy succession may be only a formal set of targets to be interpreted by organization members as they see fit (see Barton, 1979). Thus, the manager of a major policy change must beware of explicit acceptance and covert avoidance of the policy change. Also, a change in the policies of the organization may be the occasion for challenging the existing power relationships within the organization, so that a significant change in the informal organization may occur at the same time as a change in the formal tasks of the organization. This may be in some ways functional, as organizational structure should correspond to function, but may only be a manifestation of the internal political dynamics of the organization rather than a functional change.

Relatedly, organizational members trained and socialized to accept (and, indeed, promote) a set of policies may find it difficult to accept a policy succession. Ironically, if the organizational has been successful in generating commitment by its staff to its program it will be more difficult to follow through the implementation of an alternative than if the organization had been less successful. Organizational members may feel that they or their clients have been betrayed.

5.4.3   *Interorganizational dynamics*

Thirdly, as well as not being fully integrated entities themselves, public organizations do not exist alone in the world. The 'single lonely organization syndrome' may be a convenient assumption when analyzing implementation, but it may also be an unrealistic assumption (Hjern and Porter, 1979). To understand the implementation of a policy or program is to understand the interorganizational politics of the program as organizations encounter each other in the field and conflict over authority, money, and clients, and attempt to resolve their differences by some sort of political process. At the inception of a policy succession we would assume that the organizations in a network of interacting organizations exist in some sort of equilibrium. To change one aspect of this interorganizational network is to upset the entire network, and to force a readjustment of the bargaining position of all involved organizations.

Difficulties in interorganizational politics may occur in two dimensions. The most familiar, at least in the United States, concerns coordination among levels of government. The Federal government may make a variety of policy proposals to be implemented through state and local governments. But this is no guarantee that the proposals will be implemented as intended. Pressman and Wildavsky's classic study of implementation (1973) illustrates the difficulties of obtaining compliance, but this is but one of many, many similar studies which could be cited of such difficulties. It is not only in federal political systems that such conflicts arise, as the recent conflicts between the Conservative central government and Labour-dominated local governments in the United Kingdom illustrate.

The second dimension of interorganizational politics in implementation occurs between organizations within the same level of government. In these cases the conflicts are more clearly over 'turf', that *sine qua non* of bureaucratic life. Any policy succession requires a home, and there will be conflicts over which organizations will be given authority over the policy area. It is frequently the case that to minimize such conflicts the reaction of legislators and administrators will be to create new organizations. This will require the readjustment of existing networks but will not be perceived as advantaging one existing organization over another.

Thus, a failure to implement a policy succession in the intended fashion may not be the result only of the recalcitrance of the members of the implementing organization or its clients. Rather, it may result from the recalcitrance of the whole network of organizations and interests in which the implementing organization is embedded. It may well be that the organization charged with implementing the succession may be more than willing to carry out the implementation, as in the case of a succession which expands its power and authority, but it may be thwarted by other powerful actors.

5.4.4 *Extra-organizational hurdles*

The final barrier to implementation of a policy succession may be the individuals that the policy serves—at least nominally. Clients may resist the changes in 'their' programs, both as individuals and as organized groups. Such resistance is certainly to be expected when a cut in a program is forthcoming, but may also occur when less dramatic forms of change are initiated. Just as the members of the organization may feel threatened by a policy succession, so too may the recipients of the outputs of programs. It is important to remember that client groups are not necessarily just the recipients of public social programs; the concept should be extended to include other industrial, professional and labor groups who benefit from public programs.

The modern state is especially prone to having proposals for policy succession impacted by private actors, given the 'neo-corporate' characteristics of many of these governments (Schmitter, 1974; Richardson and Jordan, 1979; see Jordan, 1981 for a critique of 'corporatist' concepts). Stated simply it is argued that one of the major characteristics of contemporary political systems is the involvement of interest groups in all stages of the policy process, and the blurring of the distinction between public and private sectors. In some circumstances interest groups may be able to block a policy succession because their consent is necessary for effective implementation. As King (1975) has pointed out, the number of dependency relationships of a modern government has increased dramatically. Given that a number of public programs are directly implemented by interest groups and clients, the dependency on these groups by government for the implementation of a program has also increased.

5.4.5   *Continuing implementation*

Just as we have argued that policies are not made once and then fixed for all time, so too some policies are designed to be implemented on a continuing basis and consequently to be modified through the process of implementation (see also 2.3.4.4). This is especially true of policies requiring gradual compliance with a set of standards, or the upgrading of standards, with some ultimate goals in mind. The Clean Air Amendments of 1970 in the United States established two types of air quality standards: primary and secondary. Primary standards are those necessary to protect public health and were to be attained by 1975. Secondary standards, which were those necessary to protect vegetation, paint on buildings, etc., were to be attained 'within a reasonable time'. The attainment of these standards was to be monitored by the Environmental Protection Agency with a gradual upgrading of standards, especially for stationary sources of pollution.

In these cases of continuous implementation, policy succession is occurring as the standards are upgraded. The goals have been established in the legislation but the effective policy is being defined through the implementation process. Implementation is not only the result of the policy succession process, it is an integral part.

5.5   Outcomes and evaluation

Just as in the analysis of policymaking undertaken for the first time, the outcomes of policy succession must also be evaluated. The evaluation of any policy is difficult, but the evaluation of a policy succession may be especially difficult. Politically the question must always be raised if the change was worth the effort which had to be invested to bring it about.

5.5.1   *The bathos of policy succession outcomes*

> Plus ça change, plus c'est la même chose.
>
>   Alphonse Karr, *Les Guêpes*, 1849

Policy succession is almost certain to be disappointing. The huge political effort required to produce the succession is unlikely to be rewarded in the first month or the first year of the change. This is perhaps especially so because in order to produce the change expectations must be raised, and promises made which cannot be realized quickly, if ever. It is unlikely that the necessary coalitions at several stages of policymaking could be assembled if they were told quite honestly that marginal improvements were the best outcome which could be realistically expected. This is, of course, a problem not only with policy succession but with policymaking in general, and the great expectations which must be raised are indeed dashed in Oakland and elsewhere when the policies are put into effect. The length of time required for many policies to take effect, even if those policies will ultimately be successful, will further reduce the probability of a policy succession being regarded by analysts as a positive change in the policy area (Salamon, 1979).

5.5.2   *Destabilizing by policy succession*

> For what wears out the life of mortal men?
> 'Tis that from change to change their being rolls;
> 'Tis that repeated shocks, again, again,
> Exhaust the energy of strongest souls,
> And numb the elastic powers.
>
>   Matthew Arnold, 'The Scholar-Gypsy', *Poems* (1853)

The bathetic results of policy succession may engender a certain cynicism about the new policy, and perhaps about the entire policy area. This may then be related to one policy succession following another once a stable policy system is disturbed (Pressman and Wildavsky, 1973; Hood, 1976, p. 27). If one change cannot produce the type of result desired, it is then easier to advocate another change which may. Our analysis of organizational change in Chapter 4 found that rapid sequences of organizational successions were particularly likely to occur in wartime. The danger with a rapid sequence of changes is that none of them is given the chance to show benefits and that frequent change will pose additional costs on top of the costs associated with each change separately.

Once a stable policy area has been disturbed by a policy succession, there will no longer be a single set of entrenched interests with which to contend if one wishes to bring about a further policy succession. Consequently, forming a coalition in favor of a subsequent succession may be easier. This is especially likely when there has been a policy reversal. This may leave a significant number of the members of the organization charged with implementing the policy change anxious to return to the old way of doing things. Likewise, it may make the clients of the organization equally anxious to bring about a change in the new policy. Many social agencies who have had to cope with the enforced policy successions of the Reagan administration would clearly be in the position of desiring either a return to the *status quo ante*, or even an extension of their earlier programs.

More creatively, destabilizing a policy area which has been assumed to be settled for some number of years may encourage thinking about policy alternatives. In almost all analyses of the policy cycle, placing an issue on the agenda is a crucial step, and in policy succession once an issue is returned to the agenda after a period without direct consideration, the attention of policymakers and other concerned individuals may be brought to bear (Jones, 1977; Downs, 1972).

5.5.3   *Evaluating policy in muddied waters*

The evaluation of public policies is extremely difficult in the best of circumstances because of the difficulty of separating out the effects of a specific policy from other complex and changing factors, including other policies. Governments get both credit and blame for things they have not done. Evaluating a policy succession is even more difficult, as distinguishing the effects of replacement policies from the 'old' policies may be difficult, if not impossible. In the short term, the upheaval and uncertainty created by a policy succession may make any evaluation suspect, even though those responsible for the succession, and especially politicians, may want some immediate evidence of success. Many policy successions are marginal in their impact in relation to the previous policies, even if there has been substantial organizational upheaval, and consequently the detection of effect may be difficult. Finally, policy successions now take place in a policy environment more crowded with other organizations and programs than would have been the case at the time of the establishment of the program which was replaced, and it will be extremely difficult to distinguish the effects of the replacement program from the changing interaction of other programs.

5.6 How succession differs from innovation

If the process by which replacement policies are decided on and implemented were identical to the process involved in genuine policy innovations, then the concept of policy succession would not be worth the exploration it has been accorded in this book. What we have attempted to do in this chapter is to show that while changes involving a high degree of innovation and those involving a high degree of succession both go through a similar sequence of stages in the policy process, the nature of the activities within each stage differs according to whether succession or innovation is involved.

In Table 5.1, we present a highly simplified compendium of the key differences between the innovation and succession processes. If the distinguishing features of the policy succession process were to be summarized in one sentence, then we would point to the extent to which the policy actors, the process, and the substantive outcomes of the policy succession process are all shaped by the existing policies which succession is intended to replace (Wildavsky, 1979, Chapter 3).

The effects of existing policies are evident at each stage of the policy succession process. At the agenda-setting stage, the range of issues considered is shaped by those which have already been considered. Once a particular type of policy has been treated by the political system, the systemic agenda has been expanded to include that issue, although the previous treatment(s) of the issue may lead to the assumption that the problem has already been solved, with the

Table 5.1   A comparison of the main features of the innovation and succession processes

Policy innovation	Policy succession
AGENDA-SETTING	
Issue has to overcome initial hurdle of legitimacy	Issue has legitimacy
No established place on agenda	Possibility of routinized recurrence
No existing institution for which proposal is core issue	Service provider organizations provide institutional agenda letter-box and receptor for cross-fertilization
Problem perceived as lack of policy	Problem perceived as inadequacies of existing policy (though may be difficult to re-open issue if it is considered 'solved')
Mileage for politicians in advocating new provision	Little mileage in advocating modifications
Key role for holders of political office	Greater role for service providers and clientele groups
POLICY CHOICE	
Existing organizations have little central interest in using resources to promote proposal;frequently defensive	Organization(s) with core interest now exist and have resources to resist or promote policy
Potential clientele without structure	Clientele defined and structured (often with mandatory consultation)
For both service providers and clients *potential* benefits are at risk	For service providers and/or clients *actual* benefits may be at risk
Traditional professions well-mobilized and may perceive threat; embryo professions poorly mobilized and perceive opportunity	Professional providers exist, are mobilized and may perceive their jobs and service delivery criteria threatened
No current organizational base for 'ideologies' about service delivery	Organizational 'ideologies' about service delivery exist

Table 5.1 (*Contd.*)

Policy innovation	Policy succession
High return to investment of legislative time and credits	Greater probability of low return to investment of legislative time and credits
Possible high expenditure/resource cost (though normally at time of expanding public resources)	Often only marginal expenditure/resource cost (though often at time of constraint)

IMPLEMENTATION

Need to design completely new organization	Need to alter or consolidate existing organizational structure(s)
Need to recruit and socialize new personnel	Need to resocialize existing personnel (some of whom may be committed to previous policy) at field level as well as center
Need to devise operating rules (including informal)	Need to adapt operating rules (especially informal, which since often unwritten are difficult to rewrite)
May be some clearances required from other organizations	Strong likelihood of inter-organizational implications, including with organization administering predecessor program

IMPACT

Symbolic payoff high	Symbolic payoff low
High expectation of substantive impact; impact in practice variable	Relatively lower expectations of substantive impact; impact relative to previous programs variable but normally low (not true of policy reversals)
May be interactive effects with other existing programs, but policy space relatively uncrowded	Strong likelihood of interactive effects with other existing programs
Evaluation relatively easy (no policy compared with policy)	Evaluation more complex

consequence that political elites are less willing to take the role of advocates of policy change.

Policy succession will encounter more mobilized interests than will policy innovation. Both producers and consumers of policies will have been developed around a particular existing policy, so that an attempt at policy succession will challenge their interests. This may be contrasted with policy innovation, in which the absence of these interests permits the formation of a coalition with less direct involvement by affected interests. Also at this stage, legislators must consider the political payoffs to them for mobilizing a majority. In general, they have higher returns to their investments of time and energy when they can advocate a new policy rather than when they 'simply' try to modify an existing policy.

Implementing policy succession rather than policy innovation involves changing existing organizations rather than creating new organizations. It also involves changing the attitudes and behaviors of existing organizational members rather than recruiting and training new members. Perhaps most importantly, implementing policy succession is more likely to involve greater interactive effects with other policies and programs than is genuine policy innovation. Therefore, the interorganizational politics of accommodation and adjustment are likely to be more pronounced in policy succession than in policy innovation (see Scharpf, Reissert and Schnabel, 1978).

Finally, the impact of policymaking upon clients and the policy environment is likely to be different depending upon whether a policy innovation or policy succession is being adopted. In particular, once a policy area has once been processed through the policy cycle, expectations of benefits from future policy changes tend to be diminished by the probable weaknesses of the initial policy. Policy areas would not be candidates for policy succession if the initial policy adopted were totally salutory in its effects and capable of solving the problem addressed. Initial failures breed disillusionment about subsequent changes so that there is less idealism, and (perhaps) more realism, about the probability of significant improvements in the policy area. On the other hand, however, it will be considerably easier to isolate the effects of the policy innovation as compared to the policy succession. All the problems of repeated treatments in research design obtain in the real world of policy evaluation, so that making definitive statements about the effectiveness of a particular policy change becomes increasingly difficult as the number of different policy successions increases.

In summary, both the policy innovation and policy succession processes have hurdles which present particular difficulty. For the policy innovation process, this is primarily placing the issue on the agenda and overcoming resistance to its consideration by government at all. The absence of organizations and clienteles receptive to the particular policy issue makes government relatively insensitive to that issue. Innovations will also normally face greater long-run additional resource cost implications than successions. For policy succession, however, the principal hurdles are overcoming the inertia and defensiveness of existing organizations and clientele groups which, having identifiable benefits being provided to them, fear and resist change and policy succession.

Chapter 6
THE ORGANIZATIONAL SETTING OF POLICY SUCCESSION

> We trained hard, but it seemed that every time we were
> beginning to form up into teams we would be reorganized.
> I was to learn later in life that we tend to meet any new
> situation by reorganizing, and what a wonderful method it
> can be for creating the illusion of progress while producing
> confusion, inefficiency and demoralization.
>
> Petronius (66 AD)

6.1 Change organizations to change policy?

To some degree organizational change and policy succession are
intertwined and constitute two components of a larger change
process. The two aspects are, however, analytically distinguishable,
and it is important for theoretical development to distinguish them
and to examine their relationships. Policy succession may occur
without direct organizational manifestations, although certainly the
internal dynamics of the organization would be altered as a result of
the change in the policy being administered. Organizations may be
changed in an attempt to make them function more efficiently
without any desire to alter the substance of the policy being
administered. The majority of attempts at government reorganization in the United States over the past half-century would fit that
description (Szanton, 1981). However, the policy being administered
may be affected in more subtle ways, and indeed one purpose of
organizational change may be subtly to generate a policy succession.
For example, organizational differentiation or splitting without any
direct change in the policies being administered may make certain
policies more visible to the public, and thereby advantage or
disadvantage those policies. One obvious example is the moving of
the Department of Education out of the then Department of Health,
Education and Welfare (HEW). This had the initial and intended
effect of making the policy area more visible and improving its

chances for budgetary success (Miles, 1977). However, with the change in administrations, the independence of the Department of Education made it a more visible target for budget cutting and perhaps even organizational termination (*Washington Post*, 13 August 1981).

As well as the theoretical purposes behind understanding the linkage between organized succession and policy succession, we will want to understand this linkage from a strategic perspective. Is policy succession without concomitant organizational change pointless, or at best an inefficient use of time and resources? It could be argued that if the pre-existing organization is allowed to remain in operation that the intended result of a policy succession will be difficult if not impossible to attain. Or, are there certain types of organizations, defined both in terms of their structures and their members, which can effectively respond to policy changes imposed upon them, or in fact generate those policy changes themselves (Wildavsky, 1979, pp. 212–37; Baehr and Wittrock, 1981)? And can the desired goals of policy succession be achieved without the political struggles involved in a complete policy succession only by altering a few crucial elements of the relevant organizations? We will be attempting to provide answers to these and other questions as we discuss the organizational aspects of policy succession.

This chapter will be particularly concerned with the instances in which form follows function and organizations change along with a policy succession. Neither type of change is easy to accomplish politically, and each imposes a number of costs upon members of the organization and upon its clients. We must be concerned with the extent to which it is desirable to impose the double trouble of both types of change, as opposed to going through them sequentially. Additionally, we must be concerned with the most desirable types of policy and organizational changes to attempt, both to minimize disruption generated by the changes, and to maximize the benefits created.

6.1.1   *Is it easier to set up an organization or to change one?*

One clear option in managing a policy succession is to abolish the existing organization and to establish a new organization in its place to administer what is, in effect, a 'new' policy. Such an approach to the problem of organizational change is rather neat analytically, but may not be practical. It might be a desirable option if the purpose of the policy succession was really to terminate a policy and then generate an entirely new policy to take its place. But given our argument that policy succession is the most common form of policymaking in industrialized societies, and that 'new' policies frequently will contain elements of the old, it may be difficult to determine in what instances the termination of an existing organization should be advocated. Even if there were an answer to that question, organizations might forever be being created and then terminated. An alternative outcome would be, of course, that many organizations would be created but few would be terminated (Kaufman, 1976; see also 4.2). The policy and organizational zoo would become inhabited with an increasing number of endangered species with very little to do. Putting organizations out of business is not as easy as the critics of government would like to have citizens believe, nor perhaps as desirable, even given the existence of a number of termination policies such as 'sunset' laws (de Leon, 1978; Behn, 1978; Brewer, 1978). Thus, although there may be definite costs involved it may be more efficient to attempt to alter the existing organization than to develop an entirely new organization for each change in policies.

The real trick in changing organizations is, however, to make the old organization feel and act like a new one. Organizational change is difficult and is threatening to many people, but it is also exciting. Effective organizational change will therefore depend upon managers developing a positive sense of change rather than accentuating the defensive posture which is all too common when change is proposed (Eddy, 1981, pp. 174–98; Dalton, 1970). Creating this sense of excitement is no simple task, especially if there are organization members who have seen it all before and who regard the present change as simply one more in an on-going series of changes. Members of the Department of Energy in the United States concerned with nuclear power would be difficult to excite about any proposed change, one would surmise, given the rather tortuous organizational path they have followed from the era of the Atomic Energy Commission. Such a series of organizational changes can only engender cynicism about the causes and consequences of the change at hand which will make the task of the manager that much more difficult. Also, one might hypothesize that in instances where change has been frequent, the appropriate response may be to terminate the organization and begin with a new organization.

Of course, some criteria must be established which will assist decision-makers when they must decide on how to coordinate organizational change and policy succession. Two criteria which should be used are the extent and the type of policy succession being undertaken. First, the greater the extent of the succession, both in terms of the changes in the goals of the policy and in the methodologies used to attain those goals, the greater the need for an organizational change to be combined with the policy succession. For example, it may be difficult for many of the members of the Environmental Protection Agency, recruited during the 1970s, to administer the programs of the Reagan administration and, as a consequence, it may be desirable for the administration to reorganize the management of environmental policy if their goals are to be attained. Likewise, even if the goals of environmental protection were not to be altered significantly, a movement towards more incentive-based policies, for example, effluent charges, as opposed to direct regulation, might make it difficult for the holdovers to be effective in the organization. That may not be as much a function of their lack of commitment to a program of that type as a function of their lack of expertise in implementing a program using that methodology.

Several types of policy succession would also appear to require organizational change. Clearly, policy splitting and policy consolidation imply that new organizations would be required for adequate administration. Policy splitting may be possible to accomplish within a single organization, but if the intention is to accentuate some components of the policy over others, then the absence of organizational change may make the policy succession rather fruitless. Further, the complexity involved in non-linear changes would appear to require organizational modifications if they are to be implemented successfully.

6.1.2 *Changing organizations*

To some degree, changing organizations may be merely a cosmetic response to real problems. It has been characteristic in both the United States and the United Kingdom to respond to real, difficult problems by merely altering the organizations associated with the policy area (see Brittan, 1970, p. 468). This 'institutionalitis' has perhaps been best demonstrated in the numerous reforms of the National Health Service in the United Kingdom without addressing the underlying problems of professional control and allocation of expenditures.

This denigration of organizational change as a response to problems should not be overdone, for indeed some benefits can be obtained by changing an organization. But it does appear that, despite their difficulties, organizational responses have been used rather than confronting the policy problems directly. The organizational response has been used for several reasons. First, the organization is a visible manifestation of the problem, and it is easier to kill the messenger bearing the bad news than it is to confront the bad news responsibly. That is not only a defensive mechanism for hard-pressed politicians, but it is also a means of satisfying demands for action. The political leaders can argue that the problem has been 'solved' simply by changing the organization.

In addition, the structure of the organization is often easier to modify than substantive policies. Presidents and Prime Ministers are given considerable latitude in changing the organization of the executive branch of government, and consequently they can make a response to a perceived problem without having to become involved with the legislature, clients, service providers, and the host of other interests which are associated with the existing policy (Mansfield, 1970). This does not mean that the organizational response to the problem will generate the desired results, or that the change will be made easily by those in the organization. It is simply convenient for political leaders to use organizational change as their modal response to pressures.

Finally, it must be remembered that some politicians believe in the organizational response. This was clearly the case with President Carter, and to some extent was true of Harold Wilson and Edward Health (Johnson, 1976). At least in the case of Carter, this was the response of a political leader who did not really appear to enjoy politics, but who sought to solve problems in this rather mechanistic, engineering fashion. But it is perhaps no surprise that in an organizational society even intelligent people might regard organizational changes as the key to other types of desired changes.

The most fundamental point to be made here is that there is no academic theory, nor any set of practical proverbs, that relates organizational change to program change, policy change, or other types of transformations. Organizational change may be a necessary but certainly not a sufficient condition for some types of policy successions. Changing the organization does not of itself necessarily produce any real changes in the policies being implemented, although it can facilitate making those policy changes. Leaving the pre-existing organization in place to administer a new policy, with different goals, clients, and policy instruments may be fruitless if real change is desired. But, of course, real policy change may not be desired and changing policy without changing the organization may be a not too subtle means of sabotaging the policy succession. For the political leader organizations provide a convenient scapegoat to explain why nothing ever happens.

6.2 The bureaucratic politics of policy succession

As well as presenting difficulties for managers and administrators, policy succession may also present opportunities. The common stereotype of public bureaucrats is that of extreme caution, legalism and defensiveness. However, the more creative of the species are also capable of playing politics quite effectively. This is not, of course, partisan politics, but rather is the politics of organizational survival and growth: bureaucratic politics (Allison, 1971; Halperin, 1972; Downs, 1967). Since organizations constitute the permanent, or almost permanent, components of government, while political leaders and their policies come and go, bureaucrats must be concerned about their long-term positions in the structures of government (Heclo, 1977; Aberbach, Putnam and Rockman, 1981). Even if there is an organizational change associated with a policy sucession, that change will frequently be shuffling boxes around within the bureaucratic structures, rather than making fundamental changes within the building blocks themselves. This permanence, at least at the lower levels of disaggregation, places the organization or the agency in a position to interpret and then implement the policy successions which are adopted.

6.2.1 *How organizations interpret policy documents*

The first manner in which the bureaucracy can influence the nature of a policy succession is through the interpretation of legislation and regulations. The majority of policy documents and intended changes in policy are not so clearly defined that an agency could make only a single interpretation of them. The interpretation which the agency may make as it prepares the policy succession for implementation may be crucial for attaining the goals of that succession, and for attaining the goals of the organization. The most obvious strategy would be for the members of the organization to interpret the policy succession just as they had the old policy, and to continue to do what they had always done. The agency may simply politely ignore the intentions of the legislature or political executives and continue along their previous path, while rationalizing their actions in terms of the newly made policy. Or the agency may interpret the new policy, and the vacuum which almost inevitably accompanies the promulgation of a new policy, as an opportunity to do what they had always wanted to do but lacked the statutory authority to do. Thus, a policy succession may be interpreted to grant new and probably unintended authority to an agency which is already in operation and which can seize the opportunity.

6.2.2 *Relationships with the political executive*

The ability of an existing organization to engage in delaying and obfuscating activities places a special strain on the already difficult relationships between political executives and career civil servants. It is not uncommon that when there is a policy succession there will also be a change in the political executives responsible for the policy area. This is especially common in the United States where the 'government of strangers', composed of political executives going in and out of a rapidly revolving door, means that change in political executives is a common occurrence (Heclo, 1977). It may be true also in the United Kingdom when a change in government, or a change in ministers within a sitting government, means that a policy succession is associated with a change in the political personnel nominally in charge (Headey, 1974). The uncertainty of political leadership will tend to result in greater latitude for the organization, and its career civil servants, to have their own way in the implementation of the policy succession (Kellner and Crowther-Hunt, 1980, pp. 203–36).

6.2.3 *The strategic uses of policy succession*

The preceding sections may give the clever civil servant the idea—quite correctly—that policy succession is not necessarily something which should be feared and resisted. The cleverest may regard policy succession as an opportunity rather than as a problem. Policy succession may create uncertainty and an absence of clear authority which may enable those with a firm organizational base and administrative abilities to seize control and provide directions to otherwise vague and directionless policy statements. But there are attendant risks, one of which may be accentuating the power which the career civil servants do have over the nature of policy in practice, through their role in the implementation of the policy statements. This may make bureaucratic power more of a political issue and threaten to make politicians more conscious of their need to control the bureaucracy.

Finally, it should be remembered that organizations do not necessarily need to engage in deceptive practices in order to gain from policy successions. The ties between the agencies and legislatures writing legislation may be better than the relations between the legislative and executive elites, especially in the United States (Seidman, 1980). The policy succession may well be written to the specifications designed by the organization, rather than requiring them to interpret it in a self-serving fashion after the fact.

6.3   Personnel barriers to policy succession in organizations

> Progress is a nice word. But change is its motivator. And
> change has its enemies.
>
>   Robert F. Kennedy, Federal power and local
>   poverty, *The Pursuit of Justice* (1964)

Although the clever and creative manager of an organization may regard policy succession favorably, or at least neutrally, this may not be true of other members of the organization. Those not in managerial positions and not having the information or strategic perspectives of those positions may regard any policy change or proposed policy change more negatively. These are the foot soldiers who view the war from the perspective of the fox-hole, rather than as an exercise in tactics and map reading. Many of those in the lower echelons of the organization, even if they had the information, might not have an interest in growth or in enhancing the power base of the organization. Given the characteristics of civil service employment, for example, established pay scales, seniority and union protection, there may be little incentive for the rank-and-file members of an organization to cooperate enthusiastically in a policy succession. They may simply not see the value of any growth or change for them in their everyday working lives. In addition to this inertia, there are a number of compelling reasons to expect the workers in an organization to resist attempts to change their organizations and the policies which they administer.

6.3.1 *Recruitment*

The first barrier to policy succession is a result of patterns of recruitment. Organizations tend to recruit personnel based upon their activities. Thus, the Environmental Protection Agency should be expected to attract environmentally concerned individuals, as to some extent has the US Department of the Interior. As a consequence, any attempt to alter in any significant fashion the policies being administered by these organizations in a direction that would be less environmentally conscious could be expected to encounter opposition. The appointment of James Watt as Secretary of the Interior in 1981, and his articulation of policies allowing considerably greater exploitation of public lands than had been allowed previously, has been encountering opposition from career members of the Department. Departments and agencies which have less sensitive policy areas may encounter fewer difficulties, but any attempt to modify the program for which the employees of an organization have been recruited is likely to encounter opposition.

Another effect of recruitment on the resistance of an organization to policy succession is that certain types of professions tend to be attracted into certain types of organizations. When those professionals are recruited they bring with them a particular conception of the manner in which policy problems should be approached. Thus, for example, an agency which has recruited physicians to treat mental health problems will find it difficult to escape the 'medical model' of mental disease in favor of a more social or community-based conception of the etiology of mental disease (Foley, 1975). With the increasing professionalization of society and the public service, the possibilities of conflicts among professionals have increased when a policy succession is undertaken. Each profession defines how a particular problem should be defined and treated, and if different professions are forced to interact, they will tend to conflict over control of clients. Also, as professional rigidities tend to be enshrined in law and in practice, policy successions may be expected to encounter these institutional problems as well as the behavioral problems arising from individuals.

6.3.2   *The 'age lump' problem*

Another personnel barrier to policy succession in organizations is the 'age lump' phenomenon (Downs, 1967). As noted in 6.3.1, organizations tend to recruit their members selectively. Organizations also attempt to train their members to meet perceived organizational needs. However, as we understand from our general orientation to policy succession, those perceived needs may change. Thus, within a single organization there may be individuals who have been recruited under a number of different sets of values and policy perspectives, despite the attempt of the organization to supply a common set of values to all its members. The contemporary university may be one of the best examples of this organizational problem, as faculty members recruited during the 1960s and 1970s have rather different professional and economic perspectives from those recruited prior to the explosion of higher education during those decades.

The age lump phenomenon may be particularly troublesome when the leadership of the organization has been recruited and trained in one era, and lower echelons or subunits have been recruited under a very different set of circumstances. Mazmanian and Nienaber's (1979) study of the Army Corps of Engineers and its response to environmental protection issues illustrates this point rather clearly. The majority of the leadership of the Corps was recruited prior to the strength of the environmental movement, and found it difficult to respond favorably to the new environmental units organized to allow the Corps to respond to National Environmental Protection Act (NEPA) requirements to produce environmental impact statements. The authors do point out, however, that the Corps has had a generally successful change in its orientation, in part through changes in leadership and in part through learning on the part of the existing leadership.

6.3.3   *Organizational ideology and policy succession*

Even if the members of an organization do not self-select themselves for membership, organizations may develop an almost ideological conception of the nature of their policy problems and of the appropriate responses. Certain types of organizations tend to develop ideological perspectives on policy to a greater extent than do others. In general, we would expect organizations with more interactions with their environments, and which have interactions with that environment which would tend to weaken the internal cohesion of the organization and the enforcement of consistent standards, to be more prone to develop ideological guides to action. Thus, we would expect the development of ideological guides to action in law-enforcement agencies, financial agencies, and to some extent the military (Kaufman, 1960).

The ideological orientation to policy problems can be developed and reinforced through training and organizational socialization. Some organizations invest a great deal of effort in teaching new recruits a particular set of values about the proper means of enforcing policy, and attempt to reinforce those norms through frequent training sessions throughout the career. It is arguably more difficult to initiate a policy succession in an organization of this type, as training tends to indoctrinate members into the belief that there is but one way of accomplishing a desired end. This may explain, in part, the persistence of certain dysfunctional patterns of policy and behavior, for example, the long survival of the horse cavalry after its futility in battle in modern warfare had been proven (Katzenbach, 1958).

6.3.4 *Goal displacement*

Finally, perhaps the most serious personal barrier to policy succession to be overcome within an organization is the tendency of members of an organization to interpret any policy statement not in the context in which it was written, but rather in terms of the personal goals of the individuals themselves. This is a restatement of the classic problem of the 'displacement of goals' in organizations (Merton, 1940). This is especially important as individuals may place individual security goals ahead of purposive policy goals. Instead of attempting to accomplish anything substantive, be it through an old policy or its replacement, members of an organization may seek simply to serve their own interests. Downs (1967, pp. 92–112) has discussed this as another aspect of the age phenomenon within organizations. As individuals, and their organizations, age they become more conservative and more concerned with personal security goals than with the ostensible policy goals of the organization which they may have espoused when they were younger 'zealots' or 'advocates'. As a consequence, older organizations and older individuals are likely to be more resistant to policy succession simply because it would require changes from established conservative routines. Further, although the organization as an organization may gain from the policy succession, there may be a reluctance to make the changes because of their destabilizing nature.

Of course, a policy succession or other proposed change may be undertaken simply because of the extent to which the displacement of goals has already progressed. Change is not a good in itself, but may approach being one when a manager or political executive faces an intransigent and entrenched bureaucracy. Thus, organizational change associated with policy succession may be a healthful tonic for organizations which appear to have lost a sense of purpose. There is no guarantee that a new purpose will be found by making the change, but the change may offer more hope than doing nothing.

6.4 Organizational barriers to policy succession

As well as the individual working within the organization, the organization itself can present a series of formidable obstacles to attempted policy successions. Some of these barriers are simply aggregations of individual level barriers, but an additional set of barriers arises from the interactions of one organization with others, and from the concerted efforts of the organization *qua* organization to resist the imposition of a policy succession. Additionally, we must remember that an organization does not always exist as a single, united organization, but as a coalition of many organizations. Organizations are divided hierarchically, and field branches and the street-level members of the organization may not accept any succession which the leadership of the organization may attempt to implement (Lipsky, 1978; Kaufman, 1960). Likewise, organizations are divided vertically, and conflicts frequently arise between staff organizations which plan policy successions and the line organizations which must implement those changes. These conflicts are as old as the first organizations, but are nonetheless real and they continue to present difficulties for anyone attempting to implement a policy change.

6.4.1 *The law*

Any organization attempting to resist a policy succession has a number of powerful weapons at its disposal. Perhaps the most basic weapon is the law. A policy succession will generally take the form of legislation, but unless other previous legislation is specifically repealed, the organization can plead confusion and conflicts within the legislation, and still attempt to do what it wishes. The implementation of Comprehensive Employment and Training Act (CETA) and the many conflicting guidelines coming from Congress and the Department of Labor illustrates the difficulties arising from conflicts in laws and regulations (Van Horn, 1976). These difficulties will tend to increase as more levels of government are involved in implementing the succession and each level has some latitude to legislate in the area.

Even a single piece of legislation may be confusing and have inconsistent statements, simply because legislation arises from compromise and one means of compromise is to include all views (Derthick, 1975). The agency can then seize on which pieces of the legislation it likes and implement those, and without effective oversight there will be difficulty in having legislative intentions in a policy succession implemented.

6.4.2 *Procedures*

In addition to formal legislative statements of the purposes of the organization, procedural requirements may also allow the organization to resist attempts at policy succession. One level at which these restrictions on policy succession may arise is through the rather broad statements of procedural requirements for administrative action, such as the Administrative Procedures Act (Freedman, 1978). The constraints written into these acts may be used to limit the speed of response to any particular policy succession. To issue regulations requires a number of notifications and waiting periods for responses, and these delays can be used and abused to inhibit change.

An organization itself will also develop procedures which can be used defensively to retard change. These organizational procedures can be used first to slow down change simply by doing such things as engaging in required consultation with organized interests affected by the succession. As these groups are apt to be as apprehensive as the members of the organization, the feedback from the consultation can be used to avoid the real intent of the policy succession. A new policy which is implemented through procedures developed for other policies is unlikely to be successful in attaining its desired goals. Simply put, the use of an outmoded procedure can be a mechanism for keeping an old policy actually in operation.

6.4.3 *Interorganizational barriers*

Very few public organizations have policies and programs which are so clearly defined that they do not interact with other organizations (see 5.4.3). These interactions may be intentional and the product of negotiations among agencies, or they may be purely incidental. For example, all social programs are to some degree related, and they interact to provide a benefit level for needy clients. A change in one of these programs may place additional demands on other agencies for service, or may render another type of service superfluous. The interaction between taxation and social policy may also produce the 'notches' or 'poverty traps' which present such difficulties in the administration of social programs (Sandford, 1977, pp. 161–3).

6.4.3.1 *Poor losers*

Perhaps the most difficult interorganizational problem associated with policy succession is that of the poor loser. That is, one form of policy succession is to take authority, personnel and budget from one organization and give it to another. Contrary to many popular stereotypes, those losses are not always perceived as losses by the organization which sustained them (Goodin, 1975). But when they are perceived as having harmed the program or the survivability of the organization, then the organization cannot be expected to be cordial towards those perceived as having been the winners. If these two organizations must cooperate to make the new program work, there is the obvious possibility that the losers will attempt to sabotage the winners. The ability to sabotage may be hypothesized to be greatest when the succession takes the form of policy splitting, and when the new organization is established to carry out a portion of the program of an already existing organization. That new organization will have all the problems faced with starting up, and in addition must face the hostility of an existing and bitter organization which it needs to make the program function. For example, if President Carter had been successful in hiving veterans' education programs from the Veterans' Administration to the new Department of Education, the Department of Education could not have expected much cooperation when it had to do things such as determine eligibility for benefits.

6.4.3.2. *Threshold level synergy*

A related problem might be termed 'threshold level synergy'. That is, below a certain level of activity or interaction one organization may make little difference to another. But if one of the organizations increases certain activities above a certain, and variable, threshold the synergistic effects may be substantial and may influence the performance of the organization. The effects on a policy succession may be positive or negative, but they must be considered when planning the succession. For example, as long as the involvement of the US Department of Agriculture in promoting agricultural exports was small, there was little necessity to coordinate its activities with the Department of State, or the Foreign Commercial Service of the Department of Commerce. However, as there has been a significant increase in its activity, and in the importance of agricultural exports, the need for coordination has arisen. Further, the basis for greater conflict over bureaucratic 'turf' has been established.

6.4.3.3 *Clearances from organizations with different tasks*

Even when the functions performed by organizations are not directly competitive, interorganizational problems may still arise when a policy succession is attempted. Some of these difficulties may arise from organizations designed to coordinate and facilitate the activities of the numerous government agencies. For example, in the United States, Lawrence Lynn (1980, p. 64) points out that:

> many, and perhaps most, policy issues of high importance involve other offices, agencies, and departments in the executive branch. National health insurance, for example, involves not only the Health and Human Services Department but also OMB, the Domestic Policy Staff (DPS), the Council of Economic Advisors, the Veterans Administration, and the Departments of Commerce, Labor, Defense, and Treasury.

Financial control agencies typically provide the most serious barriers to an attempted policy succession, especially ones with the extensive range of powers granted to the Office of Management and Budget, which not only approves funding but also more mundane matters such as the nature of Federal forms. Personnel organizations can also present difficulties by simply not supplying the required personnel, or by delaying or obfuscating specialized job categories which are felt necessary. The degree of detail which exists within the American public personnel system allows substantial delay, even if the Office of Personnel Management does not want to create problems, simply because of the complexity of the procedures. Even organizations such as the General Services Administration in the United States or the Property Services Agency in the United Kingdom may create difficulties simply by not providing enough space or paper clips.

6.4.3.4 *Intergovernmental relations*
A special case of the difficulties which may arise because of interorganizational difficulties in policy succession is the relationship between central and subnational governments, and the analogous relationships which may arise between a government and the autonomous or semi-autonomous organizations which exercise some governmental powers. There have been so many examples of a local or state government in both the United States and the United Kingdom delaying, or blocking, implementation of central government policy that it is not worth recounting any in great detail (on the United States, see Bullock and Rodgers, 1976; Berke and Kirst, 1972; on the United Kingdom see Jones, 1980; Rhodes, 1981). But these clearances have to be obtained in order to make policies effective, and may not be easy to obtain. This is especially true if the central government and the subnational government are of different political persuasions. The difficulties of the Thatcher government in obtaining compliance with its expenditure policies from Labour controlled council is indicative of this general problem.

Likewise, autonomous bodies such as the Federal Reserve Board may make it difficult to alter policies in ways which the autonomous body would regard as ill-advised. The ability of the Federal Reserve Board to thwart some aspects of the Reagan administration's attempts to change economic policy is indicative of the necessity of interorganizational coordination between the 'government' and other organizations which exercise a portion of the power of the state (Peters and Heisler, 1981).

6.4.3.5 *Interorganizational problems with the private sector*
To this point we have been discussing primarily interactions of one public sector organization with another. But increasingly in modern societies policies will be made and implemented with the involvement of private sector actors (Heisler, 1974). Any policy succession which requires the cooperation of such private organizations and which does

not please the private organizations is likely to encounter difficulty. For example, when states in the United States have attempted to integrate the delivery of social service they have encountered resistance from professional organizations and private social service agencies (Edwards, 1980, pp. 135–6). Hanf, Hjern and Porter's (1978) comparison of the implementation of manpower policy in Sweden and Germany indicates that as many problems may arise from coordination with private sector organizations in meeting changing policy needs as with public sector organizations.

6.4.3.6 *The non-Lego-like nature of organizational change*
In summary, organizations and organizational tasks do not fit neatly together as do children's Lego blocks. In fact, the superior analogy may be to the game of jackstraws. If one straw is moved the wrong way the stability of the entire, randomly designed, structure is threatened. Analogies aside, there are distinct interorganizational difficulties involved in making what is ostensibly a single, simple change in a policy. These difficulties need not arise only because of political or 'turf' fights between competitive agencies. They may arise simply because so many activities of government agencies are intertwined, and because some very important organizations, such as the Office of Management and Budget or the British Treasury, are given the task of coordinating all other organizations in government. Additionally, central governments must implement their programs through subnational governments. Differences in the political affiliations and in the policy priorities of these governments will further increase difficulties in attaining central policy goals.

6.4.4 *The non-hierarchical nature of hierarchical organizations*

When organizations are portrayed in graphic form, they have a neat, hierarchical appearance. It is assumed in such drawings that those on the top of organizational pyramids do in fact control those who appear under them in the hierarchy. But in reality this may not be the case, and this is crucial for understanding why organizations can resist changes imposed upon them from the outside.

The concept of the 'informal organization' grew out of the human relations approach to organization theory (Whyte, 1959). The basic concept is that there are informal social networks which develop in organizations to supplement or to counteract the power of the formal structure. Crozier's concepts of strata isolation and parallel power relationships are another statement of the same phenomenon (Crozier, 1964). Organizations develop power centers outside of the formal structures. These in turn limit the ability of those in the management of the organization to produce the control and the positive response to policy successions that they might like. Authoritative commands may be issued, but they may be interpreted and avoided by those who have control over some aspects of the functioning of the organization. Crozier (1964) and others (Merton, 1940; Selznick, 1948) interested in this phenomenon have noted that the attempts of the leadership of organizations to impose control through impersonal rules may actually diminish their control over the activities of the organization.

Relatedly, Victor Thompson (1961) discussed modern organizations as having an increasing separation between authority and knowledge. Those at the apex of the organizations have the power to make decisions, but those at the bottom have the technical information and abilities required to make good decisions. If the lower echelons of the organization do not cooperate in the making of a policy succession, or in responding to one imposed from the outside, then the quality of the decisions which will be made will be diminished, and the need for further decisions and further successions increased. Thus 'organizations seem to be typically harder to change at the bottom than the top' (Hood, 1976, p. 27). Policy succession involves not simply (or perhaps not at all) the redrawing of boxes and lines in an organization chart but the adjustment of informal networks.

6.4.5   *How oysters cope with grit*

What are the methods by which the organization will seek to defend itself from real or perceived threats to its existence from a policy succession imposed on it? Here the most apt analogy is the oyster coping with grit. For a smoothly functioning organization with a well-defined and satisfying set of tasks a policy succession may not be a welcome occurrence. But the organization must adapt to the problem being imposed upon it, and may do so in a number of ways.

6.4.5.1   *Accommodation*
The most straightforward means of dealing with the piece of grit is to accommodate the functioning of the organization to the policy

change. This is likely to occur when the change is basically compatible—both in terms of goals and methods of service delivery—with the on-going activities of the organization, or when the policy succession is perceived as a victory for the organization. Or the organization may accommodate to a policy succession if it believes itself to be under attack either from other similar organizations or from central controlling agencies (see 6.4.3.3). Even in the best of circumstances, however, this will require good management. This will involve principally convincing the members of the organization to respond positively to the challenges presented by the policy succession.

6.4.5.2 *Absorption*

But no one should expect the organization, as embodied in its management, to respond in such a positive and professional manner to a policy succession. A somewhat less constructive approach to the policy succession is to attempt to absorb it into the on-going programs of the organization. This may be as simple as adding the new program to an old program, or deciding to administer a new program much as the old one had been administered. Unless the legislature is careful, the new program may be used primarily as a subsidy for the other programs of the agency. Thus, programs which are intended to be new and creative frequently end up being very much more of the same thing. We would expect absorption to occur in agencies which have well-defined and rather singular interests, as opposed to more multifunctional organizations. Also, organizations which have rather direct ties to clientele groups who have come to expect a certain type of program will attempt to absorb any policy succession. Finally, policy successions which are linear replacements for other programs may be more easily absorbed than other types of policy successions.

Absorptions of a program can be used to characterize the fate of the Elementary and Secondary Education Act of 1965 (ESEA). This Act was intended to provide compensatory education primarily for school districts with large numbers of disadvantaged children. In part because of the ambiguity of some aspects of the language of the legislation, and in part because it was given to the US Office of Education to administer, the program was implemented as if it were a general subsidy to education. The majority of the Great Society legislation was administered by new agencies created outside of the existing social policy networks, but ESEA was given to an existing agency with a large number of ties to local school districts (Murphy, 1973). As such, it was accustomed to administering programs equally for all school districts and regarded its role as to promote education rather than equality. Of course, some programs such as the Title I reading programs were provided only for the disadvantaged, but others were administered to spread the money quite broadly, for example, Title IV money used to purchase library and audio-visual materials. Thus, despite the importance of ESEA as the first general subsidy for elementary and secondary education in the United States, it was administered much as the Federal educational programs which had existed previously.

6.4.5.3 *Insulation*

If we return to our original analogy, and the response of oysters to grit, another means by which an organization can respond to a policy succession is to respond much as the oyster does. That is, the organization can build up of a wall of insulation around the 'grit' to prevent the new and presumably contaminating influence from irritating the entire organization. This response, then, is to build a new organization within the original organization and to separate as much as possible a new policy from the remainder of the organization. One example of this type of response is the development of the Glasgow Eastern Area Renewal Project (GEAR) within the Scottish Development Agency (SDA). The SDA was primarily concerned with general economic development in Scotland and not with urban policy, but was given GEAR to administer. It isolated the program in a special section on urban problems while the remainder of the organization was very little affected by the new addition (see Page, 1977).

The insulation response is almost the exact opposite of the absorption response mentioned above (6.4.5.2), and one option may be selected over the other on the basis of several variables. One would be the perceived viability of the new policy. If the policy is perceived as doomed from birth or as having little chance of any real success, as was perhaps true of GEAR, it will be isolated so as to protect the 'heartland' of the organization: the programs central to the purpose of the organization (Downs, 1967; Holden, 1966). Or if the policy succession is perceived as potentially conflictual relative to the purposes of the remaining sections of the organization, every effort will be made to isolate it from the mainstream of the organization, so that a friendly reorganization moving the new program can occur without threatening any of the remainder of the organization. The isolation response is particularly likely to be employed in such circumstances if the succession involves the use of a mechanism for policy delivery which is different from that employed by the rest of the organization.

6.5   Organizational costs

Although at times politicians and the popular media may talk about reorganization and organizational change as being simple and virtually costless (indeed they are often portrayed as cost-saving), such changes do have definite costs (see Hood, 1976, pp. 26–7). Each separate organizational change which is made to accommodate or resist a policy succession must take into account the costs which may be associated with that change, and attempt to determine if the costs indeed outweigh the benefits. This is especially difficult as, under Sayre's Law, the benefits of a reorganization are created immediately, whereas the costs accumulate over the long term (quoted in Miles, 1977). In his conception of reorganization the benefits arise primarily from changing the organization and loosening rigidities which have developed over time, whereas the inefficiencies and dysfunctions which may be inevitable in public organizations will tend to accumulate as an organization develops and attempts to implement a policy.

6.5.1   *Time as an organizational cost*

One of the principal costs associated with organizational change is time. It simply takes time to make a change in an organization, and the reaction of the administering agency may take longer than simply promulgating the policy succession. Depending upon the nature of the policy succession, it can be made with the stroke of a pen, but altering the functions of an organization may require substantially more time and effort. An important strategic question arises with respect to the time dimension: policy succession which requires prompt action may best be implemented without an associated organizational change, while those which require a more complete alteration of previous practices, regardless of time constraints, would best be implemented through an organizational change.

6.5.2   *Disruption costs*

Any alteration in an organization is disruptive to the members, and even if the proposed policy succession does not threaten the survival of the organization, it may threaten individuals who believe that they will be adversely impacted. The apprehension created by a proposed policy succession places an additional burden upon the managers of the organization to assuage the fears of workers, and to gain their cooperation, or at least acquiescence, in the change. For example, the proposed changes in the Customs and Excise in the United Kingdom associated with the introduction of Value Added Tax required a substantial investment of managerial time to calm fears (Johnstone, 1975).

Even in the absence of real or perceived threats, the disruption associated with a policy succession may impose substantial costs on an organization. Organizations exist as formal structures, but perhaps as importantly they also have an informal structure. A policy succession, and any associated changes in the formal structures administering the policy, may affect informal patterns of interaction and in turn affect the efficiency and effectiveness of the organization.

6.5.3   *Burdens on top management*

Although we have alluded to it previously, it should be remembered and emphasized that one of the principal costs of organizational change is the burden which it places on top management. As Samuel Brittan remarked in the context of the management of the British economy:

> The cost in confusion, and time-wasting of each organization of government machinery, is enormous. After each 'dynamic' reshuffle, ministers and officials have to spend months getting used to their new environment—which means everything from office arrangements to jockeying for position in the new hierarchies. The result is that high-level time, which should be devoted to analysis and policy, has to be devoted to demarcation and personnel problems (Brittan, 1970, p. 468).

The burdens falling on top management come from above and below. Those coming from below are perhaps more obvious. The management of the organization must use his or her own personal powers of leadership or authority to obtain compliance with the proposed policy succession. More than simple compliance should be sought, for a more grudging 'going along with the program' is not likely to obtain positive results from the change, and may be simply a disguise for the more obstructionist tactics mentioned previously. To produce a more positive organizational response to a policy succession may require more than management by authority, and there must be an attempt to develop some real commitment on the part of the members of the organization to the new policy and the new organizational structure. Obtaining that commitment in an organization which has been in existence for a number of years, and whose members have seen policies and the politicians who promoted them come and go, is an exceedingly difficult task.

It is here that the additional pressures on organizational leadership coming from above are important. Presumably the policy and organizational changes being discussed will have been initiated for some good reason, and there will be demands for the attainment of the goals (Warwick, 1975, pp. 71–6). This is especially true as the new policies will bear the trademark of a particular set of political leaders on them, and those leaders will demand performance. As the time frame within which politicians operate is almost inevitably shorter than that of career civil servants, it is quite likely that there will be demands for changes to occur quickly as the result of the policy succession. But, of course, it may be that because of the changes and the difficulties outlined above, *less* can be accomplished than if organizational change had not occurred. Clearly, then, the leader of the organization is a person in the middle, receiving demands for action from above and demands for protection and support from below. These problems are but one more reason for the common observation that effective public management is a scarce commodity, which is at times difficult to explain when it does occur (Lynn, 1981).

6.5.4 *Economic costs*

As well as the intangible costs of time and psychological disruption, an organizational change associated with a policy succession can produce real economic costs. Of course, lost time and lost performance because of poor morale will impose economic costs, but out-of-pocket costs may also arise from an organizational adaptation to a policy succession. Many of these costs appear trivial, for example, the physical costs of moving and the costs of printing new stationery, but these costs do amount to substantial sums. Frequently it is not just letterhead which must be reprinted but a number of other forms—those of the organization undergoing change and those of the agencies which must interface with that organization. Even if there is not splitting or consolidation of agencies, the need to alter activities and functions in response to policy succession will impose substantial costs on an organization.

6.5.5   *Balancing the costs and benefits of reorganization*

We have been discussing the difficulties encountered when attempting to link a transformation of an organization with a policy succession. While it is clearly desirable to do so in a number of types of cases, the costs associated with the change may outweigh the benefits produced. Clearly there must be a serious consideration of just what those benefits and costs are before organizations are changed. No reorganization is costless (Seidman, 1980), and politicians and even some administrators must be constantly reminded of that point.

6.6   Interorganizational change as an alternative to intra-organizational change

As we have been noting throughout the above discussion, organizational changes associated with a policy succession may be done within a single organization, or they may involve a number of organizations. When there is an interorganizational change it may involve either establishing a new organization or set of organizations, or it may be accomplished by shifting functional responsibilities among a set of existing organizations. Each of these types of change has its associated costs and benefits, and the choice of which type of change to seek may pose a dilemma for decision-makers.

The costs of intra-organizational change are largely borne internally within the organization and include the costs of disruption, time and managerial effort which we have already discussed in 6.5. Other organizations would be threatened relatively little by an internal change of this type, and there would still be the same constellation of organizations with which to consult when making policies which involved or had spillover effects on those other organizations.

In order to avoid these direct costs it may be decided to attempt the easier course of interorganizational change, which may include creating a new organization out of elements of others. A newly created organization, even though it may be administering wholes or parts of policies which existed previously, will lack the history and the commitment to the way things have been done in the past which makes intraorganizational change so difficult.

When the organization is genuinely new rather than simply consisting of a collection of units taken over from other organizations, the manager begins with an organizational, if not policy, *tabula rasa* and would be better able to structure the activities of the organization to meet the demands of the policy succession than in an existing organization. However, a major impediment to the internal functioning of such an organization is its very newness, and the necessity of developing both formal and informal patterns to attain the desired ends. Some have argued that this newness and lack of structuring is a principal advantage of the new organization as it allows and forces thinking about the purposes of the new structures and the best way of achieving goals (Miles, 1977; Kaufman, 1972; Kaufman, 1977). Just thinking does not accomplish the tasks, however, and structures must still be developed.

However, interorganizational change does not occur only by creating new organizations. It may occur by shifting functions or subsidiary organizations from one large organization to another. This has been a characteristic activity for many government reorganizations in the United States. Many subsidiary organizations have been transferred from one Cabinet department to another, for example, the Forest Service, the Coast Guard, the Weather Bureau. In each instance, although certain gains may have been anticipated through greater similarity of functions or coordination with other organizations, there were also decided costs involved in the moves.

Finally, as we noted in 6.4.3.1, organizations which were raided to form the new organization, or which thought that they should have been given the policy succession to administer may react in ways ranging from insecurity to downright hostility to the new organization or the organizations which were given the successions. Thus, what is gained by the interorganizational policy succession may easily be lost through external conflicts and the uncertainty generated by the change.

Clearly, from the above discussion, the type of organizational change which should be attempted will depend on the nature of the policy succession and the nature of the organizations involved. Policies and organizations with extensive external interactions which depend upon the goodwill and cooperation of other organizations would be well-advised to forego interorganizational transformations if possible. However, certain types of changes imposed by the legislature, or by the wishes of the organization itself, may require that type of change anyway. Clearly, policy consolidation, to the extent to which it involves bringing together elements of different organizations and policies, is best performed through an interorganizational change. Otherwise, one organization will be identified as a clear loser and another as a clear winner. But with an interorganizational change of that sort there is the danger that both of the pre-existing organizations may be thought to be losers to the organization.

Intra-organizational changes can best be accomplished if the policy succession is a linear one, or perhaps even a non-linear change not involving changes in elements of existing programs. The major distinction is that such a change would not involve splitting or consolidating existing activities or suborganizations. However, intra-organizational change may not be effective if an organization with a different function or methodology of service delivery is to be created within the boundaries of an existing organization. For example, the difficulties which the Department of Health, Education and Welfare (DHEW) had with the Health Care Financing Agency (HCFA) illustrate the difficulties of putting a fox in the hen house. The majority of agencies in DHEW lived by spending as much as they were allowed. HCFA was established to monitor one of the fastest growing areas of social expenditure and reduce its growth, primarily through regulation. Within the context of the executive department as the unit of organization, HCFA was a maverick, and largely unwelcome, even though the impetus for its creation came from within the department rather than from an external watchdog.

6.7 Summary

This chapter has discussed the nature of the costs and benefits of organizational change as a companion to policy succession. While the two types of change are analytically distinct, they occur together frequently, and we have analyzed several aspects of their interrelationship. One question which arises is whether one type of change can be used as a substitute for the other. Another is whether organizational change is necessary as a companion to policy succession. Finally, if organizational change is to occur, when should it be done within existing organizations as opposed to being done by creating new organizations or shifting authority among existing organizations?

As with so many other issues in policy analysis, the basic answer to the questions raised has been 'it depends'. A number of factors affect the desirability and efficiency of organizational change associated with policy succession. These include the nature of the organization, and especially its relationships with other organizations in its environment, the nature of the policy succession proposed, and the skills and commitment of the managers of the organization. The one factor which appears central to the entire analysis is the role of the agency manager in bringing about the change, be it through the formation of a new organization or the adjustment of an existing organization to an altered policy. Both organizational change and policy succession involve substantial challenges to organizational leaders.

Chapter 7

CHANGING DELIVERY SYSTEMS

7.1 Interest in changing delivery systems

In Chapter 3 we discussed various types of policy succession which may often continue to employ the same method of delivering policy (for example, replacing one or more cash income maintenance benefits by another). In this chapter we are concerned with the implications of transitions in terms of broad categories of methods of delivering public policy, such as regulation as opposed to financial incentives, or direct provision by government agencies as opposed to delivery through 'private' professionals, or organizations under contract to government. While much of the argument is inevitably concerned with broad analytical themes, our concern is not simply with comparing different methods of delivery in the abstract, but with analyzing the practical issues surrounding actual or proposed transitions between delivery methods in practice.

Relatively little has been written about the implications of alternative 'technologies' for delivering public policy (but see Bardach, 1980; Hood, 1976, especially pp. 198–203; Hastings, 1981). Yet clearly such technologies have implications for differences in the policy delivery process, the form of outputs and the distribution of outputs, and for the nature of the politics surrounding them. If the analysis of the difference between delivery systems is relatively neglected, it is hardly surprising that the implications of the transition between delivery systems is very underdeveloped, though we will refer to specific policy areas, such as health, where useful studies have been conducted.

This aspect of underdevelopment of the policy literature runs parallel to a developing political interest in the theme. Although we argued in Chapter 5 that many policy succession outcomes will be incremental relative to the previous policy, dissatisfactions with existing policies may take the form of arguing that the root of the problem lies in the basic method of delivering the policy. For example, some critics of the National Health Service in Britain argue that its problems are caused by allocating resources administratively and providing health care more or less free at the point of demand; the solution is therefore seen as lying in a system which would involve patients being charged for individual items of treatment. In the United States there have been arguments, put into practice in some areas, for a move from direct provision of education as the primary method of allocation to the issuing of educational vouchers to parents, who can then use them, plus any additional sum they choose, to 'purchase' education from a school of their choice; similarly, there have been arguments for the use of housing vouchers rather than public housing provision (see Butts, 1970). In this chapter we attempt to analyze such arguments and, in the case of health discussed in more detail below (section 7.5.3), to show that they often misperceive the fundamental realities of delivery systems in practice.

A second and related reason for political interest in changes in delivery systems is that the greater climate of constraint for public expenditure growth and government more generally has led to greater attention being paid to the possibilities of handing areas of government to the private sector, or increasing the use of charges so that pressure on taxation would be reduced. We will argue that many of the proposals do not in fact involve the termination of government involvement—they are policy successions of a special kind rather than policy terminations. For example, the proposal by the Conservative government in the UK to wind up the regional Road Construction Units and contract out the supervision of contracts (sic) is an example not of termination but of moving from direct supervision to indirect allocation through contracts.

Although the search for savings may inspire the search for apparently cheaper methods of delivering public policy, caution is required in appraising the potential benefits of such proposals, since, as much of the literature on regulation in the United States has pointed out, costs may merely be passed on to the private sector and thence to the taxpayer/citizen (see Weidenbaum, 1979, for an arguably overstated case). Further, there may be political costs to increasing regulations at a time when all forms of output, not just those drawing on taxation, are under political attack, and the prevailing mood is one of 'deregulation'. Similarly, contracting out aspects of delivery or procurement is not without problems of monitoring and accountability (see Hood, 1976, chapter 3).

In this chapter the following interrelated themes are developed in an attempt to improve our understanding of the implications of proposals to change methods of delivering public policy:

1   Transition between different forms of policy output (section 7.2).

2   Transition between delivery through 'public' and 'private' sectors, and the relationship between this and delivery through 'administrative' and 'market' methods of allocation (section 7.3).

3   The implications for changing delivery systems of the distinction between current output and over-time patterns of output (section 7.4).

4   The implications of introducing change in only part of a highly complex system of policy delivery, and the apparently counter-intuitive results this can produce (section 7.5).

5   A further development of the theme already emphasized in earlier chapters (especially Chapter 5) that the dynamics of changeover between policies are crucial, whatever the agreed merits of the proposed replacement policy. In section 7.6 this theme will be developed in a more formal manner, with specific emphasis on proposals for changes in delivery systems derived from static models.

7.2   Transition between forms of policy output

7.2.1   Classifying the forms of policy output

Ideally, we would have preferred in this section to move straight to an analysis of the implications of transition between types of policy output, but in the absence of an agreed analytical framework for analyzing systems for delivering public policy, we must begin by presenting a brief summary of the forms that public policy outputs take and the processes by which they are delivered (but see Peters and Heisler, 1981). Only by being able to analyze the key elements of such processes can we begin to offer propositions about the implications of transition between them.

While we make no claims to originality in many of the distinctions made in the classification we present below, we have found no other classification of public policy suitable for our purposes which relates the forms of policy output to the processes by which they are delivered. Despite its complexity, we recognize that this classification is a simplification of reality. The key point to note in the discussion of each type of output is that its form has implications for the nature and complexity of the delivery systems, and this in turn has implications for transition between them. This point will be taken up in section 7.2.13.

7.2.2   *Provision of cash payments*

7.2.2.1   *Provision of cash benefits to individuals*

The provision of cash benefits to individuals is the simplest, most-understood 'technology' for delivering policy outputs. Put simply, governments are good at giving away money, and the organization and procedures necessary to do this are relatively well understood (see Figure 7.1). The simplest procedures (fortunately for government, since they involve the largest sums of money) are payments under automatic entitlement programs, which require little more than simple checks of eligibility (such as contribution records or age). More complex are those programs where some element of discretion or means-testing is required. In such programs, as the histories of National Assistance and Supplementary Benefit in Britain and Aid to Families with Dependent Children (AFDC) in the United States indicate, there may be dilemmas between according a high degree of discretion to low-level officials or evolving a very complex and detailed set of rules, and between openness about criteria (with the implication of entitlement) and the genuine exercise of discretion in special circumstances.

7.2.2.2   *Provision of grants and loans to business*

The provision of funds to businesses is liable to be more complex than to individuals since it is more likely to entail judgement about future performance. It is still easy to hand over the cash, but more difficult to

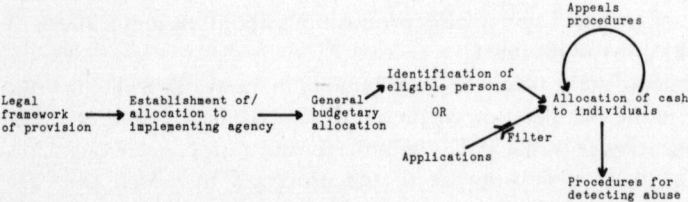

Fig. 7.1 Provision of cash benefits

ensure that the purposes for which the cash is being provided are achieved (whereas the provision of cash benefits to individuals is normally an end in itself). In principle, it is desirable that a distinction should be drawn between the provision of benefits and the provision of incentives in the form of cash payments (see Bardach, 1980), but in practice it is often difficult to assess the extent to which 'incentives' are in fact subsidies of, or windfall gains to, activities which would have taken place in any event. Some cash payments are repayable in the event that certain conditions are not fulfilled. In such cases, effective policy would require a monitoring staff similar to that required for regulatory outputs. However, the delivery agency may have considerable discretion about whether to enforce such conditions: the Department of Industry in Britain does not insist that those who have received investment grants fulfil the employment projections included in the initial application.

Where the payment is a loan (subsidized or otherwise) automatic arrangements for collecting repayments have to be established. However, whether a payment is initially made in the form of a grant or a subsidized loan may simply reflect administrative discretion or accident of legislative history. For example, the industry departments in Britain have moved away from offering soft loans under Section 7 of the Industry Act 1972 to offering interest relief grants (involving similar implied subsidy) under the same program.

Given that cash payments to business normally involve an incentive element (and we reiterate our skepticism about the extent to which such incentives are finely tuned), they bear similarities to the sort of price signalling involved in micromarket manipulation considered below (7.2.6.2). However, given our concern with delivery systems, what determines the delivery of the grants and loans considered here is the processing of applications from individuals. Micromarket manipulation refers to the impersonal price subsidy or surcharge on goods regardless of the characteristics of the purchaser or seller. Like all the distinctions we attempt in this section, this one breaks down at the margins, as when a price subsidy has to be claimed in the form of a rebate or supplement by individual businesses.

7.2.2.3 *Implications for transition*
Where programs involve the making of payments in clearly defined circumstances, the basic clerical tasks involved (on the assumption of initial systematic documentation) are readily replicable for payment

of similar benefits under replacement programs. Accordingly, there are few snags from the nature of the delivery technology from switching the entitlement basis of benefit programs (such as from contributions record to age alone, or from acreage to crops sold). All such systems will, of course, require some policing to prevent fraud. Programs involving discretion or judgement, particularly those involving payments to businesses, may require the employment of skilled persons able to assess complex applications (or even to assist the applicant to prepare them) and make judgements, such as whether a firm will be profitable if a grant for new capital equipment is given. In general, such skills may be capable of switching between programs in the same policy area, such as industrial investment incentives, but may not be applicable to policies in other areas.

7.2.3 *Provision of goods and services to individuals*

In common with the provision of cash benefits, and in contrast to certain other types of public outputs such as roads and defense (discussed in 7.2.4 and 7.2.5), some goods and services are provided in more or less discrete amount to individuals. (In terms of public goods characteristics, these goods are not supplied or consumed jointly and it is practicable, if so desired, to vary the amount provided to given individuals or even to exclude them from benefiting altogether.)

No attempt to offer a clear subdivision between goods and services is made here, on the grounds that the provision of a good is often inextricably wrapped up with the provision of the service; thus, provision of subsidized medication is related to the medical care provided by doctors and it would be nonsensical to regard them as two distinct outputs. The distinction between cash benefits and provision of goods and services refers to the final output of the policy process (though we recognize that the final output is often difficult to identify unambiguously). Thus we would distinguish between the provision of a cash incentive (output) to a firm to alter its location (outcome) from contractual arrangements between a government and a 'private' organization, say to provide health care. While incentives and contracts do have certain similarities at the relevant stages of the policy process, to view the two as identical would be to commit the fallacy of regarding the contract as the output rather than a link in the chain of policy delivery (contracting is discussed further at 7.2.12.1). This discussion emphasizes a typical and key characteris-

tic of delivery services for goods and services: they are highly
complex, normally involving intergovernmental or interorganizational funding or regulation (see Figure 7.2).

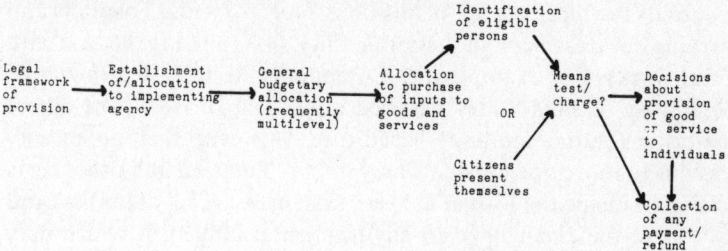

Fig. 7.2 Provision of goods and services to individuals

A second common (but not universal) characteristic of provision of
goods and services is the need for judgement on individual cases as to
who should receive provision and if so how much of what kind. This
role has frequently been allocated to professionals or quasi-
professionals who have been given a 'grant of autonomy' by the
government (Wirt, 1981) to determine the criteria for service delivery,
which normally involves the exercise of professional judgement
which is subject only to peer review short of legal action. We shall
explore the implications of complexity and the role of professions for
policy succession in the delivery of health care in section 7.5.3 below.

In general, we would argue that professions involved in service
delivery are typically not substitutable between policy areas. Indeed,
they are often highly specialized within the policy area. Because
proposed policy successions rarely challenge the role of professional
expertise, this is less of a practical problem than it would be
otherwise. Many of the other tasks involved in service delivery, such
as means-testing for eligibility, may be readily substitutable between
payment of cash benefits and provision of goods and services.

A final distinction worth drawing is between open and closed
systems for service delivery. A closed system, such as hospitals or
schools, provides a greater (though often still limited) certainty that
defined outputs will produce the desired outcomes. In some cases,
such as hospitals, clients may present themselves voluntarily to the
closed institution, but in other cases, such as mental hospitals or
schools, regulation may be necessary to ensure attendance at the
institution. Delivery through relatively closed institutions may reflect

the convenience of professionals rather than necessarily be the most effective way of treating clients. Further, attendence at institutions, particularly on a twenty-four-hours-a-day basis is very costly. Such considerations have led to calls and, in some cases, implemented proposals for 'opening up' institutions such as mental hospitals and carrying out treatment 'in the community' (as is already the case with social work). For example, the Community Mental Health Act of 1963 in the United States required movement of treatment out of institutions into community-based care. However, such policy successions to more open systems may impose financial and other costs on those outside the formal delivery system (especially families) and may leave the client open to environmental influences which may offset his or her treatment and may, indeed, have been responsible for the need for treatment in the first place.

7.2.4   *Provision of goods and services jointly (domestic)*

The previous category of outputs refers to those eventually allocated to individual clients, though there might well be externality effects, as in health and education. Many goods and services are not provided to each citizen on an individual basis, but can be utilized by a number of citizens simultaneously (see Figure 7.3).

Here we need to distinguish services which have the attributes of what economists describe as 'public goods': those where the amount consumed by one individual does not affect the amount available to others in the group, and where it is not feasible to withhold provision from any member of a group if it is provided to one of them. There are very few domestic public policies which have pure public good characteristics of this sort. The closest policies are what Rose (1976a) calls the 'defining' activities of the state, including defense, the preservation of internal order, and the provision of a currency. Such policies are regarded as being available to all citizens equally,

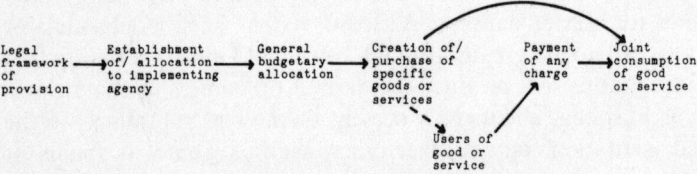

Fig. 7.3 Joint provision of domestic goods and services

without any specific action being required from the citizen. There is no question of means-testing such provision or charging individuals for the specific amount of benefit they receive. (Even this distinction breaks down: quite apart from the fact that individuals and businesses buy extra protection from employing security guards or private security firms, even public police forces may charge for specific services, such as attendance at soccer matches in Britain.)

For other types of joint provision, such as highways, water supply and sewage disposal, it is often possible to identify how much benefit an individual receives from the joint provision, and it may be technically feasible to charge him for it. In such cases the decision about whether or not to levy a charge (and thereby by implication to exclude those who are unwilling to pay) is a political one as well as one about economics or technical feasibility. The widely varying practice in terms of levying tolls on highways and major bridges illustrates both that these are not pure public goods and that decisions about levying tolls are primarily political.

7.2.5 *Provision of defense and promotion of external interests*

Although in this book we are concerned largely with domestic policies, we mention for the sake of completeness those outputs concerned with protecting and promoting the state's interests in relation to the rest of the world. As students of defense and foreign affairs are well aware, outputs such as the promotion of good relations, assistance to citizens overseas, collection of politically or commercially useful information, deterrence and the use of armed force are intangible outputs which are difficult to define unambiguously (see Figure 7.4).

Although defense is pre-eminently a provision made almost exclusively by the state, there is frequently a major role for private

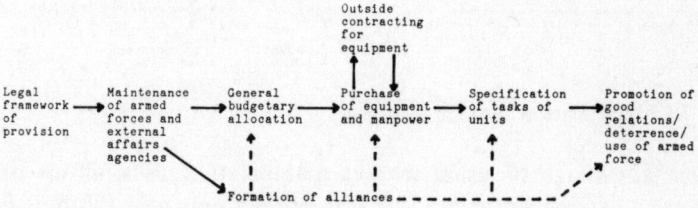

Fig. 7.4 Defense against (or promotion of) aggression

contracting in providing hardware inputs (for discussions of the implications of contracting, see 7.2.12.1 and 7.3.4). Espionage is a murky area where the state exercises many of its activities through 'disavowable' agencies or agents (Hood, 1976).

An important characteristic of modern defense provision is the way in which at all stages from agreements about budgetary allocation (for example, the NATO agreement that defense budgets should grow by 3 per cent per annum in real terms) to troop deployment, the decisions by any one state are often tied up with the joint provision for defense through alliances with other countries.

The provision of defense and the promotion of external interests are classic public goods in the sense that they are provided for all citizens collectively and it is not feasible to exclude any individual citizen from benefiting from them.

7.2.6 *Manipulation through markets*

7.2.6.1 *Manipulation of the macroeconomy through markets*
Governments have always sought to secure particular macroeconomic outcomes through intervention in economic markets (if only to manage the national debt) (see Figure 7.5). Since the 1940s governments have also sought to secure desirable outcomes in terms of economic goals such as inflation, interest rates, unemployment and growth, and intervention in markets is one means of doing this (others involve the provision of benefits, regulation and extraction). Since the early 1970s there has been less confidence among governments and economic commentators about the ability of governments to secure specified outcomes by market intervention of this sort.

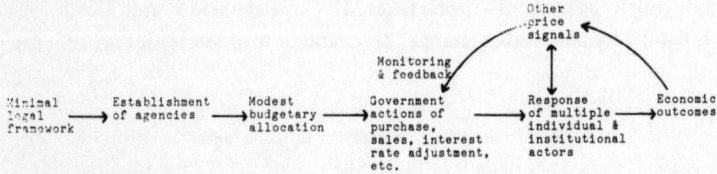

Fig. 7.5 **Manipulation through markets**

One advantage of using market manipulation as a means of delivering government policy is that it requires only a small (though preferably skilled) staff. A major disadvantage is that it relies on setting very general price signals to which firms and individuals will respond in varying and perhaps unpredictable ways or, just as important, with varying and unpredictable speeds of response (see King, 1975). As a means of reducing short-to-medium-term inflation it may be an unreliable approach. However, in contrast to regulation through a prices-and-incomes policy, market manipulation has the advantages of avoiding political opposition to such regulation and also of retaining flexibility for different circumstances (for example, shortage of skilled labor, greater productivity through new technology) which influencing price signals provides in contrast to regulation, where attempts to provide flexibility may lead to the exploitation of loopholes.

7.2.6.2 *Manipulation of microeconomic markets*

Often the purposes of government are concerned with targets too specific to be usefully manipulated through general price signals. Again, governments have had a long-term involvement in such micromarket manipulation through the building up of strategic stockpiles for use in military contingencies, or for release on to the market in time of shortage either politically induced by supplier boycotts or through more general economic circumstances.

Micromarket manipulation can also be conducted not so much because of government concern with the specific good but because of some broader purpose which the manipulation of the price of that good may serve. Because control by regulation has often been insensitive to the balance of costs and benefits, micromarket manipulation has achieved some favor as a suggested means of achieving a more sensitive influence over desired outcomes. For example, instead of attempting by regulation to limit the amount of pollution discharged by a factory into a river, the factory could be charged a price for the right to discharge its effluent and the price could be varied according to any combination of volume, the degree of pollution in the effluent, the degree of pollution already in the river at the point, and the economic benefit generated by the factory. However, the more sensitive the use of the price mechanism, the more complex and expensive it would be to administer and the greater the monitoring which would have to take place (see Linder and McBride, 1981). Many of the claimed advantages of this sort of pricing are apparent only in contrast with general and therefore insensitive rules laid down by regulatory agencies. An important advantage of pricing mechanisms over regulation is that they can be used as a means of resolving the *distribution* of economic costs and benefits, through there is no guarantee that governments will actually use them in this way rather than as an additional means of taxation (extraction).

Pricing can, of course, be used as a means of encouraging an activity by subsidizing it. (Consumption can also be encouraged by regulations compelling the price to be kept at a low level, but this may have the effect of reducing supply.) Thus, if it is felt that individuals in making purchasing decisions about, say, education, protection against infectious diseases or investments would not take into account the benefits to others (the externalities) the government may subsidize the price of these goods to increase consumption to the optimum level. In practice, as we have already noted (7.2.2.2) it is often difficult to assess the extent to which 'incentives' are in fact subsidies to activities which would have taken place in any event. Government may also make a decision that it will itself provide certain goods or services free (for example, compulsory schooling) rather than manipulate provision through markets. There is, of course, no guarantee that governments will not use price manipulation for perverse economic purposes, as numerous examples from food and agriculture attest.

In addition to micromarket manipulation to ensure that external benefits and costs are taken into account in production and consumption decisions, governments may also subsidize goods whose increased consumption the government considers would benefit the individual (merit goods) or tax those it considers to harm him (demerit goods). Price subsidies may perversely have the effect of increasing prices where supply is relatively fixed, as with some housing subsidies. Taxes may also have resource extraction purposes, as in taxes on alcohol and tobacco. Resource extraction and behavior-modification may be at cross-purposes: maximization of resource extraction would indicate concentration on goods the consumptions of which is price insensitive, whereas the whole purpose of micromarket manipulation is to secure response to price changes. Purely in terms of their economic characteristics, regulation rather than taxation of alcohol and tobacco (particularly given their imposition of external costs on non-users) would be indicated, but as the experience of Prohibition in America shows, there may be slight problems of enforcement.

One would expect finance ministers to be keener on the taxation of demerit goods (or negative externalities) than the subsidy of merit goods (or positive externalities). One notes the lack of a subsidy on fluoride toothpaste or high-fiber breakfast cereals.

7.2.7 Rule-making and enforcement

A wide range of processes involving the making and enforcement of rules covers all areas of public and private activity. It is possible here only to outline some of the major types of rule-making before going on to discuss their shared feature of complexity and some of the implications of moving from detailed rules to case-by-case adjudication, and vice versa.

7.2.7.1 Criminal law

The process of criminal law-making and enforcement involves specifying crimes, the maintenance of police or other forces to detect and apprehend lawbreakers, of courts to try cases, and of various punitive and rehabilitative agencies to carry out sentences (see Figure 7.6). In the United States there are parallel federal, state and local systems of enforcement.

7.2.7.2 Laws and regulations enforced by government agencies

Governments frequently specify the conditions under which certain activities (other than 'crimes') are permissible or mandated, ranging from whether an activity is permitted at all to the details of pricing structures. The main stages in this type of regulation in the United States are shown in Figure 7.7. There is considerable scope for variation in the extent to which specific rules are promulgated in advance or general rules only are specified in laws or regulations and adjudications then made on a case-by-case basis (for further discussion of this point, see 7.2.7.5).

7.2.7.3 Framework of civil and constitutional law

All legal systems have frameworks by which one or more private parties (perhaps including a government agency) can bring a case against another and for the resolution of the dispute between them to be achieved by the allocation of rights or the award of damages.

7.2.7.4 The complexity of rule-making and enforcement

Clearly the scope for variations in procedures among these various types of rule-making and enforcement is vast, but they all share

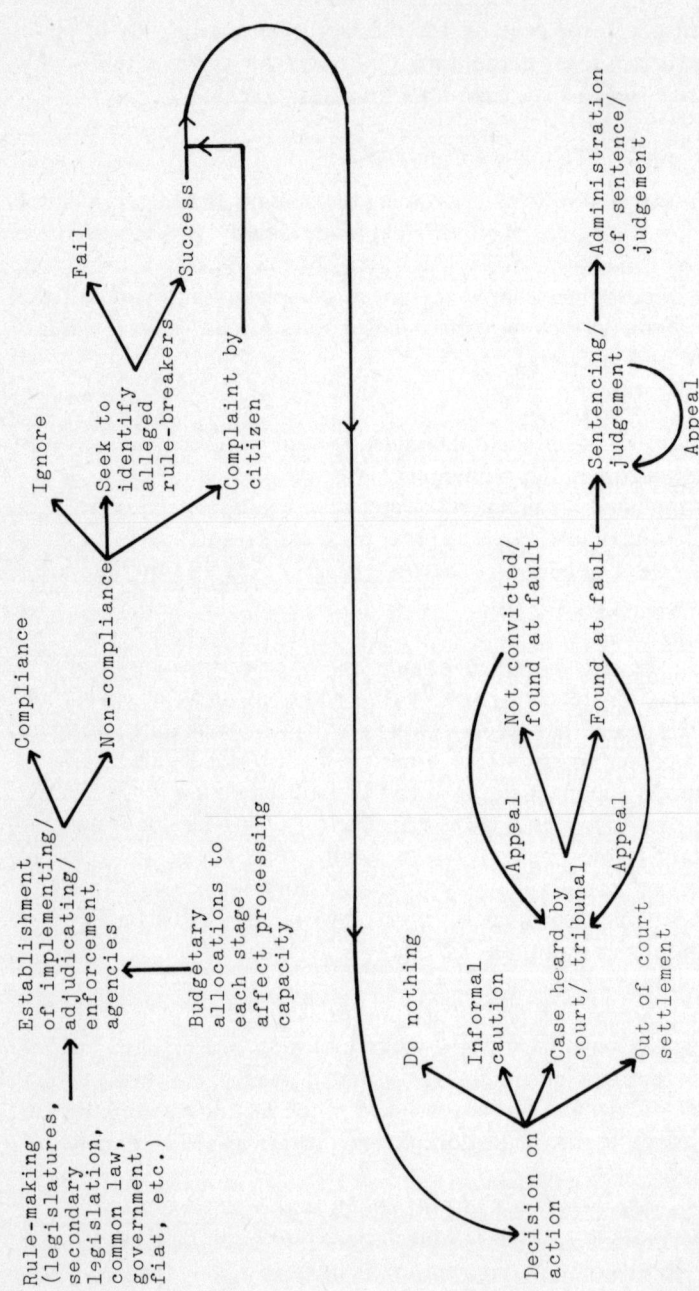

Fig. 7.6 Rule-making and enforcement

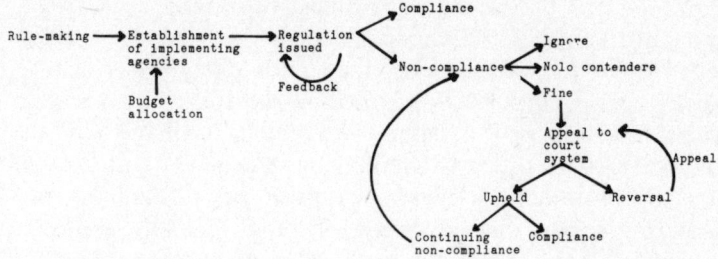

Fig. 7.7 Regulatory enforcement in the United States of America

certain features in common. The first is that the procedures for enforcement are highly complex, often involving a number of different government agencies at one or more stages. This is illustrated in Figure 7.6 which presents a simplified picture of the type of criminal law enforcement described at 7.2.7.1 above. At each stage there is scope for a range of possible outcomes, with variation in the discretion available to the government agency concerned in selecting the option. One consequence of the multiplicity of agencies involved is that the processing capacity of the system as a whole will be affected by the budgetary allocation made to any one agency. For example, cutting the budget of the agency responsible for detecting infringements may affect the number of infringements detected. The way in which any one agency carries out its processing stage may have spillover effects on the behaviour of other agencies involved. For example, if a police force felt that a court was being too lenient either in convicting or sentencing it might cease to bring forward cases where it thought it stood little chance of success, or it might resort to informal and illegal methods of punishing suspected offenders.

Because our concern is with what actually happens rather than with words on paper, we regard the output not as the rules, but as their enforcement. From the perspective of the beneficiaries of rule enforcement, this can be regarded as a service, but the *process* of delivery is oriented towards rule enforcement.

7.2.7.5 *Detailed rules versus case-by-case adjudication*
A recurring choice particularly in the regulation of businesses, is the choice between enforcement through specific rules versus rule-making through case-by-case adjudication. Specific rules have the danger of overlooking unforeseen loopholes, while case-by-case

adjudication has the related disadvantage of seeming arbitrariness and failing to give advance warning of what is permissible behavior. The 1970s saw an increased use in the United States of specific rule-making, 'leaving little to be decided in subsequent adjudication beyond the factual issue of compliance or non-compliance with the rules' (Scalia, 1981, p. 25). In addition to overcoming the problem of seeming arbitrariness, a greater emphasis on rule-making was considered to have the advantage of a more readily accessible prescription compared to case-law, a more purposive role for enforcement agencies rather than simply reacting to cases, and, at least in the early 1970s, a procedure for rule-making that was less demanding on agencies than adjudication. Many of these apparent advantages were never as great as they seemed, and the relative procedural simplicity of rule-making as against adjudication has subsequently been eroded. Scalia (1981) argues that there will therefore be a move back to a greater use of adjudication. There are few obstacles in the way of most agencies wishing to make such a switch back, just as there were initially few in the way of a greater emphasis on rule-making, since most regulatory agencies in the United States have a rule-making capacity but are not compelled to act through rule-making. It is difficult to determine what, if any, implications a switch in either direction has for the substance of what is or is not permissible. Because of the flexibility of the agencies' authority it is a relatively simple matter to achieve a transition between the two approaches to regulation (though it should be noted that this is only true from the perspective of the agency—attempts to enforce or thwart such transitions from outside would be more difficult). In such cases we are talking about a simple linear succession, with no requirement for organizational or legislative upheaval.

7.2.8 *Extraction*

The concentration of students of public policy on the public expenditure side of the budget has led to a relative neglect of the extraction of resources from citizens by taxation or other means as a type of policy output in its own right rather than merely the means of financing public expenditure. Economists are less open to this criticism, though much of their discussion of the use of extraction is abstract.

There has been some study of tax expenditures as an instrument of public policy (see Willis and Hardwick, 1978; Pechman, 1979), but it is problematic whether they should be considered under the heading of cash benefits, extraction, or a type of policy output in their own right. Because of our focus on relating outputs to processes, we choose to examine tax expenditures at the same time as extraction. Extraction inevitably involves elements of rule-making and enforcement, but its prime purpose of extracting resources from specified sources merits its consideration as a separate category.

As can be seen from Figure 7.8, the process of tax collection is much more complicated than the legislative injunction that 'A tax shall be charged' (a phrase used as the title of a book describing a case study of policy succession in taxation by Johnstone, 1975). Three main features are worth highlighting. The first is that a degree of reluctance to hand over taxes due can be expected. The government will wherever possible design its tax collection to take advantage of 'ergonomic controls' or 'bottlenecks' through which the activity to be taxed (or one related to it) has to pass (Hood, 1976, pp. 118–20). The collection of income tax in Britain is partly automatic through the Pay-as-you-earn (PAYE) system and the use of employers as tax collectors. To a considerable extent, however, tax collection relies on voluntary compliance with tax laws, both in notifying authorities of a taxable activity, self-assessment of liability and handing over taxes. The United States income tax system relies heavily on self-assessment albeit backed by checks and penalties. Such willingness by taxpayers to comply is obviously related to the perceived fairness of the tax burden both as to amount and distribution.

People may alter their behavior in response to the imposition of a tax either to avoid paying a tax (or as much tax as they would otherwise have to) or to evade it illegally. Tax avoidance would include reducing the amount of work effort because of the disincentive effect of marginal tax rates (or increasing it to make up for the loss of income) or displacing financial behavior in order to take maximum advantage of tax allowances. This displacement of behavior is most notoriously true of tax allowances on interest on house mortgages in Britain and the United States (Farmer and Barrell, 1981; Downs, 1980). Such displacement may be the intention of introducing the tax allowance in the first place, but the scale and distributional impact may turn out to be quite different from what was anticipated. However, attempts to terminate such allowances or to replace them by a more equitable system of tax credits or cash

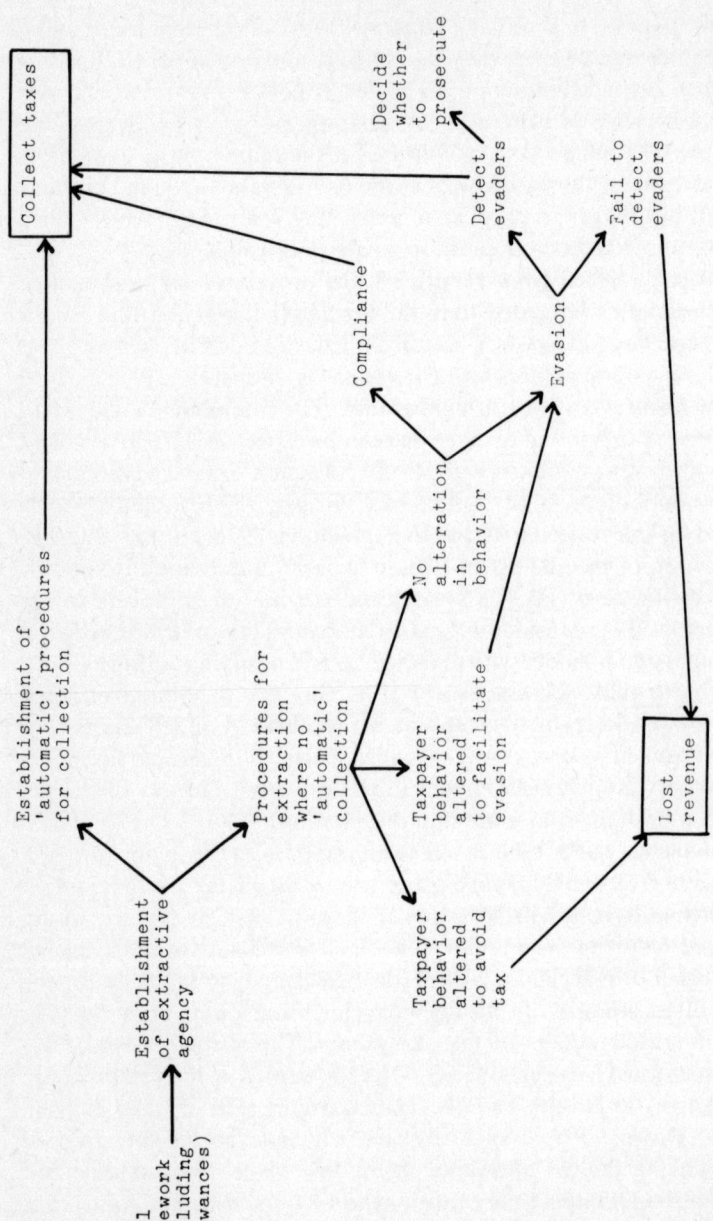

Fig. 7.8 Extraction

benefits are likely to run into the twin problems of vociferous opposition combined with fear of electoral consequences (arguably true of the reluctance of British governments to tackle the mortgage tax allowance (non) issue) and an apparent feeling that tax foregone in the form of tax expenditures is somehow not such a problem as actual cash handed out by government.

Alteration of behavior to take maximum advantage of tax allowances is perfectly legal, but behavior can also be altered to maximize opportunities for illegal tax evasion. (By contrast, 'simple' evasion consists of continuing the same economic behavior but not paying required taxes.) Thus, behavior may be switched from jobs readily subject to taxation because of the controls or bottlenecks mentioned above to freelance or 'moonlighting' activity in the cash economy, which is much more difficult for tax authorities to police (Laurin, 1980). Such displacement of activity into the black economy is much more likely if the government is taking an increasing proportion of pay or turnover of small businesses in taxation since such civic indifference is easier for the individual citizen to accomplish than political mobilization with others to secure the policy terminations or successions otherwise needed to restore his take-home pay (see Rose and Peters, 1978, pp. 205–11).

Given all these features of the tax collection process, replacements of taxes may involve substantial change in organizations and procedures. This is true even where the transition is smooth, planned and effectively under the control of the executive, as was the case in Britain with the replacement of Selective Employment Tax (SET) and Purchase Tax by Value Added Tax (VAT) in 1973 (see Johnstone, 1975). A two-year period from 1971 to 1973 was taken up in consultation and detailed preparation. The Customs and Excise department was required to expand a staff of around 2000 administering purchase tax to around 8000 to administer the new tax; in addition there was the problem of the 'hump' while the new tax had to be set up and the old tax still collected. There was no advance knowledge of the number of traders who would be registered to pay VAT. Planning the administrative structure and procedures had to take place before the details of the tax were known. The ability of taxpayers to fill in forms was overestimated and there were problems with the computer, both as a result of an industrial dispute and technical problems. These problems led to temporary make-shift arrangements in the first year of operation of the new tax. However, the replacement of SET and Purchase Tax by VAT, which was the biggest change to the British taxation system since World War II, must be recognized as a relative success story in terms of smoothness of transition. Its problems were 'merely' administrative and temporary, and in a more politicized environment for changes to taxation, as in the US Congress, there would have been a good chance that such a proposed succession would have been abandoned, delayed or drastically transformed.

7.2.9 *Licensing and certification*

The licensing and certification by government of activities conducted by others is a growing though difficult-to-measure feature of government intervention. To mention just two items in the British news the week this section was written, a number of protesters were arrested for interfering with a licensed seal-cull conducted by local hunters in the Orkneys and the use of Citizen Band radio was legalized for holders of a new license. Examples of licensing range from the trivial (the $37\frac{1}{2}$p dog licenses in Britain) to the highly important (such as licenses for oil exploration and exploitation, TV franchises, cable-television rights, etc.). Lord Thomson once described the award to him of the franchise for Scottish Television as a 'license to print money'.

Licensing by government can involve a mixture of resource extraction and regulation.

7.2.9.1 *Resource extraction*
Here the award of a license is recognition of payment of a mandatory tax. In Britain, TV licenses are effectively a form of taxation earmarked for the use of the British Broadcasting Corporation (BBC). The use of a specific license fee rather than funds voted from general taxation was intended to provide a measure of financial independence for the BBC, but this has proved a chimera in times of inflation.

7.2.9.2 *Regulation*
Here the award of a license is recognition that a project, article or activity has met standards required by government; conditions may be attached to the continuing validity of the license. In some cases, the license may be directly issued by a government department or agency, such as those for nuclear power construction in the United States. In

other cases the standards for receipt and continued holding of a license or certificate may be administered on behalf of government by a professional body or even a private firm. This is most obviously true of licenses to practice in the law and medical professions, but some odd examples of government handing over the awards of licenses or certificates can occur: for example, in Britain 'type approval' certificates needed for the importation of cars (even the reimportation of British cars) are issued by official distributors—not surprisingly, they have been reluctant to issue these to 'parallel' importers who can undercut their prices (*The Economist*, 24 October 1981, pp. 46–7)! This example illustrates the potential danger of 'contracting out' certain functions of government.

7.2.9.3   *Award of monopolistic property rights*
Certain activities such as oil exploration or TV broadcasting rights are either intrinsically monopolistic or are economically best provided by a monopoly (see Wolf, 1979). In such cases government often awards rights to carry out such activity by awarding a license on the basis of vetting applicants or putting the license/franchise out for bidding, or a mixture of the two. Such licensing is an alternative to direct state provision of the monopoly activity. Britain has moved from a system of monopoly state provision of broadcasting to mixed state and franchised private provision. However, this was achieved by setting up parallel commercial radio and television broadcasting and not direct replacement of any of the state provision.

7.2.10   *Value shaping*

Governments seek to shape the values of their citizens in a variety of ways, whose output is difficult to define and impact often impossible to determine.

7.2.10.1   *Exhortation*
Political leaders frequently urge citizens to behave in certain ways, for example, to be responsible in making pay claims. This is clearly a very 'soft' technology compared to, say, providing cash benefits, but it does have the advantage of being very cheap.

7.2.10.2   *Advertising*
Governments spend substantial sums on a variety of forms of

advertising, urging citizens to conduct themselves in a prescribed manner. This is particularly important in the health and safety field. Such advertising often is provided in parallel with rule-making on the same subject.

7.2.10.3   *Arbitration and conciliation services*
Here the government is not advocating particular substantive courses of action, nor is it concerned with enforcing its rules. Rather the concern is a process one: to promote non-conflictual modes of resolving disputes between groups of citizens by providing a forum for the resolution of that conflict.

7.2.11   *Provision of financial guarantees and insurance*
One of the big growth areas of government over the past fifty years has been the provision by government of insurance or guarantees (see Aharoni, 1981). It is difficult to measure the scale or significance of this growth, since what matters is not only the amount actually paid out by government but the 'overhang' of potential commitments. Governments have increasingly used such guarantees as an apparently 'cost-free' instrument of industrial policy. (They are, of course, not cost-free since, apart from any actual or implicit government subsidy, they represent a redirection of economic resources; see Hogwood, 1979a, pp. 124–6.)

One example of an escalating commitment on guarantees was the growth of the ceiling on shipbuilding credit guarantees in Britain from £200m in 1967 to £1000m in 1972, with provision for a further extension of £1400m. These credits and the wider export credits were provided by private banks backed by a guarantee by government. By 1971 the banks complained that interest rates had got out of line with current interest rates and the scheme was revised (Hogwood, 1979a, pp. 165–6). The effect of these new credit arrangements was that in future the element of subsidy would be made explicit, whereas under the old arrangements the banks had absorbed the extra cost of providing the credits in return for other 'favors' from the government. The cost to the government of the new arrangements turned out to be well above expectations and the system to administer them broke down.

In the United States, loan guarantees to Chrysler Corporation, the Lockheed Corporation, students, small businesses, veterans, etc. represent a huge potential liability for government, although the expenditures on a year-to-year basis for these programs have so far been very small.

Governments wishing to reduce their 'above the line' public expenditure or to make implicit subsidies more opaque may find the idea of a switch from grants or outright loans to guarantees attractive, but as the examples of shipbuilding and export credit guarantees in Britain show, such a move could in a few years backfire and produce unexpected new 'above the line' expenditure items.

Related to the concept of guarantees is the role of government in insuring business or other risks. The government will normally extract a premium for this insurance cover, but there is at least an implicit subsidy. For example, in 1975 the British government announced a scheme to protect exporters from rising costs on export contracts for capital goods; exporters or buyers were expected to bear cost increases of up to 10 per cent, but the government would cover 85 per cent of cost increases within a 10 per cent band above that level. Premium income more or less covered modest outlays up to 1980, but substantial net payments will be incurred from 1980 onwards.

There are few technical problems in introducing or switching to guarantee or insurance schemes or persuading private firms to undertake financing or refinancing of funds that would otherwise appear on the government's books. However, by the nature of such schemes the risk is transferred to government (and therefore the taxpayer), and, as our two examples from Britain show, there is no guarantee (sic) that government outgoings under such schemes will be balanced by income.

7.2.12 *Complex and ambiguous delivery systems*

Despite the extensive listing of policy outputs and delivery systems above, there are other aspects of delivery systems which cannot neatly fit into the classification above, either because they can occur in a number of delivery systems (such as contracting) or because the particular sequence of events appears to embody elements from a number of delivery systems.

7.2.12.1 *Contracting*

We have already briefly mentioned the role of contracting out the provision of goods and services at 7.2.3 and we will be returning to the theme at 7.3.4, since contracting raises interesting issues about the

relationship between 'government' and 'private organizations' in the
provision of public policy. Here we want to draw attention to the fact
that contracting can be used both to supply inputs into provision by
government agencies and to farm out the actual provision. The
distinction can be seen from Figures 7.9 (a) and (b). Contracting for
delivery of inputs (for example, weapons systems for use by armed
forces) is common in both Britain and America, but contracting out
the actual delivery of services is much more common in America than
in Britain, though there have been recent signs of interest in Britain,
with Southend contracting out its refuse collection.

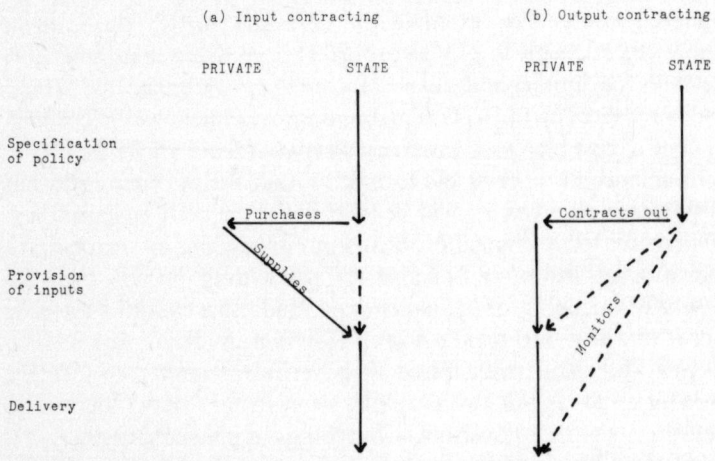

Fig. 7.9 Input and output contracting

It should be clear that contracting out does not simply involve
government signing a contract, handing over the money, and letting
the contractor get on with it. Monitoring is an essential feature of the
effective use by government of contracting. Contracting can raise a
number of problems such as determining an appropriate price,
allocating responsibility for cost overruns, and ensuring adequate
performance, to say nothing of collusion and corruption and broader
issues such as the distortion of the political system by the danger of
the emergence of a military-industrial complex (see Smith, 1975;
Adams, 1981). These problems will be most acute when government
is a monopsonist (single buyer) and there is one or only a few large
suppliers. Such problems will be reduced, though not necessarily

eliminated, where there are multiple purchasers (for example, local governments) able to contract with a number of would-be suppliers (for example, refuse collection firms); such relatively free markets make it easier to set an appropriate price, compare performance with other localities and, if necessary, to find an alternative supplier. Having stressed the problems of contracting it is necessary to draw attention to the inefficiencies which can arise with direct government supply, as with naval dockyards or construction by public employees in Britain.

A government wishing to switch from direct provision itself to contracting out provision faces all the problems associated with succession which has connotations of termination. Resistance can be expected from existing government employees, particularly unions. Problems of transition are likely to be eased when, as at Southend when it decided to contract out refuse collection, redundancy payments are made to government employees, guarantees are offered by the private contracting firm that most former public employees will be taken on, and conditions of employment in the contracting firm are more favorable than as public employees.

Once established, contracting out of provision can give the government much greater potential flexibility in planning and implementing future successions. Alternative suppliers can be considered, though in many cases (particularly for major input contractors) the government may effectively be 'locked in' to the existing supplier. Further, when a contract comes up for renewal, its terms can be modified to secure a succession. Such modification will, of course, be subject to bargaining between government and contractor rather than unilateral imposition by government, but the point remains that contracting may well give greater flexibility and avoid many of the organizational constraints on succession identified in Chapter 6 (see also 8.3.2.1).

Contracting can also provide an opportunity to 'attach' various other policy objectives, such as a decision to purchase a proportion of output from minority enterprises.

7.2.12.2 *Prices and incomes policies*
Statutory prices and incomes policies can be seen as straightforward regulation, but many government incomes policies are not set out in this way, partly to avoid the problems of enforcement and resentment which often accompany statutory policies. Such alternative 'policies'

can at one extreme involve little more than exhortation to pay restraint. Sometimes, however, governments set out targets in more detail in the form of 'guidelines', often following discussion or even agreement with unions and employers (see also 7.2.12.3). The success of such guidelines depends on voluntary compliance. A firmer policy is where government seeks to impose sanctions on firms which fail to conform to guidelines. In 1978 in Britain the Labour government compiled a 'blacklist' of firms which had broken its pay guideline and threatened to and in some cases did withdraw facilities (such as export credit guarantees) available under various items of legislation. The government abandoned its sanctions following a defeat in the House of Commons, though its policy had never had a statutory basis in the first place. In the United States, President Johnson was able to have steel prices rolled back by threatening not to buy steel from firms which broke the guidelines.

7.2.12.3 *Compacts and planning agreements*

In recognition of the fact that in many areas of economic activity governments by themselves can achieve little, governments have frequently sought to secure the cooperation of industry and unions in achieving jointly agreed aims. This can range from relatively narrow issues such as incomes policy (see 7.2.12.2) to a wider range of industrial targets (as under the 'Approach to an Industrial Strategy' under the 1974–9 Labour government in Britain) to discussions about the whole range of government policies (the so-called 'Social Contract' between trade unions and the Labour government in Britain in the mid-1970s). At one extreme such arrangements may amount to little more than institutionalized arrangements for the exchange of views (arguably true of the National Economic Development Council in Britain). At the other extreme some commentators have been concerned that implementation of policies through such arrangements amounts to 'corporatism' (for a critique, see Jordan, 1981). Our own view is that the significance of this supposed trend in Britain and the United States has been exaggerated, both because such arrangements have not actually committed themselves to many specific policies, and because when they have the outcomes have frequently failed to materialize. Nevertheless, faced with the failure of policy instruments over which they have autonomous control but which operate in environments over which they have little control, governments will frequently be attracted by the idea of seeking to improve effectiveness through cooperation with non-governmental actors, if necessary at the cost of compromising on objectives.

7.2.13 *Changing outputs may involve transition between delivery systems*

Were all these different outputs delivered by administrative structures and processes with more or less similar characteristics, the fact of variation in the form of output would be of little relevance to the analysis of policy succession. However, as the accompanying highly simplified diagrams indicate, processes relating to different outputs vary substantially in a number of ways and some elements are not substitutable.

1 The significance of laws in shaping process and outcomes.
2 The significance of budgetary allocation at various stages.
3 The complexity of the processes in terms of number of stages, options at each stage and loops.
4 The extent to which non-transferable skills are involved.
5 The degree of discretion accorded to service deliverers or enforcement agencies and their members in initiating any given unit of output and shaping its form and scale. The exercise of this discretion may be shaped to varying degrees by organizational or professional ideologies.
6 The degree of discretion open to citizens or corporations in triggering off outputs (either in the form of receiving benefits or compliance) and in shaping their form and scale.
7 The extent to which different outputs have public goods characteristics, that is, the extent to which the output is supplied jointly rather than to individuals, the extent to which individuals receive an identifiable benefit distinguishable from that received by others, and the extent to which it is feasible to vary the output to individuals, charge for it or exclude the individual from benefit altogether (this overlaps with points 5 and 6).
8 The scope for introducing 'private' elements in the delivery process, including contracting out supply of inputs or actual provision (see 7.3 and 7.2.12.1).

The implications of these features for transition between different forms of output have been discussed above. Particularly for the more complex processes, it is important to understand the process in terms of the significance of each stage for the allocative properties of the process as a whole, even for policy successions which do not involve changing the form of the output. For policy successions which involve changing the form of the output, it is clear that we cannot simply say: 'we will use the existing system for delivering cash for delivering social work services instead'.

Moves from cash to care are moves from a simple to a more complex (and arguably less certain) technology, but one which is in principle more attuned to non-financial 'needs' and getting at the 'cause' of the problem. This latter point is highly disputable, since low income may be the 'real cause' and in any case since low income is the proximate cause of the problem it may be more susceptible to treatment even when the underlying 'causes' (such as being a one-parent family) are not removed, and arguably in many cases are unlikely to be removeable by any instrument in the repertoire of state-sponsored social caring. An important feature of social work is the role of the individual social provider in deciding detailed allocations. Any switch from cash provision to social care would require the training of such service providers, and would require different skills from a program of cash benefits.

Because of the problems of social care, a reverse switch to cash may have attractions, but because we are talking about a transition from service to cash there may be special problems (many of which would also apply to a switch from specific cash grants, such as housing allowances, to general income maintenance grants). In the first place, the citizen-client will previously have been placed in a position of dependency whereby key decisions about his or her life or income are not taken autonomously. From this position the individual is suddenly expected to manage a small budget to cover all needs. Ironically, there is a good argument to be made that it is precisely at this time of a switch from a service orientation that there is greatest need for social work support. In addition there is a problem of certainty of effects; for example, whether a patient will actually take medication.

A more political problem in attempting the transition to cash benefits is that social care is likely to be delivered through professionalized or unionized personnel who will be capable of a high degree of political mobilization and will claim legitimacy in defining what the needs of their clients are and what type of delivery system is appropriate to meet them.

Although only illustrative, this discussion of switches from cash to care and vice versa does emphasize that the analysis of the *transition* between two systems of policy delivery must involve more than a comparison of the merits of the two delivery systems viewed statically or abstractly. This point will be developed more formally in section 7.6.

7.3 Allocative mechanisms in the public and private sectors

In this section we develop the analysis of allocative mechanisms in terms of the extent of discretion or choice available to producers and consumers of public policies, the relationship between choice and the public-private distinction, and the variety of mechanisms by which government can pursue public policy through, or directed at, 'non-governmental' organizations or individuals. The analysis is developed by starting with a caricature distinction between public and private sector methods of allocation and progressively removing the oversimplifications involved.

7.3.1 The caricature classification of political rhetoric

The simplest conceivable classification of the allocation of policy would be a simple dichotomy between a government allocating goods by standardized administrative criteria and a private sector allocating goods through economic markets in conditions approaching 'free' competition. Here administrative would be defined in an over-simplified ideal type form as referring to criteria derived from the internally generated rules of an organization or from external legislative or executive mandates, with these criteria being implemented through command or defined conditions for the receipt of a benefit, good or service. Similarly, market criteria would refer to allocation where multiple producers and multiple consumers, each totally free to decide whether and how much to buy or sell, would make their sales or purchasing decisions on the basis of a freely moving price which reflected relative supply and demand.

In the political rhetoric surrounding discussion of such issues, movements from public to private sector are sometimes treated as synonymous with movements from administrative to market allocation. However, a moment's reflection reveals two fatal flaws with this conflation of the public-private and administrative-market dimensions.

7.3.2 *Variation within the public and private sectors*

First of all, the extent of competition in the private sector can range from highly atomized markets where no single producer or consumer can influence the price or volume produced of a good to markets in which there is a single buyer or seller. The more conditions approach those of monopoly, as for example with utilities, the greater the extent to which the criterion used by a firm is de facto an administrative, not a market, one (Lindblom, 1977; Galbraith, 1967).

Secondly, and relatedly, the distinction between public and private does not refer to the *criterion of allocation*. Thus an activity can remain within the public sector, but the *criterion* for allocating outputs could be switched from bureaucratic/political guidelines to greater consumer choice or even transactions in markets. Similarly, responsibility for a service might be switched from a social service department to a 'private' voluntary organization, but the private organization may use *administrative criteria* for rationing its services to individual recipients. While proposals for moves from administrative to more market-oriented criteria often involve a switch from public to private sectors, the two are not logically identical. This point can be illustrated by Figure 7.10 which shows that allocative mechanisms can vary both within public and private sectors in the degree of market orientation.

Figure 7.10 or variants of it can be used to show that denationalization may simply involve a move from a public monopoly to a private one (the single arrow). Where a state monopoly was split up into two or three private companies, there would be a move

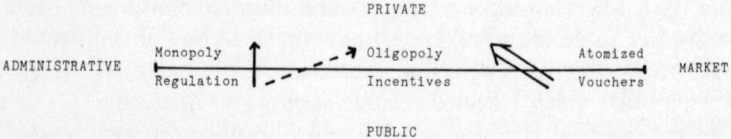

Fig. 7.10 A simple model of administrative/market and public/private distinctions (based on a diagram drawn by Chris Hull)

towards greater market allocation, but not the allocation envisaged in pure competition (the dashed arrow). It is possible for a move from public to private sectors to entail a move away from the market criterion of allocation (the double arrow); for example, the proposal that British Rail sell its Seaspeed Channel ferry subsidiary to an existing private operator would have increased the degree of monopoly on Channel ferry routes (the government accepted a Monopolies Commission report that the takeover should be barred for this reason). Another example would be where all local authorities in a metropolitan area were obliged to sell off their leisure facilities and the only buyer was a conglomerate already owning other major leisure facilities in the area.

The decision of the Reagan administration to reduce the Federal government's involvement in higher education, combined with its change in the tax laws, has had the even more perverse effect of tending to increase the degree of public sector dominance in higher education. By reducing funding for students through the student loan programs and the Basic Educational Opportunity Grant, a substantial proportion of the recipients of which went to private higher education, state-supported higher education has become the only affordable option for more students. As the tax laws now reduce the benefits of contributions to higher education, the possibility of increased funding for students through private sources also appears reduced. The net effect may well be a reduction in the proportion of students (now 19 per cent) who attend privately run colleges and universities.

Of course, the issue of public versus private is as much a matter of political psychological perception as objective criteria, and a publicly owned monopoly may be regarded as different in kind from a privately owned one, with some regarding a publicly owned monopoly as more benevolent and others vice versa.

7.3.3   *Quangos and other assorted animals*

While Figure 7.10 is valuable in illustrating the basic points that the distinction between public and private sectors is not identical to the administrative-market dimension and that this dimension can be applied *within* each sector, the analysis of allocative systems relevant to public policy needs to be developed further in a number of ways.

First of all, Figure 7.10 implies a distinction between public and

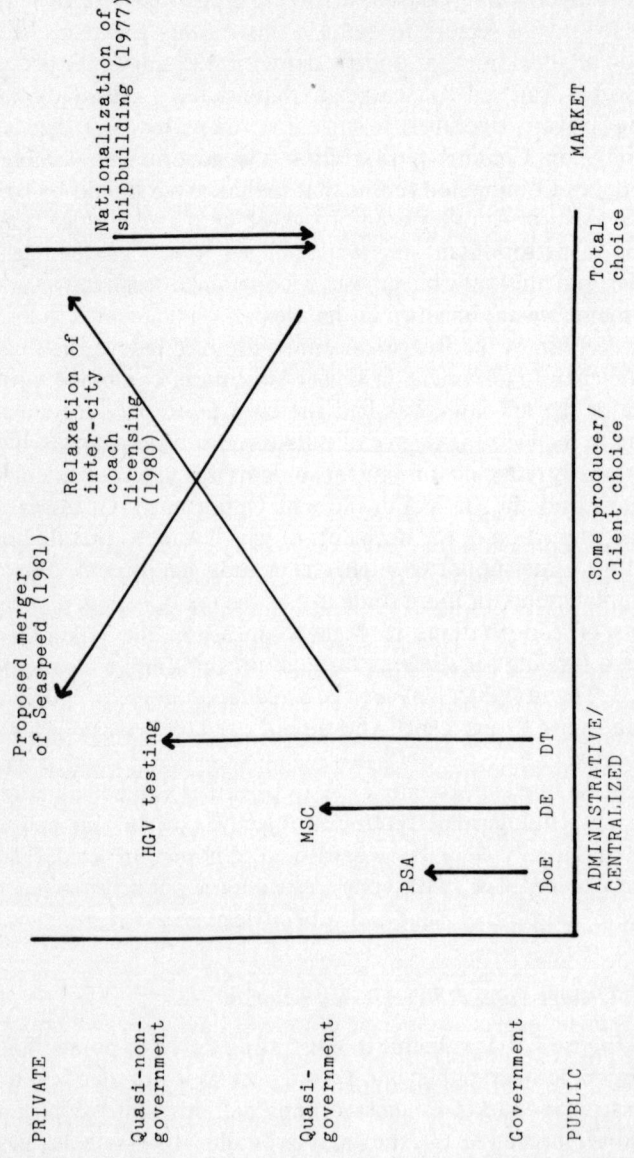

Fig. 7.11 Unpacking the public-private dimension, with British examples

Notes to Fig. 7.11: 1   DE, MSC refer to the establishment of the Manpower Services Commission in 1974 as a separate statutory body with nominees from unions and business. Formerly the functions were carried out by the Department of Employment. Originally, MSC employees were taken out of the civil service, but were later put back in.
2   DoE, PSA refers to the establishment of the Property Services Agency as a separately accountable unit within the Department of the Environment.
3   DT, HGV testing refers to the proposal by the 1979 Conservative government that the Department of Transport should cease to test Heavy Goods Vehicles and that this function should be carried out by the 'private sector' (but nevertheless under government direction and supervision).
4   The nationalization of shipbuilding is shown as two arrows, since much of the industry was already government-owned prior to nationalization. The arrow is shown as being vertical on the grounds that shipbuilding is an internationally competing industry, unlike the oligopolistic cross-Channel ferry market in which Seaspeed operates.

private sectors which does not, in fact, exist in developed Western societies. Commentators have remarked on the variety of bodies which can exist between the extremes of government departments and purely private organizations (see, for example, Smith and Hague, 1971; Smith, 1975; Hague, Mackenzie and Barker, 1975; Barker, 1982; Seidman, 1980). Such bodies can vary from government-appointed and funded bodies, through organizations regulated by government or receiving contracts from it, to organizations responsible for appointing their own leadership but partially funded by government or carrying out self-regulatory functions with the 'nod-and-a-wink' support of government. Accordingly, Figure 7.10 might be reconstructed along the lines of Figure 7.11 to make explicit the point that the public/private distinction should also be treated as a continuous rather than a dichotomous variable.

From Figure 7.11 we can see that some changes (shown as vertical changes) may simply mean a move from determination by a quasi-government organization (appointments made and organizations funded by government) to a quasi-non-governmental one, (a 'private' organization, but effectively carrying out a function on behalf of government); this may alter arrangements for appointments and accountability, but make no difference to the choice open to clients or customers or the criteria by which output is allocated.

There are a number of ironies in recent political fashions in Britain about the appropriate 'distance from government' at which activities should be conducted. When the Conservative government came into office in 1970, it was attracted to the idea of taking tasks currently carried out by government departments, and allocating them to separate units: 'But by far the best way of reducing bureaucracy is to sort through all the tasks of central government, to delegate responsibility for achieving them, *to organise at one remove from the centre*' (Howell, 1971, p. 14, emphasis added; see also Howell, 1970). A number of functions were 'pushed out' from government departments to appointed agencies, including the establishment of the Manpower Services Commission in 1974 and the Civil Aviation Authority in 1971. These moves had the not merely incidental effect of appearing to reduce the number of civil servants (see Parry, 1980; Hood, 1978). The overall effect of such changes might therefore appear to have been to reduce the 'visibility' of government activities (though employees of the Manpower Services Commission started being counted as civil servants again after a brief pause).

However, when the Conservatives came back into office in 1979, they did so on this occasion with an antipathy towards government-appointed 'quangos'—the very sort of 'hived off' body favored ten years earlier! The government commissioned a report (Plaitzky, 1980), but in the subsequent 'cull' of quangos the terminations were largely cosmetic, together with the termination of a few bodies carrying out activities which would probably have been terminated regardless of organizational form (see Hood, 1981; Barker, 1982). But the final irony was the 1979 Conservative government's commitment to 'privatization', which involved 'handing over' functions currently carried out by government to the private sector (with an implied conflation of the public-private and administrative-marḳ dimensions). Because in many cases the government would still be responsible for setting the policy framework and monitoring performance of these 'private' bodies, they would be quasi-non-governmental bodies, the original 'quangos'—about with academics had identified a number of problems of accountability—before the term 'quango' came to be applied to a quite different type of government-appointed body to which the Conservatives now appeared to feel so much antipathy (see Barker, 1982; Hague *et al.*, 1975).

The question naturally arises as to whether movements of organizations along the vertical dimension necessarily imply differences in the substance of policy delivery. Such changes are likely to involve changes in formal accountability and methods of appointment of top leadership and the mere fact of such changes, regardless of the direction of change, may produce an invigorating effect on the organization. However, very large organizations involved in largely repetitive tasks may hardly be affected by such changes at the top; in both Britain and the United States the Post Office has moved from being a government department to a corporation, but it is difficult to detect any difference in performance arising from the change itself (see Pitt and Smith, 1981, pp. 109–32).

Even when there is some reason to believe that a change was not purely cosmetic, it may be difficult to evaluate what effect a change of organizational type has made to policy delivery. Below is a balanced assessment, shot through with implied skepticism of the kind which one would expect of the best former British civil servants, of the effect of the setting up in 1974 of the Manpower Services Commission (a statutory non-departmental body) to take over and develop certain functions of the Department of Employment:

> It is not easy to evaluate how much has been gained, as a result of having the Commission in its present form, in terms of securing acceptance of change and support for new initiatives by both sides of industry, as compared with what might otherwise have been achieved by the Department of Employment. Although little impact appears to have been made in overcoming localised resistance to novel or accelerated forms of training to meet particular needs, the MSC themselves are in no doubt important gains have been made in clarifying the general climate of opinion towards youth training. . . (Plaitzky, 1980, p. 40).

7.3.4 *The multiple dimensions of organizational distance from government*

The unpacking of the public-private dichotomy shown in Figure 7.10 into the range of government, quasi-government, and quasi-non-government and private in Figure 7.11 is itself an oversimplification. In the first place, it is not possible to identify clear-cut categories covered by these labels (see Hogwood, 1979b, p. 6). Secondly, and relatedly, the distinction between public and private cannot be confined to a single dimension of 'distance from government'. The

extent to which an activity or organization can be considered public
or private can be scaled along a variety of dimensions, including
statutory and regulatory framework, ownership, finance (subdivided
into grants, loans, guarantees, etc.), contracts, and appointments to
governing boards.

There has been a tendency in political debate, particularly in
Britain, to focus on ownership as the only dimension on which
proximity to government can be measured. However, as students of
government-industry relations in both Britain and the United States
are well aware, ownership by itself is a very poor indicator of the
intensity of interactions between government and firm. The key
dimension may be contracting and the significance of this aspect of
the relationship of mutual interdependence of government and
contractor may hardly be altered by an apparently dramatic change
on a different dimension, as when the government takes the
contractor into public ownership. This is arguably true of the
nationalization of warshipbuilders in Britain in 1977. Indeed we
would go so far as to put forward the thesis that changes of ownership
will often reflect rather than determine major developments in the
relationship between government and firm. That is, those industries
which are taken into public ownership will tend to be those with
which the government has had an increasingly intense relationship
(for example, contracting, financial assistance or regulation), and
those relatively few firms which are completely 'privatized', to use the
term favored in Britain in the early 1980s, will be those where the
government has relatively low involvement in terms of financial input
or time taken scrutinizing the firm's affairs.

Different activities and organizations will vary in the extent to
which they are close to government along each of these dimensions.
Closeness to government in this sense does not necessarily imply
accountability to the government, any more than distance from
government necessarily implies accountability to clients or
customers.

7.3.5   *Dimensions of choice within and between organizations*

Just as it is a misleading oversimplification to try to compress all
forms of relationship between organizations and government into a
single vertical dimension in Figure 7.11, so it is also misleading to
show one horizontal dimension of choice. There are a number of

different types of choice within and between organizations involved in delivering public policy, each of which can be viewed as a dimension with varying degrees of choice.

7.3.5.1 *Consumer choice between alternative suppliers*

Consumers may have various degrees of choice both in principle and in practice between a number of suppliers involved in delivering more or less the same service. The degree of choice will be low if there is one central allocation system or if the multiplicity of organizations involved have functional or territorial monopolies. Even where there is in principle wide scope for consumer choice this may be limited by the information costs of finding out and appraising the performance of alternative agencies and by costs such as the need to travel longer distances to an alternative supplier. Where the supplier of a specific service or a particular mix of services and taxes and charges does have a territorial monopoly, the consumer/citizen may decide to change his residence to the jurisdiction he prefers (see Tiebout, 1956). Public services are, however, likely to be only one of a number of considerations determining selection of place of residence. More central to our concern are the high *transitional* costs associated with house moves, which may offset marginal variations in service (though in Britain and the United States these transitional costs may be offset by the ability to 'trade up' on house values, taking advantage of tax allowances).

In addition to direct financial costs which may be involved in changing suppliers, there may also be 'aggravation costs' associated with disentangling oneself from a supplier with whom one is dissatisfied and finding an alternative supplier. Particularly where the supplier is a professional, such as a doctor or lawyer, alternative suppliers may be reluctant to take on a client who has expressed dissatisfaction with a colleague, and the client or patient who is attempting to exercise choice as a means of dealing with a 'problem supplier' may find himself stigmatized by other suppliers as a 'problem client'.

7.3.5.2 *Consumer determination of output*

There is a range of degrees of choice open to consumers in determining the amount and quality of particular goods and services they will consume. In the case of classic public goods the choice open to individual consumers about the amount of the goods to be produced from which he will benefit (or suffer) is non-existent. For a wide range of individually targetted goods, such as cash benefits, the individual beneficiary also has no choice about the amount which will be offered to him. The greatest choice is normally available for those goods and services which are in principle or in practice charged for. Thus, subject to any personal budget constraint, an individual citizen can decide how much use to make of public highways, public transport, public sports facilities, etc. This assumes that the individual has sufficient knowledge about the benefits to him of different volumes and qualities of consumption.

The dimension of choice about volume and quality of output clearly overlaps with the dimension of choice between suppliers (7.3.5.1) if suppliers offer differentiated output, but suppliers may offer standard packages, or clients may have insufficient information to choose between suppliers on the basis of different mixes of quantity and quality—as opposed to variations in price or in waiting time.

7.3.5.3 *Discretion available to individual service providers*
Much of the choice in public policy provision is exercised not by consumers or clients at whom the program is directed but by individuals within the organizations delivering the policy. This is particularly important where the service is delivered by professionals, who are likely to promote the value of professional autonomy. Individual clients, either because genuine professional expertise is involved in choices between options about what is to be provided or because of professional mystification, may have little choice in practice, regardless of any formal rights. In such circumstances, neither the individual client nor the government funding the provision may have much say in determining the pattern of distribution of outputs. The implications of this for health care, and in particular for transitions between different systems of paying for health care, are explored in 7.5.3.

7.3.5.4 *Government choice in selecting service delivery agencies*
The final dimension of choice is the scope available to a central authority in selecting which agency should be given responsibility for delivering a policy. The advantages and disadvantages of attempting to change a policy through changing the organization responsible for delivering it were discussed in section 6.1, and the implications of intergovernmental switches of responsibility were discussed in 1.3.3.

The ability of bypass state governments which were themselves seen as being part of the problem was an important feature of the institutional arrangements established under the 'Great Society' programs in the United States in the 1960s. More generally, both President and Congressional committees will seek to influence the agency to which any new or changed responsibilities are given, since this may affect not only how the program may be implemented, but also which Congressional committees become responsible for legislative oversight.

In Britain the central government has a considerable degree of discretion in determining which organizations are responsible for which services, though it does not have to concern itself with implications for Parliamentary scrutiny. The British government can both establish new organizations to supplement or bypass existing ones, as with the establishment of the Scottish Special Housing Association (without specific legislative authority being required) even though local authorities already had housing responsibilities, and undertake substantial reallocations of responsibility as with the reorganizations of local government, water authorities and health authorities in 1973–5.

7.3.6 *Interaction between public and private*

The ultimate sterility of debating whether a particular service should be delivered by the public *or* the private sector is revealed when we realize that almost all public policies involve a mixture of public and private inputs. Thus, debates about policy change concern changes in the mix of public and private sector inputs. This can be seen most clearly in the case of contracting illustrated by Figure 7.9.

The important issue is therefore not a single question about whether an activity should be carried out by the public or private sector (or by administrative or market methods) but a number of interrelated questions:

1   What types of organizational arrangements are appropriate for delivering this service? This includes considerations of what type of organizations and how their jurisdictions should be defined, and how they would relate to other organizations.

2   How far should the delivery organization be accountable to government, clients and its own members? This will include con-

siderations of methods of funding and appointment of management and staff, and any sanctions which would be available.

3   How much choice should be available to the client about the value, quantity and timing of the output he receives?

4   How much, if anything, should the client pay and should this be related to amount consumed, need, or ability to pay?

5   How much discretion should be available to individual members of a supplying organization to determine the volume and distribution of outputs?

To pose these questions does not necessarily mean that it will be possible to come up with a design for a policy delivery system which will meet the requirements of the answers to all of them or pass tests of political acceptability, but at least they are the right questions.

7.4   Policy change and 'stock' and 'flow'

7.4.1 *Distinction between current output and over-time patterns of output*

If we are concerned with the pattern of outcomes of delivery systems rather than the output in a given period, we have to distinguish between policies which are concerned with building up a stock of facilities for delivering public policy (for example, buildings and trained manpower) and those which are essentially concerned with a flow of output (for example, cash grants). To be more accurate, we are concerned with the extent to which any given program embodies stock and flow elements, since all policies involve elements of both.

7.4.2 *The implications of the stock element for changing programs*

Where the stock element of a program is high, even apparently radical changes in the methods of allocating the output may do little to alter the overall pattern of distribution of output, which will continue to reflect the output of previous allocative systems. The existing stock of facilities may impose constraints on even marginal changes to new output. For example, after over thirty years of existence of the 'National' Health Service in Britain the territorial distribution of health facilities still to a large extent reflects historical patterns (see Buxton and Klein, 1978; Haywood and Elcock, 1982).

This partly reflects the pre-1948 distribution of hospitals and doctors, but it is also the result of an incremental system of budgeting which has distributed marginal additional funds largely on the basis of previous funding rather than on a more equitable target distribution. This pattern has continued with only slight modification despite attempts by central government to secure redistribution. The slower rate of growth of health expenditure from the late 1970s makes redistribution even more difficult.

Similarly, even radical changes to housing policy would be mediated by the accumulated impact of previous programs. Clearly supply of houses would not adjust simultaneously in response to moves towards greater market allocations such as selling off public housing, abolishing subsidies and tax expenditures, and removing rent and tenancy restrictions. The supply of housing is a stock, with flow alterations (demolitions, construction, conversions) only at the margin. What is more, the stock is of widely varying types of accommodation in terms of size and layout (flats, terraced houses, detached houses, etc.). The present pattern of occupancy reflects the accumulated effect of the distortions (in market terms) produced by the existing systems of subsidy and administrative allocation and regulation. The removal of restrictions and subsidies or the introduction of marketable tenancy rights would enable easier re-allocation within the existing stock, but the pattern of components of the existing stock would still reflect the accumulated effect of the past.

There is, however, one fallacious argument which might at first sight appear to be related to the constraints imposed by existing stock on future changes, and that is the incorrect lesson drawn from the expenditure already committed to a program. This improper use of the 'sunk costs' argument states that because so much has already been committed to a program or project—perhaps in the form of very expensive capital facilities—then more should be spent on the program or project to enable it to continue or come into operation (see also 8.3.2.5). The correct economic conclusion to be drawn is that additional expenditure should only be incurred if the benefits to be generated after that date at least match the additional expenditure to be incurred. Given that this sort of issue typically arises when there have been massive cost overruns, it may well be that future costs (that is, ignoring what has already been spent) would be greater than future benefits (both costs and benefits being to an extent hypothetical). Thus it may well make sense to abandon an almost completed building or dam when millions of dollars have already been spent on it.

7.4.3 *The implications of the flow element for changing programs*

Policies concerned largely with flow, that is with an output which is consumed during the period and does not accumulate in a form which shapes the delivery of future output, are easier to change, particularly at the margin, and also produce an outcome which corresponds to the scale of the change. It is relatively easy to adjust the real value of the flow directed at individuals and to add or delete new elements or categories of clientele to the program (see 2.3.4 and 2.3.5).

However, programs apparently concerned almost entirely with flow in the flow in the form of paying out cash benefits may have an important stock element underlying them. This is especially true of 'entitlement' programs, particularly those where a contribution is paid, even if the contribution bears little relationship with the entitlement to benefit. Although it may be administratively relatively easy to replace such programs, it may be politically (and perhaps constitutionally) impossible. This in-built rigidity is quite deliberate, even if the framers of the program did not work through its long-term · implications in terms of public expenditure or policy development. The building of an entitlement into a program can serve two main purposes. The first is to engender in the recipient the feeling that he is not being given a 'handout' but something he has paid for. The second is that politicians who promoted the introduction of the program want to make it difficult or impossible for anyone to attempt to reverse the decision in the future. Unfortunately this may also make it difficult to restructure the program, perhaps in a way which would retarget it more closely towards the originally intended beneficiaries.

7.5 Complex delivery systems

7.5.1 *Different criteria of allocation at each stage*

In practice, public policy often involves complex *chains* of allocative decisions which may embody different criteria of allocation at each stage (see Calabresi and Bobbitt, 1978); for example, government budgetary allocation of educational funds to local authorities, which may then allocate them administratively to individual schools which all children in the area are obliged to attend, or to parents in the form of vouchers which can be used in any school. In other words, any given policy cannot simply be indicated by a single *point* on Figure 7.13, though it may be possible to conceive of some programs as involving chains of such points. Thus, no single allocative mechanism is used, but a related series of such mechanisms.

In general, programs involving the provision of cash benefits will involve simpler chains (both in terms of length of chain and variety of different forms of allocative criteria involved) than programs involving the provision of goods and services. Where a program is complex, or policy output depends on a number of related programs, we can see that the delivery system does not simply involve a single chain or a series of parallel chains but an interlocking pattern of allocative decisions.

7.5.2 *Dramatic change may not affect key stage*

These points about policy involving chains or patterns of allocative decisions are crucial to an understanding of changing delivery systems, since proposals involving apparently dramatic changes of allocative methods may have relatively little impact if they do not affect the key point or points in the chain of allocation (the implications of this will be underlined by the health example considered in 7.5.3). It is obviously of crucial importance, therefore, to try to identify such key points in the allocative chain. Comparative analysis can make a particularly valuable contribution here—it is often amusing to observe critics of the failures of policy in one country drawing the wrong conclusions about policy prescriptions because they have failed to examine the failure of policy in other countries.

7.5.3 *The example of health*

Health policy is a good example of a highly complex system for the delivery of outputs. The detailed arrangements vary from country to country (see Leichter, 1979), but all involve the interaction of a number of components: discretion in principle open to would-be patients to present themselves for treatment, a key role for professionals at the point of delivery, and an important role for third parties (other than patients and health-care staff) in financing the health-care system (government grants and/or government or private insurance schemes). In the British case examined here, proposals for change provide a focus for making a number of analytical points.

Health care provides a useful example of how apparently dramatic changes in the mechanisms by which policy is to be delivered may fail to have the outcomes expected, and in addition may generate unexpected side-effects. Health policy can also be used to illustrate other themes developed in this chapter, such as transitions from 'public' to 'private' and 'administrative' to 'market' (section 7.3), and the implications for transition of a 'stock' element in policy (section 7.4); health is also used to illustrate the formal model of transition outlined in section 7.6.

Critics of the British National Health Service have pointed to the highly bureaucratic (both in the descriptive and pejorative senses) nature of the processes by which the volume and type of health care delivered to individual patients, particularly in hospitals, are determined (see, for example, Harris and Seldon, 1979). By replacing this hierarchical allocative mechanism with a more market-oriented one in which individual patients requested courses of treatment from doctors and hospitals of their choice and reclaimed the money in whole or in part from insurance companies or the state, it could be argued both that patient choice would be increased and that resources devoted to health care would be allocated more 'efficiently'. However, this argument is based on the assumption that effective demand for particular types of treatment is generated by patients. The evidence suggests that effective demand for particular types of treatment is in fact generated inside the health service by doctors (see Maynard, 1979; Klein, 1975, pp. 93–4). Given the substantial growth in the cost of the National Health Service since its inception and the fact that medical treatment is largely free to the consumer at the point of provision, one might be tempted to assume that increased costs had arisen from patients presenting themselves more frequently for more treatment. 'In fact, however, consumer demand has *fallen* during the 25 years that the NHS has offered a virtually free service' (Klein, 1975, p. 93). During a period when the total population of potential consumers rose by over 10 per cent, the number of contacts between patients and family practitioners fell by an estimated 25 per cent or so (a reduction of 20 million or more in the number of annual patient 'demands'), while the number of patient visits in hospital accident and emergency departments rose by only about 5 million. What has happened is that once patients have entered the health system doctors are more likely to refer them for more, and increasingly expensive, treatment. Individual patients will find it very difficult to judge the benefit of particular proposed courses of treatment. It is this which has led to the important role of doctors in determining the volume and type of medical care given to individual patients.

The two characteristics which have produced this situation—the breaking of the link between treatment received and payment by the patient, and demand to a large extent generated by service providers—would still obtain under systems of insurance or state rebate. Indeed, one of the arguments used in favor of a more market-oriented approach to health care—that it would enable additional funds to be spent on health care—might exacerbate this situation. As Maynard (1979) points out:

> The conclusion that the cost of care, the quality of care and the coverage of insurance are related is of great importance. It indicates that doctors, because of increased insurance coverage, are able to sell a more sophisticated and expensive product. The patient has no incentive to check this tendency on the part of producers, because the opportunity cost to the patient initially is zero: the insurer pays the bill.

Because of the effective domination of decisions about type and amount of health care by professionals, attempts to regulate total health costs by introducing market mechanisms such as obliging patients to pay a share of the costs would tend to have little effect other than imposing financial burdens on the patient (see Jackson and Peters, 1980). (Different considerations apply to non-medical facilities such as private rooms, etc.). Experience suggests that government would be driven to consider the imposition of *administrative* devices on top of the quasi-market allocation, such as controls in cost escalation, total cash ceilings, vetting for whether operations are 'necessary', etc. (see Aaron, 1979, pp. 106–16).

Adjustments of supply of key medical resources such as highly-trained doctors or new hospitals have a long lead time. Supplies may adjust in the long term if it is expected that the increase in funds allocated to health as a result of a more market-oriented approach was permanent. However, both economic analysis and American experience suggest that in the short to medium-term additional income will simply lead to an acceleration of the inflation of medical costs.

All these points tend to suggest that apparent moves towards greater market allocation of health care in Britain might make relatively little difference to the practicalities of the allocation of health care and if not handled carefully might even produce counter-productive results. The reason for this is the key role of the doctor as 'gatekeeper' in the allocative system (see Friedson, 1970). Under the present system, there is a long chain of political and administrative allocations by which taxation is extracted from citizens, expenditure is allocated to the health program, the health budget is allocated among Regional Health Authorities, who allocate it to districts, who allocate it to hospitals, manpower and equipment, with each level making the allocation in response to bids from below; when a patient presents himself for treatment the doctor then exercises his judgement about appropriate treatment within budgetary constraints imposed on him. Under a system of private insurance or state rebate, insurance payments or taxation would be extracted from the citizen, a patient when ill would present himself to a doctor who would exercise his judgement about appropriate treatment within any cost constraints applying, and the patient or doctor would then reclaim the money from the insurance fund or the state. Despite enormous differences in the administrative apparatus for distributing funds to the point of treatment, the key role of the professional (the doctor) in determining the output of health care in each case remains. Only if the exercise of 'clinical judgement' by doctors was challenged head on could fundamentally different allocation systems be considered. One ameliorative mechanism suggested by Jackson and Peters (1980), which would help to restrain the worst excesses of unnecessarily expensive treatment, would be to oblige *doctors* who practice in a highly deviant fashion to share in the cost of the treatment they prescribe.

It should be stressed that the health example is not being presented as a fully generalizable one. However, similar considerations apply in other policy areas where individual professionals have a key role in determining the level and nature of service delivered to individual clients. In such cases, large-scale changes to the budgetary and organizational superstructure may do little to alter the final pattern of outputs.

7.6 Assumptions and issues in the transition debate

7.6.1 *Dynamic analysis contrasted with comparative statics*

The use of abstract models in policy analysis is a common feature of a number of authors, particularly economists, who find this a useful methodology to derive proposals for policy change. As a methodology such models frequently suffer from two related major flaws as aids to practical policy analysis (defined here as analysis which will assist a real decision-maker to choose in full awareness of costs and benefits an option which can achieve authorization and implementation).

The first of these flaws is that optimization models may fail to distinguish between circumstances in which government currently has no activity directed at a particular target and those where it is already delivering such a program. What may be 'optimal' in terms of 'starting from scratch' assumptions may not be optimal bearing in mind the implications of the existence of a current program.

Further, and this brings in the second flaw of such an approach, the costs (financial and political) of transition from an existing program to a replacement program are liable to be ignored in what is essentially an exercise in comparative statics. These transition costs may or may not be greater than the start-up costs of moving from no-policy to policy, costs which are also often ignored in formal static models. We have already seen in Chapter 6 how important issues and costs involved in transition can be in real-world organizational settings.

7.6.2 *Constructing an illustrative model of transition*

Despite the danger of abstracting from practical problems, there can be value in constructing a formal model of the assumptions involved in transition between policies. First of all, such a model can clarify the analyst's mind by serving as a checklist of points which should be taken into account when attempting a transition. Secondly, for analysts trained in the use of formal models, the construction of a model of transition provides a means of communicating some of our arguments in their own language. Undoubtedly, for a decision-maker rather than an analyst the points made in the rest of this section would have to be translated into a more readily assimilable form, with emphasis on the political costs for the decision-maker if their implications are ignored.

For the purpose of presentation it is proposed to construct a simplified (and unrealistic) model of the process of transition to greater market allocation of goods currently allocated by largely administrative means. The model is constructed in the form of assumptions about the process of transition and about the outcomes of that transition. While not every statement by advocates of greater market allocation contains all these assumptions, all of them can be found implicitly or explicitly in arguments on this theme (or, at least, the implications of the absence of these conditions is not discussed). The model as presented below does not impose any cut-off point in time or degree of coverage of clientele for us to be able to say that 'transition' has been completed, but such definitions could readily be built in for specific cases.

This model can be labelled as one of 'perfect transition to market allocation'. Not all the assumptions may be relevant to all policy areas and policy areas vary in the extent to which the absence in practice of the assumed conditions poses political problems. Many of the assumptions listed below are similar to the language of classical and welfare economists, who have so far provided the most analytically rigorous models of allocation. In particular, many of the assumptions are similar to those used in the traditional 'perfect competition' model used for exposition purposes in economics ('perfect' in the technical sense of conforming to all the stated conditions rather than perfect in a normative sense). However, the model presented here also draws on insights from other disciplines such as political science and public administration (see especially the model of 'perfect administration' developed by Hood, 1976). Moreover, it is argued here that special additional issues arise in the case of some of them as a result of a *transition* from administrative allocation to market allocation.

It may readily be seen that many of the conditions set out in 7.6.3 are so tight that they are unachievable in practice. The same would probably be true of a model of transition in the opposite direction and indeed, of any 'perfect' model. The implication is not that transition is impossible or the model is useless, but that we need to assess the practical significance of not being able to meet these assumptions in proposed successions. Such an assessment is attempted in 7.6.4, following the setting out of the assumptions in 7.6.3.

7.6.3 *Conditions for perfect transition to greater market allocation*

A number of assumptions would be required in constructing a model of perfect transition to greater market allocation. As the accompanying illustrations indicate, these assumptions are often difficult to fulfil in practice.

7.6.3.1 *Voluntary demands*

Any model of perfect competition or of transition to greater market allocation must include the assumptions that consumers of a product (recipients of a benefit) can choose whether or not to seek that product and can determine how much of the product they wish to consume. In other words, the assumption is that all demands are voluntary and that this is related to the price which will be charged. These conditions do not obtain in most aspects of health care. Although to a considerable extent health problems are self-inflicted in the sense that many are the result of personal life-styles (such as smoking, overeating, lack of exercise) and although with some types of illness (such as colds and 'flu) it could be said that there is a voluntary decision to seek professional health care, it would generally be considered that *at the time of illness or injury* demands for health care are not voluntary and can be said to constitute absolute needs. Other health problems, such as black and brown lung, are occupational diseases. Thus, any absolute use of the market criterion, that is, that only those with money to back up demands for health care could receive it, would be likely to be viewed with abhorence. Hence the widespread support for state or voluntary provision or compulsory membership of state or private insurance schemes. These arrangements, however, remove the direct link between the consumer and the price he would have to pay for a particular course of treatment.

7.6.3.2 *Demand is articulated by consumers*

A second condition for being able to move to greater market allocation is that the persons receiving the good or service are identical to persons exercising effective choice (that is, that there is no separation of consumers from demand articulators). As we saw in 7.5.3, this condition does not obtain in health care because of the inability of the patient to assess the appropriateness of the proposed course of treatment; effectively demand is generated by doctors. In the case of a free market in schooling, for example, through the introduction of vouchers, demand would not be articulated by the direct consumers (the children), but their parents; this does not prevent the operation of a market, but it is worth noting that it does not operate on the basis of the actual consumers being able to demand the type of schooling they would want subject to personal budget constraints. In other policy areas, such as housing, the consumer and demand articulator would be the same, so this condition would be fulfilled. In the case of schooling, attendance is compulsory for the consumers because education is regarded as a 'merit good', which would be underconsumed if it was simply left to children or parents to decide how much education to undertake. For all merit goods unrestrained consumer choice, and therefore transition to greater market allocation, would be considered inappropriate. It should be stressed that the concept of merit goods is one that reflects political value judgements rather than merely a technical one relating to intrinsic characteristics of the good or service consumed.

7.6.3.3 *Equitable transition*
An equitable transition to greater market allocation would ensure that persons in similar financial circumstances and with similar preferences or values would be able to secure similar levels of benefit or satisfaction. This assumption does not hold with some types of moves towards greater market allocation in housing. Because of the sizeable discounts offered under the current British scheme for selling publicly owned housing, tenants buying council houses will secure substantial windfall gains relative to families on identical incomes purchasing in the private market. In future years a different type of inequity would arise if mortgage payments remained constant but rents were raised in line with inflation. In such circumstances, persons with identical incomes would be paying similar sums, but some would be paying for a capital acquisition. It should be noted that this issue of transitional justice is distinct from that of the equity of the previous and new policies, and that the logic of transitional justice may work in opposition to the logic of the proposed end state in terms of arguments about welfare and benefits.

7.6.3.4 *Overall benefit should be maximized regardless of distribution*
If maximizing the overall benefit of society is the aim of greater market allocation, then adverse distributional consequences to

particular individuals or groups can be ignored. Those adversely affected can, in principle, be compensated for their suffering (cf. the Kaldor-Hicks principle in economics and its application in cost-benefit analysis). However, in practice distributional consequences may assume greater salience than considerations of overall benefit. The abrupt removal of housing subsidies and rent ceilings could have dramatic adverse consequences for individuals who had made financial or other plans on the assumption of their continuation. This is a major political consideration militating against the introduction of such measures (even if these produced greater equity among persons in otherwise similar circumstances), though their impact could be reduced by advance announcement and phasing in.

7.6.3.5 *Supply will simultaneously adjust*

A perfect transition to greater market allocation would assume that supply will more or less simultaneously adjust in response to the transition. We have already noted that in both health care (7.5.3) and housing (7.4.2) the size and composition of the capital stock and trained manpower have accumulated over a long period and that only marginal changes in the short run are possible, leading perhaps to counter-productive results such as acceleration of costs. In the case of greater market choice among schools, perhaps through the introduction of voucher schemes, some responses could be taken more immediately than others. Schools which faced increased demand might find it relatively easy to take on teachers from schools facing a drop in demand. Additional temporary classrooms could be placed in playgrounds, though this would decrease the quality of provision and increase the costs of the school system as a whole. Classic market responses by schools facing declining rolls would be to cut costs or improve standards, perhaps at the urging of parents of remaining pupils. However, another possibility is that such schools would be faced by accelerating 'exit' of the best (and richest) pupils and staff, leaving either low-standard schools with pupils from poor families or rolls too small for continuing viability (cf. Hirschman, 1970).

7.6.3.6 *Perfect visibility of benefits*

Perfect transition to market allocation would require that the benefits to be provided by greater market allocation are perfectly visible. A weaker form of this assumption is that market-permeated benefits are at least as visible as administratively provided benefits. In the case of housing policy, the withdrawal of subsidies and rent ceilings would be relatively short-term and visible, while the benefits of more 'efficient' allocation would be long-term, more dispersed and less visible (in the sense that they can be attributed to policy). Similarly, in Britain governments of both parties have found it difficult to stand back when a firm in which they have previously been involved again faced a crisis, since the costs are specific, immediate, concentrated, and articulated by those affected, whereas the benefits of not providing (perhaps disguised) subsidy are long-term, hypothetical and dispersed. This relative visibility of administratively provided benefits explains why governments have become involved in many areas, and indicates an asymmetry in the politics of transition from one method of allocation to the other.

7.6.3.7   *Governments can ensure transition*

An ingredient often missing from economic models, but normally implicit, is that governments can actually implement their policies. Thus our final condition is that a transition to greater market allocation can (and will) result from an authoritative declaration. The 1979 Conservative government anticipated recalcitrance on the part of some local authorities to selling public housing and inserted provisions in the legislation to surmount this, but despite these provisions there have been delays in starting sales by some councils and the use of tactics to deter would-be buyers. A second problem of implementation is that a substantial move of housing from the public to the private sector depends on existing council tenants being able and willing to buy their homes. While many do wish to buy them, the bulk wish to remain in public housing (given prospective levels of rent and mortgage payments).

7.6.4   *Absence of smooth transition imposes costs*

Deviations from these assumptions matter for three reasons. These reasons will also apply to transition between other sets of allocative systems. First of all, in the absence of a smooth transition, the transition will impose direct costs itself—disruption costs, duplication costs, political costs, etc. Such transition costs may even outweigh any benefits considered to arise from the benefits of the new allocative system compared to the old (see, for example, Hood, 1976, p. 27).

Secondly, the absence of these conditions (or of less rigorous forms of them) may mean that after the transition (if, indeed, transition is successfully completed) allocation may be improved less than expected, and in some cases may even be worse than under administrative allocation, even on the criteria used to justify the general principle of market allocation.

Thirdly, neglect of the implications of these conditions or their absence may become the focus of political opposition to measures designed to promote market allocation. This may lead to *issue displacement*, that is, the political 'problem' around which debate centers becomes not the problems caused by administrative allocation, but the adverse consequences arising from the absence of one of the above conditions (see Eyestone, 1978, p. 31). An example of this would be if the debate about selling public housing in Britain moved away from the principle of increasing private ownership to debate about the desirability of windfall gains which might accrue to tenants. Where such issue displacement takes place, then governments may face increased difficulty in getting their measures accepted and may also find that even if they succeed in implementing them the criteria for evaluating the 'success' of their measures have been changed.

Advocacy of government regulation, taxation or subsidy is often justified by pointing to 'imperfections' in the way some goods are allocated in economic markets. Such advocates are sometimes blind to 'imperfections' in political markets and to the fact that the conditions for 'perfect administration' do not in practice exist (see Wolf, 1979; Hood, 1976). The inefficiencies and inequities arising from political and administrative allocation are, of course, stressed by advocates of a greater role for market allocation (see, for example, Harris and Seldon, 1977, 1979). In this section we have demonstrated that there can also be imperfections in the process of moving from one system of allocation to another.

These imperfections have two aspects. The first concerns the substantive problems and costs arising out of the transition itself; these will tend to reduce the benefits which are argued to arise from changes in methods of allocation. The second concerns failure to perceive imperfections in the allocative mechanism towards which it is intended to move; this will have implications for the long-run outcome of the transition, but, more importantly for our focus of concern, it will cause both political and implementation problems during the transition.

Brittan (1975, p. 69) rightly dismisses as a 'widespread fallacy' the view that 'the case for the market economy depends on the existence of something called "perfect competition"'. If the case for government depended on 'perfect politics' and 'perfect administration' then we would have no government! Similarly, to point, as we have done, to 'imperfections' or problems in the process of moving from one system of allocation to another does not provide a conclusive argument against such a movement. As the discussion of specific policy areas has shown, there are variations among policy areas in these 'imperfections', both in terms of 'objective' factors (allocative efficiency and financial costs) and political problems. Direct costs of transition may be considered to be outweighed by the long-run benefits of a different system of allocation. Political pressures can, in principle, be resisted, and political arguments refuted or rejected.

7.7   The politics of changing delivery systems

In this chapter we have argued that the simple comparative analysis of the hypothesized consequences of alternative delivery systems is inadequate for an understanding of the allocative implications in practice and the processes involved in moving from one delivery system to another. A starting point must be the need for greater clarification of just what methods of allocation are actually used in determining public policies. Delivery systems are often highly complex and alterations to some allocative stages may do little to affect the allocation of final output. Even dramatic changes in delivery systems may do little to alter the historical pattern of allocation—or may even produce counter-intuitive or counter-productive results.

These points have implications both for analysis and for action. What is 'obvious' and 'common-sense' about delivery systems is often not true. Very considerable care is needed in unravelling the stages of complex delivery systems and identifying which stages would be affected in what ways by proposed transitions. In 8.2 we will argue the need for explicit policy theory of the policies to be replaced, the successor policies and the process of transition between them. In applying these concepts to issues in practice, it will be necessary to separate out which features are special to the country concerned (which may mean that policy ideas from other countries will not 'take'), which features are specific to the policy area, and which apply only to the issue concerned. These points are important to the policymaker, since they will help him to identify non-bargainable elements of the design of the successor policy and more generally warn him about the implications for political difficulties at the authorization and implementation stages.

Chapter 8

CONCLUSION: STRATEGIC CHOICE FOR POLICY SUCCESSION

8.1   Policy succession as a focus for analysis and action

THIS book has argued that the majority of policymaking in advanced, industrial societies is the replacement of existing policies or programs by new attempts at 'solving' the same problems—or the problems created by previous policies. We do not claim to be the first to have noticed this characteristic of contemporary policymaking (May and Wildavsky, 1978). However, we would argue that the conventional models of the policy process either ignore this characteristic and are constructed as if all policymaking is policy innovation, or fail to identify the features which distinguish policy succession from policy innovation. Further, these models do not attempt to understand the processes through which policies may be terminated or maintained as compared to the dynamics of policy innovation.

We have attempted to take the first steps toward providing an analytical framework which will enable us to examine the features of the policy succession process which differentiate it from policy innovation, policy maintenance, or policy termination. We can use the same framework for analyzing the implications of different types of policy succession.

Policy succession in all its forms involves supplanting existing organizations and clientele groups for a new organization or set of organizations, and perhaps a new client relationship. As change is unsettling—perhaps more unsettling than embarking upon a new policy initiative—there is a need for those involved in policymaking, as much as for academics, to understand its characteristics.

8.1.1   *Policy succession as a focus for understanding policymaking*

> Change as change is mere flux and lapse; it insults
> intelligence. Genuinely to know is to grasp a permanent end
> that realizes itself through changes.

John Dewey, 'The Influence of Darwinism on Philosophy' (1909)

The implications of our analysis are not confined to a need for academics to improve their conceptualization of the policy process (or, as we would argue, policy processes in the plural). There are also implications for the would-be initiators of policy succession for the strategy and tactics which would be most appropriate for the type of policy succession being attempted. Successful policy succession cannot be taken for granted, and at the same time there is no reason to expect anything more than incremental benefits from a policy succession, particularly when dealing with social problems which appear inherently intractable. Unless that degree of realism about the difficulties of 'solving' problems pertains, we are likely to see a series of 'solutions' being offered, with none wholly addressing the original problem, and each solution in turn coming itself to be regarded as the problem. This skepticism is not a reason for not attempting to improve and perfect policies, but it is a plea for realism and caution about easy solutions for difficult problems, some of which themselves have been generated by earlier attempts to provide a solution.

In this concluding chapter we set out the implications of our analysis in the preceding chapters for those having to make difficult choices about policy succession. Our concern here is not with the 'correct' choice to make in a specific situation of policy succession, but rather with how decision-making systems might be designed to cope with some of the endemic problems which have been identified earlier in the analysis. In Dror's terminology, we will be concerned with the problems of 'metapolicymaking' for policy succession (1968).

8.1.2 *Designing for policy succession*

In addition to gaining an intellectual understanding of the dynamics of policy succession, a second task we are undertaking is more practical. This is to aid those who are advocates of a policy succession in designing that change. How can a change in policy be carried out with a minimum of disruption for both the producers and consumers of a policy? How can politicians and public managers implement desired changes in policies without creating excessive costs, both in the strict economic sense of that term and in a psychological conception of the costs of change? The possibility of implementing a policy succession in an orderly fashion is to some degree a function of the design of the pre-existing organizations and programs. For example, in an era of increased skepticism concerning government and bureaucracy, policies are being designed with built-in termination triggers. Any administrator joining such an organization, or any client becoming dependent upon its services, should have reason to question the stability of their attachment. If this decreased conception of entitlement to either employment or a service from the organization can make future policy successions more palatable to those already associated with the organization, then one of the major hurdles in policy succession will have been passed.

8.1.2.1   *Current cycle planning*
We cannot, however, reverse history and redesign programs and organizations which are already in operation without such built-in evaluation and termination procedures. The analyst or practitioner of policy succession must therefore be prepared to intervene in an existing organization in order to bring about a smooth transition from one policy to another.

One obvious trigger for such changes would be changes in the political party in office, but incrementalism in policymaking and the 'Tweedledum-Tweedledee' nature of American parties (and to a lesser extent British parties) makes any policy succession resulting from a party change somewhat problematic (Rose, 1980). But if there were to be a policy succession resulting from a partisan change it may be more palatable given that there would be a perceived mandate to produce the changes, even changes such as those of the Reagan administration which ran counter to established incremental patterns of policymaking. Also, we would argue that those attempting to produce such a policy succession should attempt to bring it about during the first year, 'honeymoon', period (Bunce, 1981).

More common than changes associated with partisan change are piecemeal changes related to changes in the external environment of the organization, the policy ideas of its members, and available technology. There is as yet no ready technology for implementing a policy succession, but only rather ill-defined ideas about what must be understood and what needs to be avoided. In a later section of this chapter (8.2), we attempt to expand that understanding and the capability for planning substantially.

8.1.2.2   *Planning for future cycles*
Policymakers would have an advantage, or course, if they began to understand that policy succession is the norm and not the exception. If this conceptual breakthrough were achieved, any future policies

could be designed to facilitate their possible replacement. A proper attention to the possibility, or probability, of future policy succession will tend to make permanence in organizations and program characteristics to be avoided rather than an assumption of those involved.

However, care must be taken to try to design a program that will have the opportunity to be successful. Excessive attention to the problems of policy succession may make any operating program doomed to failure, and may make policy succession a self-fulfilling prophecy. Also, policy succession may depend upon the organizations involved promoting their own changes, and this may be too much to ask even of individuals and organizations which are sensitized to the importance of policy succession. In short, while planning for policy succession in creating a new program or organization, it is important to understand not only the importance of change, but the importance of service delivery and the dynamics of human organizations.

8.2 Current cycle

As noted above, the most demanding form of policy succession will be the change of a pre-existing program which was not specifically designed for succession. This includes, of course, the vast majority of organizations extant at the time we are writing. The major exception would be organizations which have been designed for termination but which may be able to demonstrate sufficient social importance to justify their continuation in some form. Given that the question of their termination will be raised automatically, it is quite possible that if they survive they will survive in an altered form. But this would not be as threatening to employees or clients as an equal degree of change in an organization designed for permanence; it would merely be a welcome surprise.

8.2.1 *The need for explicit policy theory*

We ought not to be over-anxious to encourage innovation in cases of doubtful improvement for an old system must ever have two advantages over a new one; it is established, and it is understood.

Charles Caleb Colton, *Lacoon*, (1825) 1.521

If policy succession for the current cycle is to occur at all, and particularly if it is to occur in an effective manner, there needs to be an explicit theory about the characteristics of public policies. For a succession to occur, we must be able to identify the difficulties in the existing policy, the characteristics of a policy which should replace it, and the characteristics of a process which would lead from one to the other. Unfortunately, such policies do not exist in any clearly identifiable form, and we must make some preliminary estimates of the nature of such theories. Thus, much of what will follow in this section represents some speculation about the nature of policies and the policy process.

8.2.1.1 *The characteristics of the policy to be replaced*

What are the characteristics of a policy which can, and should, be a candidate for policy succession? The identification of policies requiring change or replacement is more in the province of students of evaluation research, as well as the subject of substantial value conflict (Weiss, 1972). What we are concerned about, however, is the characteristics of the policy which would make policy succession a possible outcome of the political process, and which would make any policy succession which did result less traumatic than might be true for other policies. These characteristics for any particular policy are immutable, but if there is a choice among policies which are candidates for succession, this may be a useful guide. The selection of a policy to serve as the subject of a succession attempt should not necessarily be guided by the ease of succession, unless one is seeking to gain only political advantage or a reputation for effectiveness. But there are instances in which a single policy problem may be approached by alternative paths, and an understanding of the ease of policy succession may determine which of these alternative paths to select.

From what we have written in the preceding chapters, we can develop some of the characteristics of a policy which must be considered. These include:

(a) Clientele

1   The larger and more powerful a clientele group, the greater will be the difficulty in producing a policy succession.

2   The more the clientele lacks alternative mechanisms for receiving similar or compensating benefits, the greater will be the difficulty in producing a policy succession.

3   The better organized is the clientele group, the greater the difficulty in producing a policy succession.

(b) Organization

1   The older and larger is the organization, the greater will be the difficulty in producing a policy succession.

2   The greater the development and diffusion of an organizational ideology, the greater will be the difficulty in producing a policy succession.

3   The more recently there has been a policy succession related to the organization, the greater will be the possibility of producing a policy succession.

4   The more the organization employs professionals and/or other highly trained personnel, the greater the difficulty in producing a policy succession.

(c) The method of allocation

1   Policies involving the direct delivery of services will be the most difficult to change by a policy succession.

2   Policies involving value-shaping will also be difficult to change effectively.

3   Policies in which the individual recipient has a great deal of latitude to react to the policy, for example, grants of money or incentives, will be the easiest to change.

All of the above are essentially hypotheses, but they are hypotheses substantiated or suggested by our previous discussion. They will consequently serve as a useful introduction for anyone beginning a process of policy succession.

8.2.1.2   *The characteristics of successor policies*

In addition to the necessity of understanding the nature of the policies which are to be replaced, there must a thorough understanding of the policies which would be their replacements if a policy succession is to be effective. Certain types of policy succession will be more palatable to those affected by the succession than would others, and those who would attempt a policy succession must be cognizant of these differences.

The most clearly defined factor that would make a policy succession palatable is the similarity of the replacement policy to the existing policy. This similarity need not be so much in terms of the precise operational characteristics of the policy as much as it is in terms of its coverage. That is, it may not matter so much exactly what is done as long as the same clients are served by the same or similar organizations. It is only when the losers are clearly identifiable in a policy succession that clients are likely actively to oppose the change.

The organizations involved, and their members, are likely to oppose even policies which serve the same clients, especially when those policy successions may contradict established doctrines or ideologies of the organization. This would be true in terms of the goals expressed in the policy succession, as well as in terms of the methodologies employed to achieve the goals. That is, so long as the policy succession involves doing the same type of thing, by about the same means, then opposition is likely to be minimal. However, in such a case, there may be little reason to go through the difficulties associated with a policy succession.

If this rather inoffensive linear change cannot be undertaken, then a more complex form of change may be more desirable. A linear change which involves significant changes in goals or methodologies is an obvious target for opposition, for the losers in the process will be clearly identifiable. However, if a more complex type of change is employed then the losers will be more difficult to find and the nature of their loss will also be less clear. Similarly, if something positive can be given to clients and/or organization members, even if more is taken away, then there is an improved chance of producing an effective policy succession.

8.2.1.3 *Theories of the process of transition*
As well as understanding where we are coming from, and where we are going, we must also understand the process which would be used to move a policy area from one state to the other. Chapter 5 of this book provides an exposition of the characteristics of the process of policy succession, but here we concentrate on some of the strategic choices which might be made to accelerate the process of policy succession, and make it less traumatic for the participants.

We have pointed out that agenda-setting for policy succession is at once easier and more difficult than would be true for a policy innovation. The issue at question has already been accepted as a member of the set of appropriate areas of concern for government, but there are also existing organizations and clients who may well be threatened by any policy succession. The trick of manipulating this portion of the process may be, therefore, to build a coalition among those affected by spreading the belief that something superior to the status quo may be achieved by the change. This change would have to approach a Pareto optimal move for those already affected by the policy, and produce benefits for some without harming anyone. Even if the change cannot in reality produce such an outcome (and few policy successions could), then 'partisan analysis' could be used to try to convince at least a majority that they will receive something at little or no cost (Lindblom, 1968).

Much of the same type of coalition formation must be engaged in to legitimate a policy succession. The proposed succession will face entrenched interests of both organizational members and clients, and advocates of a policy succession must use all the available techniques of legislative manipulation—log-rolling, pork barrel, etc.—to construct a coalition on behalf of the proposed change.

Finally, once a decision favoring policy succession has been reached in the legislative body, the succession will have to be implemented. This will involve working through existing organizations, or creating new organizations (6.1.1). Both of these solutions are equally right and wrong, given a variety of characteristics of the policy succession being undertaken. The advocates of policy succession must therefore understand the organizational constraints within which they work, and attempt to develop a coalition within the organization, just as was done within the legislative institutions. There is a tendency to attempt to approach the implementation problem as one of hierarchical control, without an understanding of the organizational politics involved (Dunsire, 1978, pp. 37–9). Such an approach to producing a functioning policy succession is almost certainly doomed to failure. But it is not enough to build a coalition within a single organization, for many public programs involve the cooperation of a number of organizations in order to be effective. Thus, the effective implementor of a policy succession must plan a campaign to convert associated and affected groups, as well as the organization most directly affected.

In short, the process of producing a policy succession in the current policy cycle is a difficult one. The organizations involved were created in a climate of certainty and continuity, and it may consequently be difficult to alter their behavior. At each stage of the process a delicate and difficult political process will be required to produce the change in anything approximating the form that was intended. This, however, assumes that the change will be undertaken in as gentle a fashion as possible. The alternative which we did not discuss is a more severe type of imposition using power (through the budgeting and personnel systems), rather than the political process described above. While we have reason to expect that such severe methods of producing change may be counter-productive, there may be instances when opposition is sufficiently persistent and entrenched that only such a direct approach will possibly be successful.

8.2.2   *Identification of components*

Although we may gain a picture of the dimensions of the problem(s) involved, it is perhaps impossible to develop the strategic plans which might be required for a successful policy change if the problems of the existing policy, the proposed policy, and the process of transition are discussed in the abstract and at a high level of aggregation. One means of attacking these three broad questions is to disaggregate them into their smaller components, and isolate the variables which may influence the success or failure of a proposed policy succession. Such an analysis may help specify more clearly the points of leverage for the advocates of a policy succession, and likewise identify the crucial points of defense for those seeking to maintain the status quo.

8.2.2.1   *Identifying variables, their relationships, and power weightings*
As when constructing any model of a social or political process, there is a need to specify the variables involved in the process. Even more important, it is necessary to identify the manner in which the identified variables are interconnected, and the weightings which each variable should be given in a predictive model of the outcomes of the process. Unfortunately, to date there has been relatively little analysis in the study of the policy process which would allow the construction of credible models of this sort. This lack of highly developed models, except at the descriptive and verbal levels, would appear to be a function of several characteristics of the study of policymaking. The first of these, discussed throughout this volume, is the concentration on policy initiation. The study of the initiation of policies and programs is one of the weakest areas of the social sciences. Once that initiation has been made there are a number of

well-developed approaches to the study of diffusion to help explain its spread (Rodgers, 1970; Klingman, 1980).

A second component of the lack of development of well-articulated process models is the tendency to concentrate on environmental 'causes' of policy outputs or outcomes, with inadequate attention given to the process variables which produce the outcomes (Dye, 1966; Sharkansky, 1967; Peters and Heisler, 1978). As we have demonstrated—although not in the form of a specified model—process does makes a difference and even the fundamental premises with which one begins the study of the process of policymaking will have an influence on the manner in which the policy is conceptualized.

Finally, to the extent that the details of the policy process have been examined, they have been examined through detailed case studies of discrete policy choices. Consequently, very few generalizations have been made about the relationships of process to outcomes, except perhaps for attempts to generalize about the process within a single policy area, for example, the 'health policy process' (Alford, 1977). But policy area is, as we will argue below (8.2.2.3.2), itself an important dimension for defining the characteristics of process, and a more detailed and conscious conceptualization of the importance of these differences among policy areas should be made.

8.2.2.2 *Crucial to identify non-bargainable elements in a policy succession*

When undertaking a policy succession, it is essential to identify those elements which are essentially not bargainable. This phrase has two meanings. First, no matter what the shape of some future policy may be, it must include the elements of existing policies which may not be bargainable, and any politician or other advocate of policy succession who attempts to produce a change affecting those elements will do so at his or her peril. For example, it has by now become widely accepted that social security benefits for the elderly will be indexed for the cost of living, and any modifications to social security should not tamper with that element of the program. Two rather astute politicians—Helmut Schmidt and Ronald Reagan—forgot that point at one time or another and their lapse cost them politically. Other elements of the social security system, despite its image as a sacred cow, have been subjected to modification or even termination without excessive political uproar.

A second set of constraints on bargaining for policy succession is that for a meaningful succession to occur certain elements may have to be altered. For example, with the Americal Social Security system, any significant change must include a change in the mode of financing away from the current earmarked payroll tax. Thus, to produce a positive policy succession, the advocate must decide which changes are crucial to the success of the modified policy, and must fight to preserve the elements which are deemed to be crucial, while being prepared to bargain about others.

Unfortunately, the two sets of non-bargainable constraints may allow for no possible alternatives from the status quo; those policy elements which are necessary for a useful change from the status quo may not be acceptable changes. For example, if we pursue the social security example, although any change from the status quo in that policy area should seemingly involve a change in the method of financing, the concept of social insurance and the ethic of contributions may be so ingrained that such a change would not be possible—at least not before the system went bankrupt.

8.2.2.3   *Factors affecting policy succession*
As one contemplates the policy succession process, it is important to differentiate among important elements which may have an influence on the ease of policy succession, and the success of the new policy once it is adopted. As in any situation where there are a number of variables influencing the dependent variable—in this case the adoption and success of a policy succession—it is difficult to isolate the individual effects of each variable. Nonetheless, it will be important for any advocate of policy succession to think about the following types of factors when designing a strategy for succession.

8.2.2.3.1   *System-specific features*
First, there will be factors specific to the particular political system in which the succession is being attempted which will affect the succes or failure of the attempt. For example, the federal nature of policymaking, and particularly of policy implementation, in the United States may mean that an advocate of policy succession will have to adopt a multi-level strategy if he or she is to be successful in attaining what was desired from the proposed change. It may not be sufficient to gain approval from the Federal government (be it either Congress or the

administrative agencies which make the decisions), for fifty state governments may have to be convinced of the efficacy of the proposed change, and several thousands of local governments as well. But the federal characteristic also means that the advocate of policy succession has multiple points at which to initiate the process. The multiple opportunities for change have long been enumerated as one of the advantages of federalism (although usually connected with the possibility of policy innovation), and once adopted by one government or another the policy succession may be more readily 'sold' to other governments.

Also, the relative wealth of countries, or of areas of countries, may affect their willingness to undertake policy successions, as might other socio-economic factors such as the level of education. In general, policymaking systems which are wealthier, better educated, etc. should be more willing to innovate than less socio-economically advantaged systems.

Finally, there may be simple idiosyncracies of political systems and of individual policymakers that will determine the extent and timing of policy succession. Some of these factors may be cultural and historical, and anyone proposing a policy succession to nationalize fully the railroads in the United States, as opposed to the partial nationalization through AMTRAK and ConRail, should expect very little chance of a victory. For a significant period of time, anyone desiring to alter tax policy in the United States had to make proposals which would be acceptable to the (then) Chairman of the House Ways and Means Committee, Wilbur Mills (Manley, 1970). Also, some idiosyncracies of policymaking systems may be institutional. To understand policymaking in the United Kingdom, and to predict success of any particular proposals for policy succession, one would have to comprehend the role of the Treasury in the process (Heclo and Wildavsky, 1974; Wright, 1981). The central position of that institution would definitely shape any proposal for succession.

In short, the advocate of a policy succession must understand the policymaking system within which he or she is functioning. This appears a remarkably simplistic admonition, but it is one which seemingly is forgotten frequently both by advocates of policy change and analysts of public policymaking. A policy simply being 'right' by some set of criteria is not sufficient to ensure that the proposal can be adopted and implemented within the constraints of a particular political system. Additionally, it should be noted that the political systems in question may be defined by time as well as by space, and policies which would be acceptable or unacceptable at any one time may meet with radically different receptions at a later date.

8.2.2.3.2 *Policy-specific features*

A second set of characteristics influencing the ability of an advocate of policy succession to achieve the goal of a policy change concerns the policy itself. Although policymaking and even policy succession are at times discussed as undifferentiated wholes, there are important differences in the policymaking styles of different policymaking networks, and in the constraints on those who would produce a policy succession.

One of the most important of these differences is the types of clients being served by the program. We have been making the point throughout this book that the very existence of clients makes policy succession substantially different from policy initiation. But, a client is not a client is not a client. They vary in their political influence, in their levels of political organization, and in their connection with the program. First, a program serving working-class, or under-class, clients may be expected to be able to impose a change on those clients much more readily than a program serving middle-class clients or businesses. Secondly, groups which are not truly affluent, but which have high levels of organization, can make the life of an advocate of policy succession more difficult than equally or more affluent clients who lack effective organization. The majority of the members of organized veterans groups in the United States are not affluent, but they have tremendous political clout. The example of the veterans organizations also points out that certain classes of clients can be said to have a moral claim on the public sector which may also be an obstacle for an advocate of policy succession. Children and the elderly are the other obvious examples of classes of clients who have such claims on government, and attempts to tamper with their progress will commonly produce skepticism if not overt opposition. Along with the moral claims which groups can make on government, the dependence of a segment of the society on benefits will make succession more or less difficult. The more clients depend upon the program for most or all of their income, especially if they have few options in the private market as would be true of elderly or disabled clients, then the more opposition significant policy successions are likely to encounter if they infringe any aspect of existing entitlements.

A second factor influencing the ability of advocates of policy succession to implement their ideas is the strength of producers in the policy area. Some programs, even those with large numbers of clients, have relatively few producers directly delivering the service or benefit. Social Security in the United States, with 22 million clients, employs only some 15,000 people to write its checks and process appeals. This can be contrasted with education which employs over 6 million people to teach 44 million students. Someone attempting to impose a change upon education would probably encounter more opposition from the producers of the service than would be true of Social Security, although there would be opposition to any policy successions in Social Security from other quarters.

The above discussion highlights another characteristic of producers which may affect their ability to resist a policy succession. Producers of a service to clients will, everything else being equal, be in a more powerful position than will producers who provide primarily cash benefits. Those who directly provide the service are obviously more central to the success or failure of a program than are those who only write checks and wait for the program to have its effects.

It is not just the number of producers and their relationship to clients which are important: producers as well as clients vary in their political organization and clout. Professional and highly skilled producer groups will have substantially more ability to resist efforts at policy succession than will more replaceable workers. Not only is professional training more rare than the ability to hand over a welfare check to a client, it also provides a language, a set of concepts, and a mythology which enable professionals to wield power over others. Thus, to the extent that a program employs large numbers of professionals, it will be more difficult for the advocates of policy succession to effect the change, especially one that in any way affects the power and prestige of the professional group. The professional language and training provide a barrier to the efforts of outsiders to understand and to change the policies in question.

A fourth characteristic of producers which may affect the ability to implement a policy succession is their potential location outside of government. Government buys a number of goods and services from the private sector, and obviously has less control (in a direct sense) over those firms than over organizations within government (Blumenthal, 1979). We would hypothesize that to the extent that government is dependent upon specific private sector firms for the production of a good or service, for example, defense, the ability of an advocate of policy succession to produce a specific desired change would be reduced (see 6.4.3.5). Where there are a number of alternative suppliers there will, of course, be greater flexibility (see 7.2.12.1).

Finally, organizations and programs which are more intimately connected with other organizations and programs will be more difficult to modify than those which are more free-standing (Salamon, 1981). It is difficult to identify any public program which is truly free-standing in a modern, complex government, but some are more so than others. For example, social programs and health programs are very closely interconnected, so that a change in one may involve a reexamination of all others. Likewise, defense and foreign policy are often quite closely interconnected. On the other hand, it might be possible to alter an agricultural crop support program with only minimal repercussions for other programs. Thus, an advocate of policy succession must understand not only the organization but the interorganizational context within which the change is to take place.

If we apply this abstract analysis to specific policy areas, we might argue that health policy might be among the most difficult types of policy to change, whereas a program such as Food Stamps would be among the easiest to change. Health care programs involve a direct service to clients provided by highly professionalized and powerful providers. The clients of many health programs are poor and unorganized but the clients of the largest program in the United States — Medicare — are among the groups who are generally deemed to be worthy of receiving public benefits. Any number of policy successions, unless they undertake to attack the dominance of the medical profession over the delivery of medical services — an action which would be almost unthinkable — would be unlikely to produce any significant changes in the actual delivery of services (see 7.5.3). On the other hand, Food Stamps benefit an unorganized, poor and diffuse clientele. These clients are benefited rather indirectly and the program employs few people and those that are employed are relatively easy to replace and have little specialized knowledge. As indicated by the early days of the Reagan administration, a program such as this is a relatively easy program to modify.

8.2.2.3.3 *Issue-specific differences*
Finally, the characteristics of individual issues will affect the ability of advocates of policy succession to bring about the types of policy changes they desire. Issues and proposals can be grouped by policy

areas, but each will have its own distinctive features that will affect its chances of proceeding through the entire process.

One of the most obvious issue differences is the magnitude of the change proposed. A change involving very few clients, or very few organizational members, is likely to be better received than one which is disruptive to more people. Likewise, a policy succession which involves only relatively minor changes from the existing policy is likely to encounter less opposition than a proposal expressed in terms of major changes in benefits. So, for example, changes in the tax laws eliminating the gasoline tax deduction as a part of President Carter's energy proposal, even though they affected virtually all taxpayers, produced relatively little adverse reaction because the magnitude of the change was small. This can be contrasted with the opposition which may be expected if the proposal of the Congressional Budget Office to reduce or eliminate the tax deduction for home mortgages were to be considered seriously.

Also, the type of policy succession being advocated may be hypothesized to have a definite effect upon the ability to produce a policy succession. In general, linear policy successions will be the easiest to bring about, given that a relatively clear follow-on to the status quo can be identified. Although it may be disruptive to clients and to employees, these groups know they will continue to have an organization and some level of benefits in the future. Of course, with policy consolidation and with policy splitting, it is assumed that there will be programs and organizations after the succession, but these may be expected to be substantially different from those existing previously, and consequently there will be much more uncertainty and anxiety. More complex patterns of policy change, such as partial termination and non-linear succession, may be hypothesized to create the greatest anxiety and resistance. Changes of these types provide little guidance for either clients or the members of the organization as to what the future will hold, and as a consequence are likely to encounter resistance. In part, resistance to programs involving change of the magnitude of the negative income tax, which would have rolled a number of programs into one and then have changed the method of policy delivery entirely, can be explained by this unwillingness 'to boldly go' into the unknown of policy succession.

One very obvious point about the type of policy succession should also be made; successions that involve greater expenditure will rarely be the subject of direct opposition, except from the budget agency. Of course, there may be resistance of a general sort from taxpayers who will have to pay for the proposal, but this type of vague opposition has traditionally been easy to defeat, especially when compared to the organized interests of clients and employees. In other cases a succession that means 'more' may mean more regulation, and in such cases 'clients' and agency employees may be on opposite sides, though where the proposal comes from outside the regulatory agency, agency members may oppose it as disturbing the existing relationship.

The timing of a policy succession is also important. The timing elements are of two types. One is related to the electoral cycle, especially if the advocate of policy succession is an elective politician. At the beginning of the term of office, the 'honeymoon' period, it is easier for a politician to argue that he or she has a mandate for change and to press for the adoption of a policy succession. The success of the Reagan administration in pushing through rather significant policy successions (and terminations) during its first year in office by using this mandate theory is indicative of the ability of timing to influence the effectiveness of policy successions.

A second aspect of importance of timing is in reference to the individual policy itself. In general, it could be hypothesized that if a policy area has undergone a recent policy succession, it would not be ripe for another. There will be a tendency to give the one change a grace period in which to determine what, if anything, has been gained by imposing the first succession. It might be argued that in many areas of social policy, such as Model Cities and the War on Poverty, this grace period was not long enough. The problems being addressed by these programs were of such a magnitude, and had solutions which may be reached only after generations of intervention. Thus, the relatively rapid imposition of one change after another in the programs was perhaps unwarranted simply on the basis of few demonstrable results during the first years (Aaron, 1978).

But there is an important corollary to the general point concerning timing. It should be noted that once a stable coalition in support of an organization or program has been upset by a policy succession, the particular policy area may undergo a series of successions. Once change begins it may be difficult to contain within the boundaries originally intended, and initial attempts at policy succession may be the preface for a termination. The history of the Peace Corps, and its eventual transformation into VISTA (Volunteers in Service to America), although certainly hastened by ideological differences during the Nixon administration, might be seen as an illustration of this corollary. Another means of understanding this corollary is that in the original succession there is likely to be a significant pro-termination lobby which would accept succession only as a poor second choice. In such a situation, there is a good chance that there will be attempts to re-open the discussion and to produce an eventual termination. Also, as different individuals involved in the decision would be likely to have different 'non-bargainable elements' (8.2.2.2), and as some are almost certain not to achieve their ends in the first round of succession, they will be interested in re-opening the discussion of the policy area and producing further successions.

Finally, there are simply idiosyncratic elements in a particular policy which will influence the ability of an advocate of policy succession to produce the desired change. Some events in the relevant environment, for example, the influence of the Three Mile Island accident on enforcement standards of the Nuclear Regulatory Commission, may influence patterns of policy and organization. Or some elements of a policy or organization may be so highly regarded, for example, the FBI within the Department of Justice, that any attempt to tamper with them will almost certainly be unsuccessful. In short, advocates of policy succession must fully understand the particular policy with which they are working in order to be able to anticipate as many of the pitfalls as possible and produce the succession as desired.

8.2.2.4 *Interaction of specific variables in producing successions*
Distinguishing among the various influences which impact an attempt at succession is important for practitioners of government as well as for those interested in the theoretical aspects of policy change. It is important to understand that the various influences described in 8.2.2.3 are (relatively) independent, and may interact either positively or negatively. For example, an attempt to change a program which was delivered as a transfer to a program which is more labor intensive might be well received in a climate of high unemployment and a growing professionalism on the part of the service providers. If all the factors are aligned to favor a policy succession then the probabilities

for pushing through such a change are quite good. But if they are not so favorably aligned, and some factors are favoring a change and others are in opposition, then the advocate of change should be more cautious, or at least prepared for a good fight. The decision on whether to proceed with the attempt at succession would have to be made on the assessment of the analyst and/or advocate of the weightings of the various factors, the necessity of the change, and the gains of delay. Waiting a short time, for example, until after an election, after a predicted economic upswing, or changes in other programs, may make change a much easier undertaking.

8.2.3   *Planning ahead and following through*

> However hard we try to bring in the new it comes into being only in the midst of clumsy deals.
>
> Peter Weiss, *Marat/Sade* (1964), 1.15.

8.2.3.1   *Mapping the bridges in advance*

It has been the thrust of this and preceding chapters that, while the outcome of a particular issue cannot be predicted with guaranteed accuracy, it is possible for analysis to identify possible obstacles and in some cases to produce checklists of factors which will shape the succession (see, for example, 8.2.1.1). The policymaker who likes to live for the moment or campaign for his point of view regardless of the odds will no doubt prefer to tackle these obstacles as they arise. For the policymaker who would prefer to select an option with a good chance of success or would like advance warning of potential obstacles, our (admittedly limited) knowledge of the factors shaping the policy succession process opens the possibility of strategic choice: that is, following analysis at the beginning of the policy process of the implications at all stages of the policy process, the selection both of the preferred option and of the strategy which will best ensure its adoption (subject to compromise on bargainable elements).

Strategic planning in this sense might seem likely both to add to the burdens of already busy decision-makers (even if advisors carry out much of the analysis, the decision-maker still has to consume it) and, if the analysis is to be conducted at the beginning of the policy process, to introduce an additional delay into policy-making. However, planning ahead can also be an aid to easing the burdens of politicians by telling them that some proposed changes which would embroil them in a lot of political conflict and administrative difficulty might not be worth the effort. We would not, of course, suggest that high-risk strategies should never be attempted. A high risk of failure may be accepted for issues of central political importance. But at least advance calculation of such risks provides important information in calculating how to allocate scarce political resources of personal attention and ability to mobilize others.

These concerns might not seem to be proper ones for policy analysis, but we plead guilty of wanting to be relevant to the dirty political world in which policymaking is about winning rather than about being optimal.

In a sense there is nothing new in the type of planning ahead being discussed here, since it is already the best practice among advisors to decision-makers. British civil servants are especially adept at advising ministers about obstacles to their proposals (particularly where they conflict with the 'departmental' view). However, all too often such advice is based on immediate political concerns and on 'folk-knowledge' about how policies work, rather than on an appraisal of the factors which we have argued in this book are crucial in determining both process and outcome in policy succession.

8.2.3.2 *You still need to cross them*
Once a decision has been made about what political resources will be brought to bear at each stage to promote a particular succession proposal, there is still the need to ensure that this will actually be done in the right way, and at the right time. It is all too easy to be deflected from attention to a particular proposal, since it will be a rare politician who has only one issue at a time to cope with. Apart from the normal danger of allowing the daily in-tray to dictate the allocation of political attention, a sudden crisis on another issue may deflect attention from an important though less crisis-ridden stage of the policy succession.

Although many of the potential obstacles to a policy succession proposal can be anticipated in advance, there is always the danger that unforeseen opponents will arise or that obstacles, although anticipated, may be more difficult to surmount. (The converse, that the passage of the proposal may be smoother than anticipated is also possible, particularly if scenarios are deliberately pessimistic.)

Since both these kinds of problems are possible, though their occurrence for any given proposal is unpredictable, it will be desirable to build in to the planning of the succession campaign some slack in terms of timing and allocation of political resources. Flexibility of response is a necessary feature of any form of planning, otherwise the whole plan would collapse with the first unanticipated obstacle. Such flexibility must also include a continuing reappraisal of whether changing circumstances indicate the adoption of an alternative option or even the abandonment of the proposal altogether if it now appears that the increased political resources needed to overcome an obstacle are greater than the benefits to be secured by the proposal would merit. Such flexibility differs from a purely reactive approach to policymaking in that the tactics adopted in the present are constantly related to the future bridges which still have to crossed and particular care is taken not to be locked in to options for the sake of an easy political life now which will cause problems at later stages. The test of a good policy is not just whether people can agree on it (see Lindblom, 1959) but whether it can subsequently be put into practice.

8.2.3.3 *Taking two steps to move one*

Strategic considerations may indicate that a proposed succession should be tackled in two or more separate but related campaigns perhaps separated by time. There are two circumstances where this might be appropriate. In the first case, the total volume of change might be too much for the organizations concerned to cope with in one period; it may be better to ensure that one type of change, which may be a necessary precondition for further movement towards the eventual targets, is successfully secured before tackling the next. For example, the Conservative government in Britain split British Telecommunications from the Post Office in 1981, but did not attempt to force British Telecom to meet external competition until after the split had been accomplished. The other circumstance under which a split campaign may make sense is where the political opposition to each of the stages taken separately is less vociferous than it would be if all the change was attempted at one go. Particularly if the second or subsequent stages are those which are likely to arouse most opposition (either at the legislative or implementation stages) it may make sense to secure the first stage so that if the battle over the second stage is lost there is no need to have to start again from square one.

There is, of course, the danger with this strategy that its impetus might be lost after the first stage. The fact that the first stage has been secured is no guarantee that the subsequent stages will be easy, but there will always be the temptation for busy decision-makers who have achieved this particular milestone to turn their attention to other pressing matters.

8.2.3.4   *Remember you've crossed the bridges*

This leads us on to one of the greatest threats to effective policy succession: the dangers of success. It is all to easy for the by now battle-weary proponent of succession to assume that after a victory he can relax. However, as all the attention paid to implementation over the past decade has shown, legislative victories do not necessarily ensure effective implementation. Continuing intervention by political leaders and top management may be necessary to ensure that a program is actually put into effect and that the necessary clearances from other organizations are obtained (see especially Bardach, 1977).

However, even after implementation appears to have 'taken' it should not be assumed that the program will then continue to operate under automatic pilot. Particularly where the organization concerned does not see its own definition of its goals as being served by the program there is the danger of the various forms of absorption discussed at 6.4.5. Alternatively, program outputs may continue to be generated according to program design, but the outcome may not meet expectations because of changes in the social and economic environment or in the interaction effects with other government programs. Continuing review of the program (especially if its level or form of activity is not fully reflected in annual budget appropriations) will be necessary if an unwanted succession or partial termination is not to occur unnoticed.

Particular care must be taken to ensure that successes remain successes and that the lessons of successful campaigns are fed into the planning of future attempts at succession. It is just as important that the lessons of failures should also be remembered either as a warning of types of succession which should not be attempted or to indicate how obstacles might be overcome the next time. Lack of active (that is, feedback-generating) collective memory of past policy attempts, whether successes or failures, is one of the major pathologies of public policy, and in a time of rapid policy change can even give rise to 'rediscovering the same solutions' (see 8.4.2).

8.3   Future cycle

8.3.1   *Designing on the assumption of policy succession as norm*

To this point, we have been discussing the advocate of policy succession faced with a set of existing policies, and attempting to find ways of changing that constellation of policies. This is all that can be expected given that the existing policies have not been designed for ready change. However, on a practical level, it would be advisable for those who advocate public solutions to the problems faced by society to begin to design their policies with a greater sensitivity to the problems which future generations of policymakers will have when they almost inevitably will attempt to alter the policy. It is only human to want to leave a monument of some sort to one's work, but one generation's monuments may be the next generation's mausoleums. Even policies which are generally regarded as successes may be faced with such rigidities that they inhibit even greater successes. For example, the Social Security program in the United States is widely regarded as a success, but the payroll taxes and the insurance concept, of which Franklin Roosevelt had been so proud, are becoming something of an albatross for the program (Leuchtenberg, 1963, p. 133).

8.3.1.1   *Changing problems*
A first factor influencing the need to design for policy succession is that the problems which the society is encountering will change. The transportation problem in the United States in the 1950s was building enough highways for all the automobiles to be able to drive into the city, for the owners of those automobiles to be able to work, and for them to be able to return home to the suburbs in the evening. The Highway Trust Fund, which earmarked the gasoline tax for the construction of highways, enshrined this definition of the transportation problem. The transportation problem in the 1960s and 1970s increasingly became defined as getting people out of their cars and onto mass transportation. But the trust fund and earmarked tax meant that a large share of the transportation budget was not available to fund subways, busses, or whatever. A policymaker in any one time is rarely so well informed or perceptive as to be able to ensure that the manner in which he or she perceives a problem will be

enduring, and consequently should design in flexibility when devising solutions.

This is by no means a plea for incrementalism, as it may be interpreted to be. Small steps may promote as much inflexibility as major overhauls of a policy area. In fact, rather paradoxically, it could be argued that incremental decision-making tends to build in more inflexibility than does more synoptic decision-making. An incremental solution for an existing policy problem—which may be the policy itself—tends to imply that the basic framework of policy delivery is adequate and only minor adjustments need be made in order to make the program function well (Dror, 1968). The more incremental changes there are the longer there is an apparent acceptance of the underlying paradigm, the more rigidities are likely to be built into the service delivery system, and the less amenable to change clients and organization members will become. On the other hand, a major policy change may be necessary to instill a new paradigmatic structure for the policy and may imply greater flexibility than 'jiggling and poking'.

Rather than being a plea for incrementalism, this is a plea for strategic thought in the design of new policies, or the redesign of existing policies. There is a need to understand the essential elements of the services to be provided, the organizations which will deliver those services, and the clients who will benefit from them. With those elements fully understood, and the need for flexibility also understood, the policymaker has some hope for designing policies which, if not successful, will be amenable to change.

8.3.1.2 *Changes in the prevailing wisdom about solutions*
As well as the nature of the problems changing, the conventional wisdom about how to address the problems also changes. For example, the conventional wisdom about using harsh punishment for prisoners changed in the 1960s to a more lenient and 'rehabilitative' solution to the problem of corrections. In the early 1980s, the accepted solutions are changing back toward having somewhat harsher conditions. Prison programs, and even the physical structure of the prisons themselves, designed under one of these conceptions of the appropriate maner of handling criminals, may be useless under other definitions of the appropriate solution.

These types of sea changes in the conception of the appropriate technology for 'solving' problems have occurred numerous times in education, for example, the 'new math', and in social policy where the technology for producing desired results is less certain. The certainty which surrounded economic policy in the 1950s and 1960s, when it was assumed that the Keynesian system allowed 'fine-tuning' of the economy, has now been shattered by events and the growth of monetarism. Perhaps especially in policy areas such as these care should be exercised when designing a policy to make policy succession an easier goal to attain.

8.3.1.3 *Changes in the resource base*
In addition, the resources available for confronting the problems of society also change. The experience of most Western, industrialized nations following the oil embargo in 1974, and continuing into the 1980s, is that policies built on the premise of affluence have to be reexamined. It is not just the reduction of financial resources which can present problems for government, but the exhaustion of real resources as well. Policies built on the assumption of cheap energy, or cheap natural resources more generally, simply make no sense any more. To some degree, the environmental program in the United States (and elsewhere) was built on the assumption of cheap energy, and as a consequence its advocates have been forced to reexamine many of its premises as energy and other natural resources have become more obviously scarce.

From the strategic perspective, governments may face at least two types of strains on resources which will influence their ability to pursue certain types of policies. One is a strain on governmental resources, without any strain on real economic or natural resources. This is the case of Proposition 13 in California or Proposition $2\frac{1}{2}$ in Massachusetts. At least in the case of California there was continued availability of resources in the economy but the voters acted to deny those resources to government. In the anticipation of situations such as this, policies should be designed so as to be able to transfer clients and functions to the private sector. This might be done through attempts to coordinate public and private programs even during times of affluence and the development of flexible organizational relationships that would facilitate the 'privatization' of certain activities. In this case, the total use of resources might be changed very little; the difference would be in who was spending the resources.

The second and more severe problem arises when there is a reduction, or at least a slowing of growth, of real resources. In this instance, mechanisms may have to be found which use less to perform the relevant activity, as in perhaps switching from the direct delivery of a service to the use of incentives to those who might want to provide it by voluntary means or the use of suasion (see 7.2). There may be a need to design programs in a modular structure, not dissimilar from that implied in zero-base budgeting, in order to be able to deescalate efficiently the level of service delivery. However, the advocate of succession should not assume that those resisting a succession are fools. Those opponents will resist the development of the modular structure, understanding its implications for partial termination and succession. Thus, perhaps the most crucial fight in a succession campaign will be over procedure and organization rather than substance.

8.3.1.4   *Changes in demand*

Finally, demand for certain types of policy outputs may change (see 2.3.4.7, 2.3.5.3). The policy problem may be defined as the same, but the number of citizens demanding the service may decline. A change in demand is especially important when the service in question is relatively capital intensive and a reduction in demand will produce a great deal of excess capacity. Conversely, an increase in demand for a service of this type will require a long time to implement as the capital stock will have to be produced. But even for labor intensive services, there are a large number of individuals who may be trained to deliver a certain type of service but whose jobs may be threatened by a reduction in service, or who must be trained if there is an increase in demand.

If the demand for a service is increased or reduced significantly, there may also be a significant modification not only in the volume, but also in the type of service provided. For example, at a low volume of service, it may be possible to deliver services directly, whereas when volume increases government may choose to change to a transfer program to achieve the same goal. Likewise, if a transfer or incentive program experiences a reduction in demand, there may be pressure to switch to more labor-intensive direct delivery of service. This may be justified in terms of providing superior services to the clients, but in reality it may be a means of protecting the jobs of those already working in the program.

Clearly, if one is planning ahead for succession, it may be easier to design programs such as transfers or incentives that do not employ either large numbers of individuals or large capital plants. By reducing these fixed costs (politically if not legally) any changes in the program can be effectuated much more easily. Of course, some programs must be delivered by public employees directly and still others are better delivered by public employees. But if succession is considered as a primary design element in a program, and if there is known to be fluctuation in demand, it may be better to design programs that do not require large cadres of public employees.

8.3.2 *Designing for future policy successions*

Some definite problems arise when a policy is designed for ease in future successions. Neither workers nor clients are prone to appreciate a program which perceived by those making the policy decisions as only a temporary measure to meet the problem. No matter how loosely the legislation for a program is written, both workers and clients will attempt to solidify their positions and create permanence, or at least the illusion of permanence. Civil servants will seek to gain tenure and will attempt to make some aspects of their program essential for the functioning of other programs. Clients will organize and attempt to develop and entitlement ethos about their program (Bell, 1974). In addition to the understandable attempts of individuals to protect themselves, other problems will arise when legislation and organizations are designed explicitly to make future policy successions easier to implement.

8.3.2.1 *Balancing current-cycle enforcability versus future cycle adaptability*

One of the design problems associated with planning for policy succession is balancing the enforcability of a program during its current cycle against the ability to produce effectively a policy succession in future cycles. The more enforcable a piece of legislation is during the current cycle, the clearer will be the guidelines for action and the greater will be the precision of the training of the employees. The members of the organization implementing the legislation will be trained to carry out their tasks in certain ways, and clients would come to expect certain types of benefits and behaviors from the organization. But the precision that would assist in implementation of one program would also make succession that much more difficult to bring about in the future.

Another manner in which designing programs which balance enforcability and adaptability presents problems is that programs designed for adaptability, which consequently may have less enforcability, may produce the impression that any program in the particular policy area is doomed to be ineffective. Thus, a program balanced too heavily on the side of ease of policy succession may make it too easy for a program or organization to be terminated. While not specifically designed for succession, many of the programs of the War on Poverty did prove difficult to enforce, and this did spread the impression that any programs directed at such sweeping social change would be ineffective. This, in turn, lead to a greater ease in terminating them (Aaron, 1978; Steiner, 1981).

Another interesting aspect of the trade-off between enforcability and policy succession concerns the choice of instruments to implement the policy. As we noted above, policy instruments which involve hiring large numbers of personnel are more difficult to modify later. However, where there is a staff charged with implementing the program it is likely that this method of service delivery would produce greater compliance with the laws than other methods of service delivery. Contracting out a service may be the most flexible means of providing it, although control over the provision is weakened substantially. A contract can be terminated much more readily than can a tenured civil servant, and the provision of the service by a contract agency may make it appear less an entitlement (see 7.2.12.1). But, as noted previously (8.2.2.3.2), although change is possible, the direction of that change is less amenable to control by government than a change within its own programs or organizations.

Not all transfer programs or incentive programs are easy to change, however, as they may involve creating entitlements for the recipients. In addition to building public housing, both the United Kingdom and the United States provide significant housing subsidies to their citizens through the tax system. At least in the United States, it may be easier to change the program of direct delivery of services than to modify the tax incentives.

8.3.2.2 *Can we make organizations responsible for promoting succession of their own programs?*

Organisations are used in the delivery of public policies because of their permanence and predictability. As Biller put it, '. . . organizations have as one of their principal *strengths* the ability to resist change and termination—that is, persist in the face of information that may warrant discontinuity' (1976, p. 137). Thus, any strategy for policy succession must develop some means of coping with the tendencies of organizations to resist changes in their programs and structures. It would appear that if policy succession is to become a less traumatic event for everyone involved, some means of more actively involving the organization in the process must be designed. The perception that the entire cost of any policy succession will be borne within the organization, the general inertia of organizations, and fear that any change may threaten the existence of the organization and the jobs of its members all combine to limit the role of organizations in promoting policy succession. Few organizations have reached Wildavsky's ideal of the organization which:

> would be self-evaluating. It would continuously monitor its own activities so as to determine how well it was meeting its objectives or even whether those objectives should continue to prevail. When evaluations suggested that a change in objectives or programs to achieve them was desirable, these proposals would be taken seriously by top decision-makers who would institute the necessary changes without vested interests in continuing current activities (1979, p. 213).

Much of organizational life in government appears designed to prevent just such patterns of self-evaluation and flexibility from developing. How can the incentive structures of governmental organizations, and the individuals who compose them, be altered to make policy succession a more acceptable alternative to the preservation of the status quo at all costs?

The major disincentive to proposing changes in existing programs is that an individual or a set of clients will lose the property rights they have vested in the existing programs. Some means must be designed either to reduce the property rights, or to make the threats to them less real. Mechanisms such as the Senior Executive Service in the United States, which both limit the connection of the civil servant to the organization and provide incentives for effective performance of all types—including policy succession—may reduce the attachment between the fate of the individual and the fate of the organization.

Rather than being tied to a single agency, members of the Senior Executive Service (SES) are moved around among agencies for shorter periods of service to allow them to use their administrative talents without becoming attached to any particular agency or policy. Their career advancement is determined less by their success in getting a budget accepted than by their ability to administer programs, and consequently they can more readily accept change or termination than can someone who is directly tied to one agency and one agency only (Fesler, 1980, pp. 151–8). In addition to the rather vague incentives of career advancement, the members of the SES have the more immediate incentive of the ability to earn up to $20,000 in bonuses if their work is deemed especially meritorious. These types of incentives can provide the career leadership of an organization with a powerful set of incentives to facilitate change.

The SES plan was designed for the very upper echelons of the civil service, but similar mechanisms for lower tiers of the organization would not be unthinkable. It is those lower tiers who may perceive the greatest threat from any change, lacking the education, fungible skills, and broader outlook usually associated with those at the top of the organization. Of course, in the United Kingdom, the generalist tradition in the upper civil service, although deplored by some, does provide the flexibility for those officials.

Similarly, many public organizations which produce goods and services may be able to use market systems, or modified markets, to provide incentives for adjustment to changing conditions. This might involve financial incentives for individuals and for the organization as a whole. For example, many organizations collect fees for their services but have little or no incentive either to be effective in collecting those fees or to cut their own costs because they cannot retain any 'profits'.

Likewise, they have no incentive to innovate and improve their services because they are evaluated to a great extent by their case load and the size of their budget rather than by their economic efficiency. Trying to make essentially non-profit organizations at least profit conscious in the public sector will present a number of problems. These problems will be both political and administrative, but there does appear to be promise in using the market as a means of involving the organization in policy succession and removing the negative connotations associated with any form of policy change.

8.3.2.3 *Internal motivations for policy succession*
Another approach to reducing resistance to policy succession is to develop stronger internal motivations for the succession. This will, of

course, involve overcoming the apprehensions which change, and especially change affecting the individual's livelihood, is likely to engender. One means of overcoming the resistance to change is through training and socialization. But to use training to promote policy succession will require altering the manner in which training in organizations has traditionally been conducted. We noted previously that most training in organizations tends to teach and preach that there is one proper way of achieving the goals of the organization. It may be possible to teach instead, if not cynicism, at least some skepticism about the manner in which the organization functions. This is, of course, more easily done in the upper echelons of the organization where, through better education and greater security, greater detachment and skepticism may already exist. Also, we would expect younger employees, who have not yet invested many years of their lives in the organization and who have some of the impetuosity and flexibility of youth, to be more willing to question the traditional approach of the organization to its problems and to accept policy successions.

A number of approaches have been advanced for promoting policy succession and organizational change. For example, there is the pioneering work of Lippit and his colleagues in using consultants as 'change agents' who would go into an organization, to aid the organization in identifying its own need for change and to assist in developing the mechanisms for change (Lippit, Watson, and West-ley, 1958). Also, beginning in the 1940s, the National Training Laboratories have experimented with group-oriented approaches to organizational change, largely referred to as 'sensitivity training' (Schein and Bennis, 1965). This method concentrates its attention upon the internal dynamics of small groups, but then helps the members extrapolate from that experience to the larger organizational setting. A more extensive approach to these change problems within organizations goes under the label of 'organizational development', or 'OD' (Eddy, 1970). This approach 'goes beyond traditional training and consulting projects and attempts to help an organization establish and conduct a long-range process of self-evaluation and constructive change and renewal' (Eddy, 1981, p. 184). As this array of methods exists for changing the internal dynamics of an organization, it would appear logical that they could be applied to the problem of changing the policies which the organization administers. Changing the goals of the organization is a fundamental form of organizational change, and if the above methods (among others) have proven useful in the pursuit of changing behavior within an organization with (relatively) stable goals, they may be applicable to the more difficult problem of goal change. Of course, to the critics of these approaches, they are more theology than scientific methods of approaching the problems of organizational change, but they do offer some promise if used appropriately and with awareness of their limitations.

The above discussion points out a fundamental problem in the process of policy succession. The problems of designing a 'better' policy are formidable, but the more important problems may be those 'non-scientific' problems of securing the adoption of the changes by individuals and by organizations. We have some mechanisms, albeit rough, for evaluating the value of a proposed policy, but we have no known methodologies for evaluating the probability of its being accepted and successfully implemented.

These strategies appear most appropriate in organizations which have external reference groups that can inform them that their performance is no longer adequate. Professional organizations may serve this purpose for some organizations, while clients or suppliers may do so for others. Also, and relatedly, organizations in which the relevant technology or ideas of best practice change rapidly may have to undergo goal examination and planned change more often than others. Finally, more integrated and homogeneous organizations can undertake this type of change more readily than can more conflictual organizations.

8.3.2.4 *Designing policy succession triggers*

One feature of the design of policy succession and of organizational changes is the design of policy succession triggers when constructing the initial legislation, or when making another succession. Such triggers have already been designed for policy termination through devices such as 'sunset' laws, and there is no reason that analogous devices could not be developed for policy succession. These might be termed 'eclipse' laws, as rather than attempting to produce the end of a policy or organization, they are designed only to see that it is transformed into another if not effective.

In the design of eclipse laws, if there were to be such a thing, care must be taken to remove as much as possible elements threatening to the organization which might prevent the law from being implemented. As it is now, because of the threatening elements of sunset legislation, its provisions are rarely applied vigorously. On the other hand, if there is to be no real threat to the program under review, then there may be little reason to follow through with the effort required in a 'sunset' review. The design of eclipse laws, therefore, must be intended to place some stress on the organization, perhaps through phased reductions in budgets if changes are not made, rather than through threatening the existence of the organization.

The basic idea of sunset laws has been a periodic review of organizations and their programs, but it may be worthwhile to build in less periodic triggers as well. Several factors might be considered as means of selecting organizations for review. One is simply size: if we are concerned about making changes which may improve the efficiency of government or reduce its costs, then one obvious criterion for choice is the size of the budget and the staff. Secondly, not only the absolute size of the budget, but change in the size of the budget is an obvious criterion. If a budget is increasing rapidly, this may be a sign of success of the program or it may be an indication of a poorly designed program taking on too many clients or spending money ineffectively. Also, it is important to note not only changes in the budget which implements a policy, but also the changing environment within which the policy functions. Although the social indicators movement has not developed to the level once anticipated (Olson, 1963; Gross, 1966), changes in major indicators of demand for services can be used as triggers for reviews of programs. For example, rapid changes in the birth rate after World War II and the Korean conflict could have been used as a trigger to review existing programs of elementary and secondary school construction, teacher training, and even post-secondary education.

Finally, it is important to devise more systematic methods of feedback between local authorities and central governments. In both the United States and the United Kingdom a great deal of central government policy is implemented through local authorities, but the evaluation and feedback loops are sometimes not developed sufficiently to permit criticism and suggestions for policy successions to flow freely. The major monitoring of grants tends to be financial, and the few policy-based indicators of the effectiveness of the programs tend to be crude. There is a consequent loss of a great deal of useful information which might guide the improvement of the policies being administered. For some policy areas, the only monitors are the auditors (Stoner, 1978), who are arguably not qualified to make policy decisions.

Organizationally, the implementation of eclipse laws may already exist through the budgetary process and through legislative oversight committees (at least in the United States). The task then may be strengthening those organizations so that they can consider the alternatives to existing policies more systematically. The strengthening of the policy analytic capabilities of the Congress should help in such transitions. The existence of greatly expanded Congressional staffs and the development of the Congressional Budget Office provide Congressmen the means to make more extensive surveys of policy alternatives (Fox and Hammond, 1977; Ogul, 1981). The General Accounting Office, which reports to the Congress, has also extended its role from a strictly financial control organization to a body advising on the possible alternatives to existing policies (Mosher, 1980). In the United Kingdom, the House of Commons has a very long way to go to develop any systematic capability for developing policy alternatives, although the new Select Committees may offer some hope of such developments.

Although eclipse laws are not so dramatic in their potential effects as sunset laws, some of the problems encountered with those laws should also be expected. One is the possibility of overloading the decision-making bodies so that the proposed changes may not be able to be reviewed adequately (Brewer, 1978). Further, if termination or succession is to be a major consideration of agencies, these become the major agenda items of the organization and it cannot fulfil its real goals (de Leon, 1978). Change is important, but excessive emphasis on change may make it, or termination, appear inevitable.

8.3.2.5 *Beware of big solutions*

Finally, when designing for policy succession, it would be well to avoid the 'big solution' to the problem. The danger is that when an all-out effort is made to solve a problem, the sunk costs may become so immense that subsequent policy successions become impossible. The Vietnam war is perhaps the most significant example of the tendency of governments to continue to waste more money and lives in attempting to bring a big solution to fruition. But there are any number of other examples. The sunk costs involved in a big solution are both economic and personal. After millions of dollars or pounds have been spent on a project and little has resulted, it is only human to think that if only a little bit more is spent the whole problem will be solved (see 7.4.2). Likewise, individuals who have invested a substantial portion of their working lives in attempting to solve a problem with one program will be reluctant to admit failure and to go on to the next solution. The trick, therefore, is to design experimentally-oriented solutions to problems where appropriate, and to attempt to phase in the solution to the problem.

The concern for the danger of 'big' solutions should not be interpreted as a plea for incrementalism. One can encounter real difficulties of scale when attempting to avoid the big solution. It may be true, in fact, that solutions below a certain size relative to the magnitude of the problem will never be successful. The size factor here may be relative to the cost or extensiveness of the problem, or it may be geographic. An attempt to solve a problem when the source of the problem is a least partially mobile can only work if there is a nationwide program. Attempts by local governments to control pollution, for example, can be predicted to have as a major effect driving industry out of the locality. Likewise, attempts to attack major social problems such as poverty in a piecemeal fashion may be expected to produce little result.

8.3.3 *Changing the climate of policymaking*

Now understanding some of the goals of designing institutions and policies for their eventual succession, and understanding some of the difficulties in so doing, we should examine the means of changing the conditions under which policies are made. The underlying concept in all the mechanisms discussed below is to build as much flexibility into policies and organizations as is possible. We have already noted that flexibility is desirable but that too much flexibility may endanger the ability of existing policies to function, and may make succession inevitable rather than the product of a conscious choice. With those caveats in mind, we should examine some of the means of producing change in policy.

8.3.3.1 *Changing perceptions*
One of the barriers which must be overcome if policy succession is to be a more acceptable outcome for the policy process is largely psychological. Both employees and clients have come to regard any

public program as virtually permanent. Consequently, any attempt to alter or terminate an existing policy in favor of an alternative will be greeted with apprehension and/or hostility. There is a need, therefore, to teach both sets of people that change is a natural component of the policy life-cycle, and further that many changes may be positive. Change through policy succession may make the work of the employees easier or more effective, and may improve the quality of services delivered to clients. Of course, it will be difficult to convince members of both groups of the efficacy of changes being proposed.

One means of changing perceptions is to be completely honest with those whom the change may affect. There has been a tendency in government to attempt to restrict information and to 'doctor' the news in order to prevent adverse reactions. This has by now become so common that few official pronouncements of good news are likely to be accepted at face value. Being truthful has obvious moral benefits (Bok, 1979), but may have the effect of coopting those whom organizational leaders wish to influence. By telling clients or employees the truth, and asking them how to respond to the change, the leadership of the organization can effectively involve them in change.

Additionally, the leadership of an organization may want to employ the techniques of organization development described earlier when attempting to change perceptions (8.3.2.3). This will be more effective in dealing with the difficulties presented by employees than those presented by clients, but should be useful in involving the member of the organization in the change. Again, this may be cooptive but should aid in the transition from one policy to another.

There may also need to be some change in the macro-climate of policymaking. The leadership of an organization may have as much difficulty in adjusting to change as do the members of the organization or its clients. Any change in a program, especially one initiated from outside, may be perceived as a failure of the leaders of the organization. To save face, the leadership may resist change rather than cooperating with the changes and attempting to make them more effective. In the world of the public bureaucracy bigger is generally better than smaller, and stability is generally better than change. Until some of those perceptions can be altered it may be difficult to obtain the type of leadership for policy succession which will be required.

8.3.3.2 *Changing incentives*

But there are more than psychological barriers to policy succession that may need to be overcome. As most political systems function, there are few incentives for an organization to engage in policy succession, especially if it may result in less money or fewer staff. Any money which an agency is able to save in a given year is not retained by the agency but reverts to the general fund. If agencies were allowed to retain at least a proportion of the money saved from terminating a policy or program, or even carry it over to the following financial year, they would have some positive incentive to cancel or replace questionable programs. This might reduce the cost savings from such policy successions, but would certainly ease the transition from one policy to another.

More generally, arrangements could be made to ease adverse transitional or distributional impacts of termination among staff, clients, and the localities of any facilities. Such arrangements might include redundancy payments or guaranteed redeployment for employees, alternative utilization of facilities so that closure would not have an adverse economic impact on a locality, or assistance to localities where facilities are being phased out. Again, such arrangements would reduce the financial benefits of termination or succession, but would have definite policy benefits. They would at least make the incentives offered to a policymaker neutral when considering whether to engage in a policy succession, so that the case may be able to be decided on the merits of the issues rather than the difficulties which a succession might present for organization members and clients. Even more positive incentives, such as those offered by the Senior Executive Service (see 8.3.2.2), may change the balance of incentives in favor of change, at least for senior administrators.

8.3.3.3 *Changing the nature of institutions*

The manner in which organizations in the public sector are designed can also facilitate policy succession. There is a tendency to assign individuals to one post in an organization, to train them for that post only, and to maintain a relatively rigid structure within the organization. Organizations should be designed, however, with the possibility of succession in mind. Consideration might be given to a greater use of internal matrix designs for organizations. This can ensure that members have continuing positions in the organization but have the

flexibility to establish (and terminate) project teams or task forces
(Davis and Lawrence, 1977).

Although such an internal organizational form may be desirable
from the perspective of policy succession, it is not clear how many
policy problems could be tackled by such means, nor how the
problems it might have for accountability might be overcome. The
matrix form of organization might be quite appropriate for innovative or project-based policymaking (Peters, 1982), but not for more
routine policies serving large numbers of clients. But paradoxically it
is just the latter type of policy which may be most in need of policy
succession. Further it is only human to advocate a flexible matrix
organizational format for everyone else's policy areas, but to want a
more institutionalized and permanent organizational structure for
your own pet policy.

An alternative to the matrix form of organization is to develop a
staff of 'salvage specialists' who are trained in reallocating
resources freed by policy successions or terminations to other
positions where they can do the most good (Biller, 1976, pp. 146–7).
This may alleviate some staff reluctance and uncertainty engendered
by the succession process and can help to overcome internal
resistance. As noted above with incentives, if the organization can be
made to believe that it will not of necessity lose everything as the
result of a succession, its members will be much more likely to accept
the change.

8.4   Problem-solving or problem-causing?

8.4.1   *A cycle of solutions becoming problems*

> This planet has—or rather had—a problem, which was this:
> most of the people living on it were unhappy for pretty much
> of the time. Many solutions were suggested for this problem,
> but most of these were largely concerned with the movements
> of small green pieces of paper, which is odd because on the
> whole it wasn't the small green pieces of paper that were
> unhappy.
>
> And so the problem remained; lots of people were mean,
> and most of them were miserable, even the ones with digital
> watches.

Douglas Adams, *The Hitchhiker's Guide to the Galaxy* (1979)

One of the most depressing aspects of public policy is the way in which solutions to problems frequently cause problems themselves. There are a number of ways in which this can arise. The first is issue displacement, by which the treatment of the problem is itself seen as a greater problem by at least some of those affected. The classic example of issue displacement is the attempt to secure desegregation of schooling in the United States by transporting children to more distant schools, a solution which became the emotive issue of 'bussing'. Attempts to improve dental standards by fluoridation of water supplies in Britain have been vigorously resisted by those who reject the health arguments or are opposed to the principle of government imposition of mass medication. Growing resource-cost implications also fit loosely into this category as with the seemingly inexorably rising cost of the Common Agricultural Policy in the European Communities.

In other cases, the problems arise from perverse effects of solutions, all too many of which were introduced on a mass scale before their disadvantages were apparent and which, for reasons we have discussed at length in this book, are often difficult to reverse because of entrenched interests or 'stock' effects. Attempts to solve the problems of poor housing led to the construction of tower blocks in both Britain and the United States which have become so uninhabitable that they have had to be blown up. Peripheral housing estates in Britain with poor facilities have become seedbeds of vandalism, at the same time imposing extra transport costs on their inhabitants and leaving behind in the remainder of the area from which they have been decanted a population which is typically less able to fend for itself. Regulations designed to protect the consumer may end up depriving the consumer of the benefits of competition. Regulation of energy prices in the United States has led to occasional shortages, gross waste of energy resources and a prolongation of the inevitable adjustment to higher prices. The setting of minimum wages, designed to help avoid exploitation, may lead to greater young unemployment, particularly among ethnic minorities. The list is depressingly endless. Most of these solution-caused problems were unforeseen, though in principle foreseeable. We should be able to anticipate such problems to a greater extent in future, both because of the lessons we can learn from those past (and in some cases continuing) mistakes and because there is now a healthy skepticism about the avilability of problem-free solutions.

The final category of solution-caused problems is more difficult to diagnose, anticipate or cure, but arguably is the most significant to the increasingly program-crowded environment of policy succession. These are problems which arise not from the effect of any one program in isolation but from the interaction of a number of fragmented solutions. Although often not recognized as such a problem, the pattern of housing subsidies in Britain and the United States (both direct and through tax expenditures) has uneven but generally perverse income distribution implications. The interaction of income tax and social security payroll contributions with a wide range of income-related benefits leads to the phenomenon of the poverty trap, by which extra gross earnings may produce little or no net increase, or even a reduction, in income. Such interaction-caused problems are particularly difficult to treat because tackling individual programs may have no effect, be quickly eroded or even produce perverse results because of the complicated nature of the interaction effects as they impact on individuals.

In the face of such problems two reactions, both equally wrong, are possible: resigned pessimism and 'gung-ho' policy succession campaigns. Given the number and scale of solution-caused problems, a certain pessimism about the extent to which alternative policies can both tackle the original problem and avoid the pathological effects of the solution is in order. We would go so far as to endorse the slogan 'There are no problem free solutions'. However, the ubiquity of problems does not mean that problems are uniformly distributed across solutions. Analysis can help to identify potential replacement programs which will either better tackle the original problem or avoid the unwanted side-effects, even given the costs associated with pushing through a policy succession.

But the existence of solution-caused problems does not of itself justify a 'policy-succession or bust' attitude. In some cases (but not many) the particular mix of solutions and associated problems resulting from an existing program may be the best that can be hoped for. There is also the danger that a policy succession designed to remove the solution-caused problem may overlook the very problem that the original solution was designed to cure; that initial problem may by now have disappeared (perhaps as a result of treatment by the 'unsuccessful' program), but all too often at least some aspects of the initial problem will remain. There is a need to avoid badly thought-out policy successions: just because the proposed replacement policy will avoid the problems of the initial policy does not mean that it will either be better at tackling the original problem or may not have solution-related problems of its own. Such a badly prepared succession may trigger off a series of subsequent successions as new dissatisfactions with each program emerge. Dissatisfaction with the adverse effects of a program may trigger off a new succession before the benefits of the program have been given a chance to take hold.

8.4.2 *Rediscovering the same solution*

> As a dog returneth to his vomit, so does a fool return to his folly.
>
> *Proverbs,* 26 : 11

It may seem fanciful to suggest that in such circumstances there is a danger that a sequence of problem-causing successions may eventually lead to the rediscovery of the original 'solution'—perhaps without it being realized that this had already been tried before and had been judged to have failed. However, we do not need to rely on speculation about how such problems might arise in the future. Past experience, alas, already provides us with lessons (or rather illustrations, since they only become lessons if we learn from them).

One example is from a United States foreign aid program. This is not a worst case example, since the authors (Paddock and Paddock, 1979) had asked key officials in what by consensus was considered to be the most promising region of the world for optimistic lessons for development assistance. One of the authors was particularly pleased to be told that he should visit an experimental station at Los Brilliantes in Guatemala, since in 1956 he had been involved in selecting Los Brilliantes as a site for a substation to augment work at Chocola, which was an agricultural experimental station designed to become a major agricultural center concentrating on the problems of crops like coffee and also a training center for farmers and agricultural extension agents. Paddock was told that Los Brilliantes was engaged in promoting the introduction of rubber and citrus as new crops to diversify away from coffee. However, when he visited Los Brilliantes the place seemed dead and he was told that the Guatemalan farmers were interested in planting rubber only as long as AID (Agency for International Development) provided soft loans. On driving the short distance to Chocola, Paddock found it nearly abandoned, with only a single staff member with limited training. There had been no cooperation for years between Chocola and Los Brilliantes because of jurisdictional problems between AID and the Guatemalan Ministry of Agriculture (which had taken over responsibility for Chocola from AID's predecessor).

> Chocola is an illustration of one tragic aspect of our development work: *AID has no memory.*
>
> AID programs are constantly scrapped, abandoned, or started anew, or forgotten. Budgets are cut and then, as an alibi, Washington primly says that it is time for the local government to 'take over'. The local government, however, usually has neither the money nor the talent (nor, sometimes the interest) to take over. Thus another orphan program joins the graveyard.
>
> New foreign aid directors arrive in the capital, sweep the decks clean, and begin anew. Back home a President is elected and his new foreign aid administrator also sweeps clean. No one takes the time to learn. What preceded? Did it fail? Did it succeed? Why?
>
> A long-time AID friend says, 'Every morning we wake up and laboriously reinvent the wheel' (Paddock and Paddock, 1979, p. 31).

However, before academics start to smirk at this exhibition of bureaucratic pathology, they should know that the lesson is not yet ended. During the course of his research Paddock discovered that Iowa State University had been commissioned to make an analysis of the role of agriculture in the development of Guatemalan economy. Paddock knew that Iowa State had actually been involved in running a research center in Guatemala from 1945 to 1955, but when he wrote to the authors of the report, published in 1969, he discovered that they had not consulted any of the reports published during the course of that earlier program, even though that overlapped with the period with which the report was concerned. 'Thus, like AID, Iowa State, too, has no memory' (Paddock and Paddock, 1979, p. 35). The Guatemalan government accepted one of the recommendations of the 1969 Iowa State University report, the idea of placing more emphasis on basic grain cereals, particularly corn; this resulted in a multi-million dollar US loan to Guatemala. Meanwhile, for the past ten years the corn seed stock from the old Iowa State research center had been sitting in a storeroom since AID's predecessor had stopped funding the program.

We pointed above (8.2.3.4) to the particular danger of reinventing the same (failed) solution when there is a rapid sequence of policy successions. As we saw in Chapter 4, war seems to lead to an increase in such successions. While we earnestly hope that the specifically wartime lessons of the following example will not be required in practice, it is worth considering the experience of departmental responsibility for shipbuilding in Britain in the two World Wars (see Hogwood, 1979a, pp. 241–2). Before 1916 shipbuilding had not been under the wing of any government department and during World War I was greatly penalized as a result of the danger of requisitioning of ships and shortage of labor and materials (Chester and Willson, 1968, p. 62). In December 1916, the Ministry of Shipping was established and this was given responsibility for supervising shipbuilding. A program for constructing standard ships was introduced, but responsibility for shipbuilding did not remain with the Ministry of Shipping for long, since following considerable losses of ships during the early months of 1917 a great increase in the rate of construction was necessary. It was considered desirable that a single department should be responsible for both naval and civil shipbuilding, and this was achieved by transferring responsibility for the building and repair of merchant ships to the Admiralty in May.

A few weeks after the outbreak of World War II a new Ministry of Shipping was established (the old one having been disbanded in 1912). This took over all the shipping work of the Board of Trade and was also made responsible for merchant shipbuilding. 'This latter arrangement, however, worked no better than it had in the early months of 1917', and in order once again to place all shipbuilding under one control responsibility for merchant shipbuilding and repairs passed to the Admiralty in February 1940 (Chester and Willson, 1968, p. 95).

These examples point to the need to ensure collective memory among policymakers about past programs—what has actually been done, whether it seemed to work, and why the program or project was discontinued. The storage of information is not enough—its retrieval and utilization is important. This can be a particular problem if there has been a sequence of rapid organizational successions. There is a general problem of time: it would take longer than most civil servants are in any one post to read up all the details of preceding programs, and in the meantime current policymaking must proceed. Encapsulated summaries of program histories as described in the appendix to Chapter 2 would be one way of providing a very highly compressed guide to specific past changes which might be worth further exploration. But the greatest aid to avoiding coming full circle would be for decision-makers not to assume that they are the first to propose a particular type of program; others may have proposed such a program in the past and put it into effect, and the residues of their program may still be in place as a forgotten monument to their endeavor.

8.4.3   *No longer possible 'to boldly go'*

> Space—the final frontier. These are the voyages of the starship *Enterprise*, its five-year mission to explore strange new worlds, to seek out new life and new civilizations, to boldly go where no man has gone before.
>
> Introduction to *Star Trek*, TV series

Many policy changes in the past have been concerned with launching government into tackling new problems and involving itself in new activities. The launching of many of the social programs in the United States in the 1960s had more in common than a coincidence in time with the launching of men into space, to walk on the moon where no man had walked before (Nelson, 1978). These programs, such as Model Cities, the Jobs Corps, or Head Start, were based on some previous models but represented bold initiatives to fight a war on the enemy of poverty. But most policymaking in the future will not be able 'to boldly go' at all, because the policy space into which it would venture is already occupied by functioning programs and the debris of unsuccessful programs. Policymaking in the future will be increasingly concerned with accommodating to the functioning programs and avoiding the debris of the past programs (as well as their shortcomings) rather than about launching completely new adventures in policy. In this book we have been offering advice on how to engage in this increasingly important form of policymaking: policy succession. However, we must be careful lest this 'wisdom' become simply another set of impediments which real-world decision-makers must overcome on their way to effective policy decisions.

8.4.4   *Skepticism, realism, hope and determination*

Determined, dared and done.

Christopher Smart, *Song of David*, 1763

All the analysis we have conducted suggests that policy succession is and will continue to be a difficult and uncertain enterprise, with the visible payoff frequently seeming hardly worth the effort. The opportunity to make the task of achieving future policy successions easier by designing current policy proposals on the assumption of future succession may not be seen as an opportunity but an additional burden to a policymaker concentrating on the difficult enough task of getting the current change through.

None of the techniques we have looked at provides solutions to these problems; at best they provide aids in some circumstances. Matrix organizations may or may not become more common relative to traditional organizational forms, but they offer relatively little help as a means of removing the obstructions to change in the public sector. Termination and succession triggers built in to legislation are no more than that—triggers, not automatic guided missile systems. For triggers to contribute to effective change, the gun has to be picked up and aimed at one of a number of often blurred and moving targets by a political gunfighter with the necessary speed and skill. In the combination of strategy and skills required, policy succession is like a cross between three-dimensional chess and 'Space Invaders'.

Policy analysis cannot cure policy problems: only politicians can. We may blame politics for many of the problems of public policy, but improvements in public policy can only come about by taking into account the features of the policy process necessary to carry them through. Suggestions about the design of policies can help to restructure the political process, but ultimately the best guarantees of successful policy succession are politicians with determination and the willingness to use analysis both as political ammunition and to improve policy design.

REFERENCES

Aaron, H. (1978) *Politics and the Professors.* Washington, DC: The Brookings Institution.

Aaron, H. (1979) 'The domestic budget', in Pechman, J.A. (ed.), *Setting National Priorities: The 1980 Budget,* Washington, DC: The Brookings Institution, 99–159.

Aberbach, J., Putman, R. and Rockman, B.A. (1981) *Politicians and Bureaucrats.* Cambridge, Mass.: Harvard University Press.

Adams, G. (1981) *The Politics of Defense Contracting: The Iron Triangle.* New Brunswick, NJ: Transaction Books.

Advisory Commission on Intergovernmental Relations (1979) *Citizens Participation in the American Federal System,* A-73. Washington, DC: GPO.

Advisory Commission on Intergovernmental Relations (1980) *The Federal Role in the Federal System: The Dynamics of Growth: A Crisis of Confidence and Competence,* A-77. Washington, DC: ACIR.

Aharoni, Y. (1981) *The No-Risk Society.* Chatham, NJ: Chatham House.

Alford, R. (1977) *Health Care Politics.* Chicago: University of Chicago Press.

Allison, G. (1971) *Essence of Decision.* Boston: Little, Brown.

Altmeyer, A.J. (1968) *The Formative Years of Social Security.* Madison, Wisc.: University of Wisconsin Press.

Arnold, R.D. (1979) *Congress and the Bureaucracy: A Theory of Influence.* New Haven: Yale University Press.

Ashford, D.E. (1981) *Policy and Politics in Britain: The Limits of Consensus.* Oxford: Basil Blackwell.

Baehr, P.R. and Wittrock, B. (1981) *Policy Analysis and Policy Innovation.* Beverly Hills, Calif.: Sage.

Bardach, E. (1976) 'Policy termination as a political process', *Policy Sciences,* 7, 123–31.

Bardach, E. (1977) *The Implementation Game.* Cambridge, Mass.: MIT Press.

Bardach, E. (1980) 'Implementation studies and the study of implements'. Paper delivered at the 1980 Annual Meeting of the

American Political Science Association, Washington, DC, 28–31 August 1980.

Barker, A. (ed.) (1982) *Quangos in Britain*. London: Macmillan.

Barton, A.H. (1979) 'A diagnosis of bureaucratic maladies', *American Behavioural Scientist*, 22, 483–92.

Behn, R.D. (1978) 'How to terminate a public policy: A dozen hints for the would-be terminator', *Policy Analysis*, 4, 393–413.

Bell, D. (1974) 'The Public Household—on "Fiscal Sociology" and the Liberal Society', *The Public Interest*, 37 (Fall), 3–52.

Berke, J.S. and Kirst, M.W. (1972) 'Intergovernmental relations: Conclusions and recommendations', In Berke, J.S. and Kirst, M.W. (eds.), *Federal Aid to Education*, Lexington, Mass: Lexington Books, 386–96.

Biller, R.P. (1976) 'On tolerating policy and organizational termination: Some design considerations', *Policy Sciences*, 7, 133–49.

Blumenthal, B. (1979) 'How many people really work for the Feds?', *National Journal*, 5 May, 730–3.

Bok, S. (1979) *Lying: Moral Choice in Public and Private Life*. New York: Vintage.

Bothun, D. and Comer, J.C. (1979) 'The politics of termination: Concepts and process', *Policy Studies Journal*, 7, 540–53.

Braybrooke, D. and Lindblom, C.E. (1963) *A Strategy of Decision*. New York: Free Press.

Brewer, G.D. (1978) 'Termination: Hard choices, harder questions', *Public Administration Review*, 38, 338–44.

Brittan, S. (1970) *Steering the Economy: The Role of the Treasury*. Harmondsworth, Middlesex: Penguin.

Brittan, S. (1975) *Participation without Politics*. Hobart Paper 62. London: Institute of Economic Affairs.

Bullock, C.S. and Rodgers, H.R. (1976) *Coercion to Compliance*. Lexington, Mass.: Lexington Books.

Bunce, V. (1981) 'The life cycles of presidencies'. Paper presented at Annual Meeting of Midwest Political Science Association, Cincinnati, Ohio.

Butts, R.F. (1979) 'Educational vouchers: The private pursuit of the public purse', *Phi Delta Kappan*, September, 7–9.

Buxton, M.J. and Klein, R.E. (1978) *Allocating Health Resources*. Research Paper No. 3, Royal Commission on the National Health Service. London: HMSO.

Calabresi, G. and Bobbitt, P. (1978) *Tragic Choices*. New York: Norton.

Cameron, J.M. (1978) 'Ideology and policy termination: Restructuring California's mental health system', in May, J.V. and Wildavsky, A. (eds.), *The Policy Cycle*, Beverly Hills, California: Sage, 301–28.

Caves, D., Christensen, L. and Swanson, J. (1981) 'The high cost of regulating US Railroads', *Regulation*, 5(1), 41–6.

Chester, D.N. and Willson, F.M.G. (1968) *The Organisation of British Central Government*, 2nd ed. London: Allen and Unwin.

Clarke, Sir Richard (1975). 'The machinery of government', in Thornhill, W. (ed.), *The Modernisation of Government*, London: Pitman, 63–94.

Cmnd 6393 (1976) *Public Expenditure to 1979–80*. London: HMSO.

Cmnd 7841 (1980) *The Government's Expenditure Plans 1980–81 to 1983–84*. London: HMSO.

Cobb, R.W. and Elder, C.D. (1972) *Participation in American Politics: The Dynamics of Agenda-Building*. Baltimore: Johns Hopkins.

CPRS (1977) Central Policy Review Staff, *Population and the Social Services*. London: HMSO.

Crossman, R.M. (1978) 'Voting behaviors of HSA interest groups: A case study', *American Journal of Public Health*, 68, 1191–4.

Crozier, M. (1964) *The Bureaucratic Phenomenon*. Chicago: University of Chicago Press.

Cullingworth, J.B. (1979) *Essays on Housing Policy: The British Scene*. London: Allen and Unwin.

Dalton, G.W. (1970) 'Patterns of Organizational Change', in Dalton, G.W. *et al.*, (eds.), *Organization Change and Development*, Homewood, Ill.: Irwin.

Davis, H., and Salesin, S. (1979) 'Evaluation and change', in Datta, L.E. and Perloff, R. (eds.), *Improving Evaluations*, Beverly Hills, California: Sage, 257–71.

Davis, K.C. (1979) *Discretionary Justice*. Urbana, Ill: University of Illinois Press.

Davis, S. and Lawrence, P. (1977) *Matrix Management*. Reading, Mass.: Addison-Wesley.

de Leon, P. (1978) 'A theory of policy termination', in May, J.V. and Wildavsky, A. (eds.), *The Policy Cycle*, Beverly Hills, California: Sage, 279–300.

Derthick, M. (1975) *Uncontrollable Spending for Social Service Grants*. Washington, DC: The Brookings Institution.

Dexter, L.A. (1981) 'Undesigned consequences of purposive legis-

270   *Policy Dynamics*

lative action: Alternatives to implementation', *Journal of Public Policy*, 1, 413–31.

Downs, A. (1967) *Inside Bureaucracy*. Boston: Little, Brown.

Downs, A. (1972) 'Up and down with ecology—the issue attention cycle', *The Public Interest*, 28, 38–50.

Downs, A. (1980) 'Too much capital for housing?' *The Brookings Bulletin*, 17(1), 1–5.

Dror, Y. (1968) *Public Policymaking Reexamined*. New York: Intext Educational Publishers.

Dunsire, A. (1978) *Control in a Bureaucracy*. Oxford: Martin Robertson.

Durham, A.B. and Marmor, T.R. (1978) 'Federal policy and health: Recent trends and differing perspectives', in Lowi, T.J. and Stone, A. (eds.), *Nationalizing Government*, Beverly Hills, California: Sage, 285–9.

Dye, T.R. (1966). *Politics, Economics and the Public*. Chicago: Rand McNally.

Easton, D. (1979) *A Systems Analysis of Political Life*, revised edition. Chicago: University of Chicago Press.

Eddy, W.B. (1970) 'Beyond behavioralism?: Organization development in public management', *Public Personnel Review*, 22, 169–74.

Eddy, W.B. (1981) *Public Organization: Behavior and Development*. Cambridge, Mass.: Winthrop.

Edwards, G. (1980) *Implementing Public Policy*. Washington, DC: Congressional Quarterly Books.

Etzioni, A. (1976) *Social Problems*. Englewood Cliffs, NJ: Prentice-Hall.

Eyestone, R. (1978) *From Social Issues to Public Policy*. New York: John Wiley.

Farmer, M.K. and Barrell, R. (1981) 'Entrepreneurship and government policy: The case of the housing market', *Journal of Public Policy*, 1, 307–42.

Fesler, J.W. (1980) *Public Administration: Theory and Practice*. Englewood Cliffs, NJ: Prentice-Hall.

Finer, H. (1941) 'Administrative responsibility in democratic government', *Public Administration Review*, 1, 335–50.

Fiorina, M. (1978) *Congress: Keystone of the Washington Establishment*. New Haven: Yale University Press.

Foard, A.A. and Fefferman, H. (1966) 'Federal urban renewal

legislation', in Wilson, J.Q. (ed.), *Urban Renewal*, Cambridge, Mass.: MIT Press.

Foley, H.A. (1975) *Community Mental Health Programs: The Formative Process*. Lexington, Mass.: Lexington Books.

Fox, W., Jr. and Hammond, S.W. (1977) *Congressional Staffs*. New York: Free Press.

Freedman, J.O. (1978) *Crisis and Legitimacy: The Administrative Process and American Government*. New York: Cambridge University Press.

Friedson, E. (1970) *Professional Dominance*. New York: Pantheon.

Galbraith, J.K. (1967) *The New Industrial State*. Boston: Houghton Mifflin.

Goodin, R.E. (1975) 'The logic of bureaucratic backscratching', *Public Choice*, 21, 53–68.

Goodin, R.E. and Waldner, I. (1979) 'Thinking big, thinking small and not thinking at all', *Public Policy*, 27, 1–24.

Grey, C. (1982) 'The Regional Water Authorities', in Hogwood, B.W. and Keating, M. (eds.), *Regional Government in England*, Oxford: Clarendon Press, 143–67.

Griffith, J.A. (1974) *Parliamentary Scrutiny of Government Bills*. London: Allen and Unwin.

Gross, B. (1966) 'The State of the Nation', in Bauer, R. (ed.), *Social Indicators*, Cambridge, Mass.: MIT Press, 58–92.

Hague, D.C., Mackenzie, W.J.M. and Barker, A. (eds.) (1975) *Public Policy and Private Interests: The Institutions of Compromise*. London: Macmillan.

Hall, P., Land, H., Parker, R. and Webb, A. (1975) *Change, Choice and Conflict in Social Policy*. London: Heinemann.

Halperin, M. (1972) 'The decision to deploy ABM: Bureaucratic politics in the Johnson Administration', *World Politics*, 24, 40–79.

Handler, J. (1978) *Social Movements and the Legal System: A Theory of Reform and Change*. New York: Academic Press.

Hanf, K., Hjern, B. and Porter, D.O. (1978) 'Local networks of manpower training in the Federal Republic of Germany and Sweden', in Hanf, K. and Scharpf, F.W. (eds.), *Interorganizational Policy Making*, Beverly Hills, California: Sage.

Hanf, K. and Scharpf, F.W. (eds.) (1978) *Interorganizational Policy Making*. Beverly Hills, California: Sage.

Harris, R. and Seldon, A. (1977) *Not from benevolence. . . .*Hobart

Paperback 10. London: Institute of Economic Affairs.

Harris, R. and Seldon, A. (1979) *Over-ruled on Welfare*. Hobart Paperback 13. London: Institute of Economic Affairs.

Hastings, A.H. (1981) *Strategies Used to Equalize Access in Federal Education and Health Programs*. Washington, DC: The Brookings Institution.

Haywood, S.C. and Elcock, H.J. (1982) 'Regional Health Authorities: Regional Government or central agencies?', in Hogwood, B.W. and Keating, M. (eds.) *Regional Government in England*, Oxford: Clarendon Press, 119–42.

Headey, B. (1974) *British Cabinet Ministers*. London: Allen and Unwin.

Headey, B. (1978) *Housing Policy in the Developed Economy*. London: Croom-Helm.

Heclo, H. (1974) *Modern Social Politics in Britain and Sweden*. New Haven and London: Yale University Press.

Heclo, H. (1977) *A Government of Strangers*. Washington, DC: The Brookings Institution.

Heclo, H. and Wildavsky, A. (1974) *The Private Government of Public Money*. London: Macmillan.

Heidenheimer, A.J., Heclo, H. and Adams, C.T. (1975) *Comparative Public Policy: The Politics of Social Choice in Europe and America*. New York: St Martin's Press.

Heisler, M.O. (1974) 'The European polity model', in Heisler, M.O. (ed.), *Politics in Europe*, New York: David McKay, 27–89.

Heisler, M.O. and Peters, B.G. (1978) 'Comparing social policies across levels of government, countries and time', in Ashford, D.E. (ed.), *Comparing Public Policies*, Beverly Hills, California: Sage.

Hirsch, F. (1976) *Social Limits to Growth*. Twentieth Century Fund (London: Routledge and Kegan Paul, 1977).

Hirschman, A.O. (1970) *Exit, Voice and Loyalty*. Cambridge, Mass.: Harvard University Press.

Hjern, B., and Porter, D.O. (1979) 'Implementation structure: A new unit of administrative analysis'. Paper presented at the 1979 Annual Meeting of the American Political Science Association.

Hogwood, B.W. (1979a) *Government and Shipbuilding: The Politics of Industrial Change*. Farnborough, Hants.: Gower (Saxon House).

Hogwood, B.W. (1979b) 'The tartan fringe: Quangos and other

assorted animals in Scotland', *Studies in Public Policy*, No. 34, Glasgow: Centre for the Study of Public Policy, University of Strathclyde.

Holden, M. (1966) 'Imperialism and bureaucracy', *American Political Science Review*, 60, 943–51.

Hood, C. (1976) *The Limits of Administration*. London: John Wiley.

Hood, C. (1978) 'Keeping the centre small: Explanations of agency type', *Political Studies*, 26, 30–46.

Hood, C. (1981) 'Axeperson, spare that quango. . .', in Hood, C. and Wright, M. (eds.), *Big Government in Hard Times*, Oxford: Martin Robertson, 100–22.

Hood, C. and Dunsire, A. (1981) *Bureaumetrics: the Quantitative Comparison of British Central Government Agencies.* Farnborough, Hants.: Gower.

Howell, D. (1970) *A New Style of Government.* London: Conservative Political Centre.

Howell, D. (1971) *A New Style Emerges.* London: Conservative Political Centre.

Jackson, S.M. and Peters, B.G. (1980) 'Making costly physicians accountable', *Policy Analysis*, 6, 235–8.

Johnson, N. (1976) 'Recent administrative reform in Britain', in Leemans, A. (ed.), *The Management of Change in Government*, The Hague: Martinus Nijhoff.

Johnstone, D. (1975) *A Tax Shall be Charged.* Civil Service College Studies No. 1. London: HMSO.

Jones, C.O. (1977) *An Introduction to the Study of Public Policy.* Belmont, California: Wadsworth.

Jones, G.W. (1980) *New Approaches to the Study of Central-Local Relationships.* Farnborough, Hants.: Gower.

Jordan, A.G. (1981) 'Iron triangles, woolly corporatism, or elastic nets: Images of the policy process', *Journal of Public Policy*, 1, 95–123.

Jordan, A.G., Richardson, J.J. and Kimber, R. (1977) 'The origins of the Water Act of 1973', *Public Administration*, 55, 317–34.

Katzenbach, E.L. (1958) 'The Horse Cavalry in the Twentieth Century: A study in policy response', *Public Policy*, 6, 120–49.

Kaufman, H. (1960) *Forest Ranger: A Study in Administrative Behavior.* Baltimore: Johns Hopkins.

Kaufman, H. (1972) *The Limits of Organizational Change.* Alabama: The University of Alabama Press.

Kaufman, H. (1976) *Are Government Organizations Immortal?* Washington, DC: The Brookings Institution.

Kaufman, H. (1977) 'Reflections on administrative reorganization', in Pechman, J. (ed.), *Setting National Priorities*, Washington, DC: The Brookings Institution, 402–8.

Kellner, P. and Crowther-Hunt, Lord (1980) *The Civil Servants: An Inquiry into Britain's Ruling Class.* London: Macdonald.

King, A. (1975) 'Overload: problems of governing in the 1970s', *Political Studies* 23, 284–96.

Klein, R. (1975) 'The National Health Service', in Klein, R. (ed.), *Inflation and Priorities*, London: Centre for Studies in Social Policy, 83–104.

Klingman, D. (1980) 'Temporal and spatial diffusion in the comparative analysis of social change', *American Political Science Review*, 74, 123–37.

Lambright, W.H. and Sapolsky, H.M. (1976) 'Terminating federal research and development programs', *Policy Sciences*, 7, 199–213.

Laurin, U. (1980) *Undersökningen om Skatter i Sverige.* Uppsala: Statsvetenskapliga Institutionen, Uppsala Universitet.

Leemans, A.F. (ed.) (1976) *The Management of Change in Government.* The Hague: Martinus Nijhoff.

Leichter, H.M. (1979) *A Comparative Approach to Policy Analysis: Health Care in Four Nations.* Cambridge: Cambridge University Press.

Leruez, J. (1975) *Economic Planning and Politics in Britain.* Oxford: Martin Robertson.

Leuchtenberg, W.E. (1963) *Franklin D. Roosevelt and the New Deal 1932–1940.* New York: Harper and Row.

Levine, C.H. (1978) 'Organizational decline and cutback management', *Public Administration Review*, 38, 316–25.

Levine, C.H. (1980) 'More on cutback management: Hard questions for hard times', in Levine, C.H. (ed.), *Managing Fiscal Stress*, Chatham, NJ: Chatham House.

Lindblom, C.E. (1959) 'The science of "muddling through"', *Public Administration Review*, 19, 79–88.

Lindblom, C.E. (1968) *The Policy Making Process.* Englewood Cliffs, NJ: Prentice-Hall.

Lindblom, C.E. (1977) *Politics and Markets: The World's Political-Economic Systems.* New York: Basic Books.

Lindblom, C.E. (1979) 'Still muddling, not yet through', *Public Administration Review*, 39, 517–26.

Linder, S. and McBride, M. (1981) 'The hidden costs of regulatory reform'. Paper presented at Association for Public Policy Analysis and Management, Washington, DC. October 1981.

Lippitt, R. Watson, J. and Westley, B. (1958) *The Dynamics of Planned Change*. New York: Harcourt, Brace and World.

Lipsky, M. (1978) 'Implementation on its head', in Burham, W.P. and Weinberg, M. (eds.), *American Politics and Public Policy*, Cambridge, Mass.: MIT Press, 390–402.

Lovell, C.H. and Tobin, C. (1980) 'Mandating — a key issue of cities', *Municipal Year Book*, 73–9.

Lynn, L. (1981) *Managing the Public's Business*. New York: Basic Books.

Manley, J.F. (1970) *The Politics of Finance: The House Ways and Means Committee*. Boston: Little, Brown.

Mansfield, H.C. (1970) 'Reorganizing the Federal Executive Branch: The limits of institutionalization', *Law and Contemporary Problems*, 64, 461–95.

May, J.L. and Wildavsky, A. (eds.) (1978) *The Policy Cycle*. Beverly Hills, California: Sage.

Maynard, A. (1979) 'Pricing, insurance and the National Health Service', *Journal of Social Policy*, 8, 157–76.

Mazmanian, D.A. and Nienaber, J. (1979) *Can Organizations Change?: Environmental Protection, Citizen Participation and the Corps of Engineers*. Washington, DC: The Brookings Institution.

Merton, R.K. (1940) 'Bureaucratic structure and personality', *Social Forces*, 18, 560–8.

Miles, R.E. (1977) 'Considerations for a President bent on re-organization', *Public Administration Review*, 37, 155–9.

Moe, R. (1979) *The Federal Executive Establishment: Evolution and Trends*. Washington, DC: GPO.

Mosher, F. (1980) *The GAO*. Boulder, Colorado: Westview.

Munnell, A.H. (1977) *The Future of Social Security*. Washington, DC: The Brookings Institution.

Murphy, J.T. (1973) 'The education bureaucracies implement novel policies: The politics of Title I of ESEA', in Sindler, J.T. (ed.), *Policy and Politics in America*, Boston: Little, Brown, 165–98.

National Council of State Planning Bodies (1980) *America in Ruins*.

Washington, DC: National Council of State Legislatures.

Nelson, R. (1978) *The Moon and the Ghetto*. New York: Norton.

New Society (1976) 'Killing a commitment: The cabinet versus the children', *New Society*, 36 (17 June 1976), 630–2.

OECD (1969) *National Accounts of OECD Countries, 1950–1968*. Paris: OECD.

OECD (1981) *National Accounts of OECD Countries, 1960–79*. Paris: OECD.

Ogul, M. (1981) 'Congressional oversight: Structures and incentives', in Dodd, C. and Oppenheimer, I. (eds.), *Congress Reconsidered*, Washington, DC: Congressional Quarterly.

Olson, M. (1963) *Towards A National Social Report*. New York: Russell Sage.

Olson, M. (1965) *The Logic of Collective Action*. Cambridge, Mass.: Harvard University Press.

Paddock, W. and Paddock, E. (1979) 'So hard to remember, so easy to forget', in Peters, C. and Nelson, M. *The Culture of Bureaucracy*, New York: Holt, Rinehart and Winston.

Page, E. (1977) 'The transformation of decisions into activities: The Scottish Development Agency as a case study'. Unpublished MSc Dissertation, Department of Politics, University of Strathclyde.

Parker, R.A. (1967) 'Social administration and scarcity: The problem of rationing', *Social Work*, 24 (2), 9–14.

Parry, R. (1980) 'United Kingdom public employment: Patterns of change 1951–1976', *Studies in Public Policy*, No. 62, Glasgow: Centre for the Study of Public Policy, University of Strathclyde.

Pechman, J.A. (1979) 'Tax expenditures', in Pechman, J.A. (ed.), *Setting National Priorities: The 1980 Budget*, Washington, DC: The Brookings Institution, 225–9.

Peters, B.G. (1978) *The Politics of Bureaucracy*. New York: Longman.

Peters, B.G. (1982) *Public Policy in America: Process and Performance*. New York: Franklin Watts.

Peters, B.G. and Heisler, M.O. (1981) 'Government: What is growing and how do we know?', *Studies in Public Policy*, No. 89, Glasgow: Centre for the Study of Public Policy, University of Strathclyde.

Phyrr, P.A. (1975) 'The zero-base budgetting process', in Dudick, T.S. (ed.), *How to Improve Profit-Ability through More Effective Planning*, New York: John Wiley.

Piachaud, D. (1980) 'Taxation and social security', in Sandford, C., Pond, C. and Walker, R. (eds.), *Taxation and Social Policy*, London: Heinemann, 68–83.

Pitt, D.C., and Smith, B.C. (1981) *Government Departments: An Organizational Perspective*. London: Routledge and Kegan Paul.

Plaitzky, Sir Leo (1980) *Report on Non-Departmental Public Bodies*. Cmnd 7797. London: HMSO.

Porter, D.O. and Hjern, B. (1978) 'Implementation structures: A new unit of analysis'. Paper presented to 1978 Meeting of the American Political Science Association.

Pressman, J.L. and Wildavsky, A. (1973) *Implementation*. Berkeley: University of California Press.

Radin, B. (1977) *Implementation, Change and the Federal Bureaucracy*. New York: Teachers College Press.

Rhodes, R.A.W. (1981) *Control and Power in Central-Local Relations*. Farnborough, Hants.: Gower.

Richardson, J.J. and Jordan, A.G. (1979) *Governing Under Pressure: the Policy Process in a Post-Parliamentary Democracy*. Oxford: Martin Robertson.

Rodgers, E.M. (1970) *The Diffusion of Innovations*. New York: Free Press.

Rodgers, F. (1980) *A Guide to British Government Publications*. New York: H.W. Wilson.

Rodgers, H.P. and Bullock, C.S. (1972) *Civil Rights Laws and Their Consequences*. New York: McGraw Hill.

Rose, R. (1976a) 'On the priorities of government: A developmental analysis of public policies', *European Journal of Political research*, 4, 247–89.

Rose, R. (ed.), (1976b) *The Dynamics of Public Policy*. New York: Sage-Halstead.

Rose, R. (1980) *Do Parties Make a Difference?* Chatham, NJ: Chatham House.

Rose, R. (1981) 'What if anything is wrong with big government?', *Journal Of Public Policy*, 1, 5–36.

Rose, R. and Peters, G. (1978) *Can Government Go Bankrupt?* New York: Basic Books.

Rourke, F.E. (1979) 'Bureaucratic autonomy and the public interest', in Weiss, C.H. and Barton, A.H. (eds.), *Making Bureaucracies Work*, Beverly Hills, California: Sage, 103–12.

Salamon, L.B. (1979) 'The time dimension in policy evaluation: The case of the New Deal Land Relief Programs', *Public Policy*, 27, 129–83.

Salamon, L. (1981) 'The question of goals', Szanton, P. (ed.), *Federal Reorganization: What Have We Learned?*, Chatham, NJ: Chatham House, 58–84.

Salamon, L.B., and Walmsley, G.L. (1976) 'The federal bureaucracy: Responsive to whom?' in Rieselbach, L.N. (ed.), *The Responsiveness of American Institutions*, Bloomington, Indiana: Indiana University Press, 151–88.

Sandford, C. (1977) *Social Economics*. London: Heinemann.

Scalia, A. (1981) 'Back to basics: Making law without making rules', *Regulation*, 5 (4), 25–8.

Scharpf, F.W., Reissert, B. and Schnabel, F. (1978) 'Policy effectiveness and conflict avoidance in intergovernmental policy formation', in Scharpf, F.W. and Hanf, K. (eds.), *Interorganizational Policy Making*, Beverly Hills, California: Sage, 57–112.

Schein, H. and Bennis, W.G. (1965) *Personal and Organizational Change through Group Methods*. New York: John Wiley.

Schmitter, P. (1974) 'Still the century of corporatism?', in Pike, F.B. and Stritch, T. (eds.), *The New Corporatism: Social-Political Structures in the Iberian World*, South Bend, Indiana: Notre Dame University Press, 85–131.

Scott, K.E. (1981) 'The uncertain course of bank deregulation', *Regulation*, 5 (3), 40–5.

Seidman, H. (1980) *Politics, Position and Power: The Dynamics of Federal Organization*, 3rd edition. New York: Oxford University Press.

Selznick, P. (1948) 'Foundations of the theory of organization', *American Sociological Review*, 13, 25–35.

Sharkansky, I. (1967) *Spending in The American States*. Chicago: Rand McNally.

Smith, B.L.R. (ed.) (1975) *The New Political Economy: The Public Use of The Private Sector*. New York: Halsted Press (London: Macmillan).

Smith, B.L.R. and Hague, D.C. (eds.) (1971) *The Dilemma of Accountability In Modern Government*. New York: St Martin's Press (London: Macmillan).

Staaf, R.J. (1977) 'The growth of the educational bureaucracy: Do teachers make a difference?', in Borcherding, T.E. (ed.) *Budgets and Bureaucrats: The Sources of Government Growth*, Durham, North Carolina: Duke University Press, 148–68.

Steiner, G. (1981) *The Futility of Family Policy*. Washington, DC: The Brookings Institution.

Stevens, R. (ed.) (1970) *The Statutory History of the United States*. New York: Chelsea House.

Stoner, F.E. (1978) 'Federal auditors as regulators: The case of Title I of ESEA', in May, J.V. and Wildavsky, A.B. (eds.), *The Policy Cycle*, Beverly Hills, California: Sage, 199–214.

Subcommittee on Intergovernmental Relations (1977) *Sunset Act of 1977*. Hearings on S. 2 before the Subcommittee on Intergovernmental Relations of the Committee on Governmental Affairs, United States Senate, 95th Congress, 1st Session. Washington, DC: GPO.

Szanton, P. (1981) *Reorganization*. Chatham, NJ: Chatham House.

Tarschys, D. (1977) 'The problem of pre-planned society'. Paper presented to 1977 Annual Meeting of American Political Society.

Thoenig, J-C. (1978) 'State bureaucracies and local government in France', in Hanf, K. and Scharpf, F.W. (eds.), *Interorganizational Policy Making*, Beverly Hills, California: Sage, 167–97.

Thoenig, J-C. and Friedberg, E. (1976) 'The power of the field staff', in Leemans, A.F. (ed.), *The Management of Change in Government*, The Hague: Martinus Nijhoff.

Thompson, V. (1961) *Modern Organizations*. New York: Knopf.

Thurow, L. (1980) *The Zero-Sum Society*. New York: Basic Books.

Tiebout, C.M. (1956) 'A pure theory of local expenditures', *Journal of Political Economy*, 64, 416–24.

Van Horn, C.E. (1976) 'Implementing CETA'. Paper presented to Annual Midwest Political Science Association, Chicago, Illinois.

Walkland, S.A. (1968) *The Legislative Process in Great Britain*. London: Allen and Unwin.

Warwick, D.P. (1975) *A Theory of Public Bureaucracy: Politics, Personality and Organization in the State Department*. Cambridge, Mass.: Harvard University Press.

Webster, D. (1980) 'Why Labour failed on housing', *New Society*, 49 (17 January 1980), 117–18.

Wehrmann, G. (1978) 'A policy in search of an objective', *Public Administration*, 56, 425–38.

Weidenbaum, M. (1979) 'The high cost of government regulation', *Challenge*, November/December 1979, 32–9.

Weiss, C. (1972) *Evaluation Research*. Englewood Cliffs, NJ: Prentice Hall.

Whyte, W.F. (1959) 'An interaction approach to the theory of organizations', in Haire, M. (ed.), *Modern Organization Theory*, New York: Wiley, 154–82.

Wilcox, C. (1968) 'The regulation of industry', in Sills D.L. (ed.), *International Encyclopedia of the Social Sciences*, New York: Free Press and Macmillan.

Wildavsky, A. (1978) 'A budget for all seasons? Why the traditional budget persists', *Public Administration Review*, 38, 501–9.

Wildavsky, A. (1979) *Speaking Truth to Power: The Art and Craft of Policy Analysis*. Boston: Little, Brown. (Published in Britain in 1980 as *The Art and Craft of Policy Analysis*. London: Macmillan.)

Willis, J.R.M. and Hardwick, P.J.W. (1978) *Tax Expenditures in the United Kingdom*. London: Heinemann for the Institute for Fiscal Studies.

Wirt, F. (1981). 'Professionalism and political conflict: A developmental model', *Journal of Public Policy*, 1, 61–93.

Wolf, C. Jr. (1979) 'A theory of nonmarket failure: Framework for implementation analysis', *Journal of Law and Economics*, 22, 107–40.

Wright, M. (1981) 'Big government in hard times: The restraint of public expenditure', in Hood, C. and Wright, M. (eds.), *Big Government in Hard Times*, Oxford: Martin Robertson.

Wurzburg, G. (1979) 'What limits the impact of evaluations on federal policy?', in Datta, L.E. and Perloff, R. (eds.), *Improving Evaluations*, Beverly Hills, California: Sage, 35–41.

INDEX

281